Managing the Training Enterprise

Manuel London

Managing the Training Enterprise

High-Quality, Cost-Effective Employee Training in Organizations

Jossey-Bass Publishers
San Francisco • Oxford • 1989

MANAGING THE TRAINING ENTERPRISE
High-Quality, Cost-Effective Employee Training in Organizations
by Manuel London

 Jossey-Bass Inc., Publishers
350 Sansome Street
San Francisco, California 94104
&
Jossey-Bass Limited
Headington Hill Hall
London OX3 0BW

Library of Congress Cataloging-in-Publication Data

London, Manuel.
Managing the training enterprise : high-quality, cost-effective employee training in organizations / Manuel London.
p. cm.—(The Jossey-Bass management series)
Bibliography: p.
Includes index.
ISBN 1-55542-183-0
1. Employees—Training of. I. Title. II. Series.
HF5549.5.T7L558 1989
658.3′12404—dc20 89-45573
CIP

Manufactured in the United States of America

The paper in this book meets the guidelines for permanence and durability of the Committee on Production Guidelines for Book Longevity of the Council on Library Resources.

JACKET DESIGN BY WILLI BAUM

FIRST EDITION

Code 8957

The Jossey-Bass Management Series

Consulting Editors
Human Resources

Leonard Nadler
Zeace Nadler
College Point, Maryland

For David Zahav London

Part Three: Enhancing Long-Term Training Effectiveness

Preface

Training and development play a strategic role in the successful operation of an organization and in the career success of its employees. Each individual's employment security hinges on being prepared to meet new skill requirements as job opportunities change, and training and development are critical to such preparation.

The purpose of *Managing the Training Enterprise* is to examine how organizations educate employees and to consider policies and programs for improving this educational process. The book covers organizational training strategies, learning methods, ways of structuring training departments, the process of allocating funds and other resources to training, and the role of training as a communications vehicle in the organization. Also treated is an often-ignored part of employee education—training management and administration. This area includes developing business and operations plans, budgeting and expense tracking, and measuring and evaluating training effectiveness. The book also examines long-term employee development programs, training for quality improvement, directions for retraining and redevelopment, and development for training professionals.

While primarily directed at training managers, training directors and department heads, corporate officers overseeing training departments, and managers who are members of training advisory boards, this book is also for those managers in a variety of staff disciplines and line functions having responsibility for training employees. Secondarily, the book is for training professionals, such as program developers, instructional technologists, and instructors. Graduate students in instructional design and related disciplines who are interested in training administration can also benefit from the book.

Many training administrators, especially those new to their jobs, may not have much prior experience in training nor an advanced degree in the field. The discussions of how people learn, cost analysis, program evaluation, and advanced training technologies should be helpful to them. Training administrators with a background in training may benefit especially from the discussions of local training, client relationships, vendor relationships, competitive assessment, and union/management programs, all of which may be more familiar to line managers who are appointed to administrative positions in the training organization.

The topics covered are generically applicable to technical and managerial training and are also applicable to a variety of organizations in the public and private sectors, including businesses, government agencies, and nonprofit organizations. While many of the examples are from large and midsize organizations, the concepts discussed are applicable to small organizations in which there are one or a handful of people responsible for training. Several themes run through the book:

- How organizational change, technological advancements, and labor force trends affect training needs
- The use of adult learning principles in employee education
- Training as a transition process and ways to enhance learning effectiveness in different transition stages
- Education as a continuous learning process
- Ways to integrate employee training and development programs with organizational objectives
- The use of comparative data from other organizations for competitive assessment
- The value of measuring the effects of training
- Ways to reduce the cost of training
- Ways to enhance the quality and effectiveness of training

- The importance of providing developmental opportunities for training professionals
- The use of advanced technologies for self-paced education.

The book describes a variety of learning methods using multiple media, including computer-based and video disk training and audio teleconferencing. Self-paced learning tools and instructor-led classroom training as well as measures of success for program development and delivery are also considered. The ideas and recommendations in the book are practical and readily applied. Examples stem from many leading firms, such as Ford, IBM, AT&T, Digital Equipment Corporation, Motorola, and Merck. Each chapter concludes with a section on policy opportunities and recommendations.

Emphasis is placed on enhancing training quality. Quality improvement processes are described as ways to encourage participation of training professionals in guiding organizational education policies and programs, thereby ensuring their contribution to organizational and individual employee goals and facilitating working relationships among different training functions (such as program development, instructional technology consulting, and program delivery).

Many organizations are faced with reducing overhead costs to increase competitiveness and overall effectiveness. The employee training function is usually, and properly, viewed as overhead because it does not deal directly with end users of the organization's products and services. Nevertheless, employee training represents an investment in the organization's current viability and future success. With that in mind, this book describes ways of analyzing the training gap in the organization (the difference between how much and what types of training are needed and how much and what types of training the organization plans to provide). The book also demonstrates ways to calculate and reduce unit training costs to deliver high-quality education for the least amount of money.

The book highlights the roles of training professionals, describing different ways of organizing the training function (for example, centralization versus decentralization) and presenting ways to encourage and support "local training"—programs designed and delivered by local department managers. The book also addresses the extent to which organizations want to hire and develop training professionals and rotate line managers and subject matter experts into training jobs.

Overview of the Contents

The book is divided into three parts. Part One reviews the need for training, types of training, and ways organizations provide training, including learning methods and organizational structures. Chapter One introduces the book by reporting on the extensiveness of employee education and how training departments fit into the organization's structure and contribute to its goals. New directions for employee training illustrate the scope of education provided in organizations. Changing demographics of the labor force suggest the importance of providing training for older workers and preparing younger workers for skills that will be needed in the future. Principles of adult learning are described as a basis for structuring educational processes and generating a continuous learning environment.

The second chapter demonstrates the diversity of what employees learn in organizations. The chapter describes how varying degrees of organizational change affect the learning process. A sudden job shift can be a frame-breaking change that sets up a "make-it-or-break it" situation. Or a business simulation can be an incremental change that allows trial-and-error learning. The chapter also describes alternative advanced technologies, including computer-based training, interactive video disk, PC teletraining, and teleconferencing. Learning laboratories, artificial intelligence methods, job aids, and on-the-job training are covered along with traditional face-to-face, instructor-led classroom training. These alternative methods are compared on their application of adult learning principles.

Chapter Three outlines sixteen different roles in a training department—including director, curriculum manager, program developer, instructor, and instructional technologist. Examples of alternative organizational structures for different size training departments are outlined as are mechanisms for enhancing relationships between the training department and its customers and suppliers. Ways to improve relationships among people within a training department are recommended, and the pros and cons of centralized training departments are discussed. The chapter emphasizes the importance of management's support for employee education and provides examples of innovative and flexible local approaches to training.

Part Two considers important administrative functions, including how to formulate training business plans, develop a training budget, conduct cost analyses, and measure training effectiveness. Chapter Four is about the development of strategic and operations plans for the training department. Strategic planning is viewed as an active, ongoing process that involves the training department's clients in establishing their training needs and envisioning ways to meet these needs. One aspect of developing training plans is analyzing the training gap—the training required owing to employees' lack of skills; changes in the work force (such as new employees and transfers); and new technology and products, changes in procedures, and other aspects of organizational evolution. The chapter describes ways to assess and reduce the training gap.

Chapter Five focuses on tracking the financial impact of the training department's plans, addressing budget preparation and methods for comparing the unit costs of alternative training media. Suggestions are made for improving the efficiency (and lowering the unit cost) of training development and delivery. The second part of the chapter considers methods for conducting competitive assessments as a basis for evaluating cost-effectiveness. Competitive assessments also provide new ideas for improving employee education. Competitive data include information from other training organizations on training costs, types of training, needs assessment procedures, evaluation methods, training media, and organization structures and strategies for providing training. The chapter describes how to collect comparable information (that is, data consisting of similar components). Examples of training operations in several major organizations are given and methods for conducting performance analyses to determine when and whether training is needed are examined. The chapter concludes with recommendations for a policy for charging back training costs to client departments and ideas for cutting costs and assessing the impact of these reductions on the organization.

Ways to measure and evaluate the effects of employee education are the subject of Chapter Six. The chapter describes the clients for training data (training managers and line supervisors) who want to know whether students acquired the new knowledge and skills taught. Examples are given of how to use employees' training records for establishing individual and group development plans. The chapter includes samples of student opinion surveys, client satisfaction measures, and tests of performance and behavior change after training. Also offered are ways to calculate indexes of the effectiveness of training development and delivery and suggestions on how to report this information to the organization. The second part of the chapter describes how to use the measurements to evaluate training programs. Three types of research designs are covered: experimental research for isolating the effects of relevant variables and eliminating contaminating effects; action (process) research for evaluating programs as they are implemented and for using the information to make improvements; and correlational research examining relationships among characteristics of training programs, characteristics of the students, and training outputs.

Part Three concentrates on ways to enhance training effectiveness by developing training professionals and making training an integral part of the organization's objectives. Chapter Seven outlines the importance of professional development for training personnel. The chapter addresses the value of rotational assignments in the training department for line personnel and personnel from other departments and argues for hiring training experts (people with advanced degrees in training-related disciplines) who want long-term careers in training. Methods for generating competency models for training professionals are described along with sample models and ways to use these models for certification processes and mastery paths. The importance of memberships in professional associations is evaluated.

Chapter Eight considers how the training department supports the organization's strategies and uses tools and processes to improve training efficiency and effectiveness. These tools include the development of an education policy for the organization and ways to improve the organization's overall performance standards by integrating training with other human resource programs and by enhancing the standards applied to the use of these processes. Another topic considered is the use of training for quality improvement efforts and the application of quality improvement teams and techniques in the training department. Training is also shown to be essential to the retraining and redeployment of employees as skill requirements change and organizations restructure. Finally, training is considered as an intervention for organizational change; by altering management and leadership style, employees are empowered, their responsiveness to client demands is enhanced, and skill acquisition and career changes are encouraged.

Chapter Nine concludes the book, providing an overview of critical issues and future directions for training management. Challenges deal with introducing new technology; partnering with other organizations, including educational institutions, to provide employee education; meeting the educational needs of an international firm; integrating employee training and training for external customers; devoting training resources to high-impact jobs (positions critical to organizational success); linking management development and technical education; and taking a systems approach to training. The chapter recommends that training contribute to the success of the organization and that training content follow directly from the organization's strategies. The training department provides the necessary resources, including designing the most cost-effective methods and providing alternative educational processes to suit employees' abilities and preferences. Employees must be clear about the organization's expectations for development, and managers are responsible for communicating these expectations to their employees. However, the responsibility for learning rests with each employee.

Four resources are provided at the end of the book. Resource A describes the various administrative roles that may be required in a training department. Training administration is an overhead cost for the training department and thus should be as simple, cost-effective, and responsive to client needs as possible. Resource B compares information from Motorola and IBM to illustrate the type of data available on premier training programs. Resource C examines the plusses and minuses of different degrees of rigor in program evaluation and provides examples of different evaluation designs. Resource D offers a set of guidelines for career development for training professionals, including a career planning process and alternative career paths for training professionals.

Acknowledgments

Many of the ideas and examples in this book come from my experiences as the manager of planning and management systems for a large technical training organization in AT&T. I am grateful to Michael Goodman for providing the opportunity to gain these experiences and for offering his insights, direction, and encouragement of my personal and professional development. He has been a valuable role model for me and an inspirational leader for all the employees in the training organization. I am also grateful to my team, the managers responsible for many of the subjects in this book. I want to thank especially Nina Barbato, Ron Baughman, Phil Gallagher, and Gail Solomon. I truly value their friendship, dedication, and their creative and effective work. I am also grateful for the support of David Chudnow, Linda Condrillo, Isabel Desousa, Fran Duva, Glenn Hagmann, and Jim Tanner. Barbara Albon, Joan Ausmann, Linda Flanigan, and Joe Wolensky provided many insights on quality processes and administrative systems for training. I am grateful to Robert Almquist and Raymond Pardee for helping make the distinction between training commitment measures and operational indicators, as discussed in Chapter Six. My peers and clients were also a source of learning about training strategy, effective communications, and responsiveness. These included Don Felker, Jim Icardi, Kathy Marsico, Jim Stanton, and Bob Stein, who helped make my work a challenge and a pleasure.

I benefited greatly from the helpful comments of several reviewers. My thanks to Leonard Nadler, Zeace Nadler, Larry Pace, and A. William Wiggenhorn. Last but not least, I am grateful to my wife, Marilyn, and my children, David and Jared, for their patience and encouragement during the many evenings, weekends, and vacation days of writing. I dedicate this book to my son David for his love, his lively and engaging personality, and his prodding me with an anxious desire that I finish this book. Now we can all go fishing together.

Stony Brook, New York Manuel London
August 1989

The Author

Manuel London is professor and director of the Center for Labor/Management Studies in the Harriman School for Management and Policy at the State University of New York at Stony Brook. He received his A.B. degree (1971) from Case Western Reserve University in philosophy and psychology and his M.A. (1972) and Ph.D. (1974) degrees from the Ohio State University in industrial and organizational psychology. Before coming to Stony Brook in 1989, London worked for AT&T for almost twelve years in a series of human resource assignments. His last AT&T assignment was manager of planning and management systems for the Network Operations Education and Training Department. From 1974 to 1977, London taught in the business school of the University of Illinois at Urbana.

London's main research activities have been in employee development and career decisions. He has also conducted research on the relationship between work and nonwork behavior and has written on ethical issues in personnel decisions. He was a consulting editor for the *Academy of Management Journal* and is now a member of the editorial boards of *Personnel Psychology*, the *Journal of Applied Psychology*, *Administrative Science Quarterly*, *Human Resource Management Review*, and the *Journal of Management Development*. He has written more than thirty papers and thirty book reviews and is the author of *Managing Careers* (1982, with S. A. Stumpf), *Developing Managers* (1985), *Career Management and Survival in the Workplace* (1987, with E. M. Mone), *Career Growth and Human Resource Strategies* (1988, edited with E. M. Mone), and *Change Agents* (1988), for which he received the American Society for Personnel Administration 1989 Book Award.

Managing the Training Enterprise

1

The Need for Enhanced Training Opportunities

Why do corporations establish training departments? What is their role in training and educating employees? What is the link between training and accomplishing organizational objectives? These questions, addressed in this opening chapter, are central to the development and operation of training organizations in business, government, and nonprofit organizations, and their answers will lead to a discussion of how a training organization's mission and values are established, the sources of training, and the importance of training throughout an employee's career. The chapter examines the need for employee training and the role of corporate training in adult education.

Defining Training, Education, and Development

Training refers to learning focused on the employee's present job (Nadler and Nadler, 1989). That is, training is aimed at improving the skills or providing the knowledge currently required or useful to the employee. A training program generally has a very specific objective—to focus on one or more skills, areas of knowledge, or abilities. A training program may last several hours or one or more days or be a sequence of units or courses.

Unlike training, which imparts specific skills and knowledge, *education* implies preparing to deal with the unknown. Education generally involves learning basic principles and constructs that can be applied to synthesize information, extract relevant data, make judgments, and take action. As such, education is learning focused on a future job. This is sometimes referred to as *retraining* (a somewhat confusing term because it assumes there has been some previous training that could apply to improving current performance) (Nadler and Nadler, 1989).

Continuous education refers to an organizational philosophy of providing opportunities for training and education for all employees regardless of career stage. The term emphasizes that learning occurs continuously, that there is always room for improvement and personal growth, and that one should always consider acquiring knowledge and skills that might be valuable in the future. Continuous education may be thought of as a value that organizations demonstrate by providing and supporting learning for all employees and that individuals demonstrate by taking advantage of learning opportunities throughout their careers.

The term *development* is learning that is not job focused. It refers to the long-term personal and professional growth of the individual. *Human resources development* refers to organized learning experiences provided by employers within a specified period of time to enhance performance and personal growth (Nadler and Nadler, 1989). A development program may consist of training courses, workshops, discussion groups, and special assignments and job experiences. It may be guided by corporate initiatives to prepare people for advancement or to ensure that employees have the opportunities needed to maintain and expand their skills.

The Organization as a Major Source of Adult Education

U.S. corporations spend approximately $40 billion annually on formal education and training (C. Lee, 1988), which is broken down as follows: $27 billion (68 percent) for training staff salaries, $3 billion for seminars and training conferences, $5.4 billion for training facilities and equipment, and $5.6 billion for training materials and services purchased from consultants and vendors. In addition to the total spent on formal training, another $140 billion is spent on informal on-the-job training (Chmura, Henton, and Melville, 1987). IBM alone spends about $500 million each year in employee training, and AT&T spends about $350 million.

Corporate training is the largest system of adult education in the U.S. About 70 percent of employee education takes place in corporations, and the other 30 percent takes place in vocational and technical schools, community colleges and universities, and government programs. Many union agreements include programs to retrain surplus employees and to provide education for workers to enhance their skills and their marketability in case they need (because of layoff) or desire a career change.

Who Gets Trained? A recent survey of U.S. organizations having 100 or more employees (1,496 organizations in the representative sample) examined the types of employees who receive training (Feuer, 1988; Gordon, 1988). The study found that more than 73 percent of the organizations provide training to middle managers and first-line managers who receive an annual average of thirty-three hours of formal training (that is, structured learning activities as opposed to informal on-the-job training). More than half of the organizations provide training to executives, senior managers, professionals, and office/administrative employees, who receive on the average between eighteen and thirty-five hours of training per year. Between a third and a half of the organizations provide training to salespeople, production workers, and customer service people, who receive between thirty and forty-three hours of training per year.

Companies also provide training to customers and to suppliers. Motorola, for instance, recognizes that its success depends on its customers' and suppliers' successes, and thus Motorola views its customers and suppliers as partners in confronting global competition. The firm trains customers in how to use and maintain their products and trains suppliers in the quality standards expected in the purchase of products and services. Companies such as Xerox, Motorola, and Ford train suppliers in such areas as statistical process control, manufacturing design, and other aspects of product control and delivery.

Types of Training. The content or subject matter for training is varied. For instance, there is training to orient a new employee to the organization, training of new supervisors in managerial skills, and training for experienced managers who are moving into new positions. There is technical training of all sorts, for example, in data systems and engineering. There is training for how to use or how to repair products and training in customer interface skills and in disciplines such as finance, marketing, and public relations. Some training is aimed at supporting organizational initiatives such as business strategies or quality improvement.

The survey of organizations with one hundred or more employees, referred to above, demonstrated the diversity of training offered by firms (Gordon, 1988). The study reported that about 80 percent of the firms provide supervisory or management skills training including new employee orientation. About 72 percent provide communication skills training. Three-fourths offer technical skills and knowledge training. Other types of training (and the percentages of organizations offering them) include programs in customer relations (64 percent), clerical/secretarial skills such as word processing (60 percent), basic computer skills (59 percent), executive development (56 percent), and sales (48 percent). Forty-six percent of the organizations offer wellness training, for example, programs in smoking cessation, substance abuse, stress reduction, and physical health. Other topics are employee-labor relations and outplacement/retirement planning (offered by 45 percent and 24 percent of the firms, respectively). About a third of the firms offer courses in strategic planning, quality control, and finance. Twenty-four percent offer remedial basic education. About half the organizations offer courses to train trainers.

Management training has become very popular because organizations increasingly view management skills as critical to enhancing the organization's competitiveness. Companies send managers to university short courses and MBA programs so they will gain new perspectives, have opportunities to interact with other managers, acquire job-specific and state-of-the-art knowledge and skills, be rewarded, and be prepared for the next job (Saari, Johnson, McLaughlin, and Zimmerle, 1988).

Other types of development are more long term in nature and

do not depend on classroom training within or outside the organization. An example would be a development program for high-potential managers. The program may select highly qualified recent college graduates and place them in a series of positions that gives them line management and staff experience in a variety of departments. As a result, these management trainees learn the business, the organizational culture, and the role of supervisor. This program may be accompanied by mentorship programs that match the trainee to an experienced and successful higher-level manager who provides advice and perhaps evaluates the trainee's capabilities. (See London, 1985, for more descriptions of development programs for educating generalist managers.)

A similar type of development program for technical staff members from an operations department is a rotational assignment in the firm's research laboratory. One such program takes the brightest technical managers and puts them through seven months of classroom training provided by the company's laboratory researchers and local university professors. The trainees then are placed on a seven-month job assignment in the laboratories. Graduates return to their home departments in more advanced assignments that require interaction with the laboratories. The program enhances the technical manager's expertise and sensitivity to the role of research and development in operations planning and new product design. Small companies that cannot afford to send technical managers off for seven months may use short-term assignment on a research and development (R&D) project.

Adult training and education is big business, for several reasons, all of which are important to the continued viability of the organization. Workers need updated skills as technologies change. Managers need to fine-tune their supervisory and peer relationship skills. Leaders need to understand how to better guide the strategies of their organizations. Training is a vehicle for organizational change in that it educates employees about new corporate strategies and better ways to operate. For instance, the movement to enhance the quality of products and services to meet foreign competition has led to new ways of operating, including quality circles and participative management. Employees need to be trained in the meaning of quality, how to measure it, their role in enhancing it, and how to work in quality improvement groups.

Training is a way to socialize new employees in the goals and values of the organization and to communicate the expectations the organization has of managers as they move to higher organizational levels. Corporations involved in mergers and acquisitions use training to bring together employees from the different organizations and to emphasize how the new combined corporation will do business. The training may focus on the culture of the dominant organization, as when General Electric used training programs in its Management Development Institute in Crotonville, New York, to integrate RCA employees into its corporate structure and culture. This training was one means, along with special task forces and other team efforts, of enhancing collaborative working relationships.

Training can strengthen the organization's culture within the context of a changing business environment. Management forums provide a way to discuss the competitive marketplace and showcase new products and services. These forums bring people together from different departments to work on how they can improve their relationships and build networks and alliances rather than work at cross purposes.

Linking Training and Human Resource Systems

Training and development may be viewed as elements of a larger human resource system. The goal of human resource programs and policies is to ensure that the organization has the right people performing jobs where and when they are needed. The term *right* refers to the match between the job requirements and the individual's skills, knowledge, and background. Matching people to jobs and improving this match through training is a continuous and dynamic process because organizations' needs for people change and because people's job needs and career goals change.

An organization's human resource department must deal with multiple, and sometimes conflicting, interests. While the department must help the organization accomplish its objectives, it must also be an advocate for the employees. The department's programs ensure employees' safety, contribute to their productivity, and promote their satisfaction with their jobs and the organization.

A human resource department's activities may be grouped into strategies, such as leadership (succession planning and management staffing), learning (training and development programs), and careers (staffing, coaching, career planning). Many operational functions are related to these strategies, such as job evaluation, job vacancy announcements, payroll processing, the performance appraisal process, compensation and benefits, and organizational development consulting, to name a few. The learning system has multiple components, including technical and managerial training. Training may be aimed directly at enhancing the individual's knowledge and career goals and at increasing supervisors' skills in working with subordinates to set performance goals, give feedback and recognition, and structure rewarding jobs.

How Training Fits into the Organization's Structure

While training and development may be viewed as part of the organization's overall human resource development effort, they may not be included in the human resource or personnel department. More likely, training will take place in different departments as needed. Some training may be applicable to the entire organization and be directed or guided by the human resource department. Other training may be unique to specific departments and may be run by these departments.

In most firms, training is a support function. It is essential to the operation of the business, but it is not the product or service offered by the organization to the outside world. Some corporate training organizations can become a line of business, selling their services outside the organization. Other training organizations can be separate business units, selling their services inside the organization and competing with outside training companies that also wish to provide training to the corporation.

Linking Training and Organizational Objectives

Just as training and development complement human resource objectives, both training and human resource initiatives must support the organization's goals. Increasingly, human resources are viewed as a strategic resource for a corporation, since a technological advantage often does not last long. Competitors quickly match or outdo each other in bringing their products and services to market. The quality of those products and services is often a determining factor in the success of an organization. Given equal technology, the skills, abilities, and motivation of the employees make the difference in the marketplace. Consequently, as executives develop business plans, they must also formulate human resource plans to ensure that employees have the needed skills, understand the business needs, and want to contribute to the success of the enterprise.

Human resource strategies tie the needs of the individual to the needs of the organization so that both sets of needs can be met simultaneously. The individual benefits when the organization is successful, and vice versa. Compensation plans, promotion policies, training programs, and all personnel efforts must be aimed at helping the organization and its employees achieve organizational and job goals. Training and development plans and programs must be developed as an integral part of the business planning process. The organization's overall training plan should be part of the business plan. These plans should be constructed together and monitored simultaneously.

IBM's systems approach to education delineates the line manager's responsibility for establishing the business need for training and for developing training plans based on this business need. The training department then is responsible for providing the resources to carry out these plans. Specifically, each business unit, with the help of the company's education department, annually reviews the business direction of the unit, examines skill requirements for key jobs, considers the inventory of skills in the current employee body, and then develops training plans for each employee. (Company policy dictates that every employee will have a training plan, which must be revised each year.) The plans are developed by comparing training records to curriculum paths in the course catalog for each key job and are then aggregated to form the training plans for the business unit. Measurements of training completed indicate the extent to which the plans are carried out.

The Cost of Training and Education

Along with business and operations plans comes budgeting and expense tracking. Training (learning that is focused on the present job of the learner) is generally considered an expense, in that money is paid out and some specific goods or services are expected in return. Education (learning focused on a future job of the learner) is an investment, with all the risks that investments entail. In both cases, the costs must be identified, budgeted, and tracked. The cost of training must be weighed against the cost of not training. This includes the cost of repeat work made necessary by employee mistakes owing to lack of skills. A part of this cost is lost credibility with customers and the consequent loss of repeat business.

Because training is intended to contribute to organizational goals, managers have been concerned increasingly with the effects of training. Meaningful measures are essential if training managers are to be held accountable for their areas of responsibility. There are varying degrees of evaluation rigor. The most common type of measurement, and the easiest to administer, is student satisfaction with the training program. More difficult to measure are the lasting effects of the training on job performance and the cost-effectiveness (utility) of the training program compared to other methods (such as recruiting and hiring people already possessing the needed skills). Other measures are concerned with tracking the different elements of training, such as course development.

New Directions for Training

A recent review of corporate education and training examined how training contributes to a firm's competitive future (Chmura, Henton, and Melville, 1987). Given a continuously changing economy and fierce competition and rapid technological change, training is a way to advance skills and increase knowledge of competitors, especially foreign cultures and markets. A static or slowly growing work force requires making the best use of the current work force. A changing work force (due to high turnover or rapid growth) requires an awareness of new worker values and new training needs, such as increased remedial training for workers lacking basic skills. A participative, quality-oriented environment relies on training to help people work collaboratively. Training is a way to ensure employment security by providing new ways for people to contribute to the organization when their current job changes or is eliminated.

Jeffrey Sonnenfeld of the Harvard Business School offers a list of training objectives to illustrate the increasing scope of education and training (cited in Chmura, Henton, and Melville, 1987, p. 17), including:

- Teaching entry-level skills
- Orienting newcomers
- Creating advanced skills hard to locate in the labor market
- Attracting and retaining talent
- Retraining dislocated workers
- Meeting equal-employment-opportunity goals
- Improving work-group effectiveness
- Reinforcing a company's culture
- Changing a company's culture
- Providing skills to high-potential managers
- Reinvigorating burned-out workers
- Improving job productivity.

Training is a vehicle for communicating organizational goals. For instance, since employees are a captive audience, courses can be used as an opportunity to explain and reinforce business goals, to tie the purpose of the training to the department's and organization's objectives, and to help employees recognize the contribution they make to the organization. Examples of corporate messages that can be integrated into training programs are the importance of quality and of customer satisfaction. For instance, AT&T printed its major business strategies in a brochure for instructors to use as a discussion guide in technical training courses. AT&T also printed quality principles on wallet-size plastic cards for distribution and discussion in classes. Motorola uses training to break down communication barriers that slow up production by mixing people from different disciplines in the classes (Gray, 1988).

Also, technical training is mixed with management instruction to expose workers to the roles supervisors play in such areas as empowering subordinates to make their own decisions.

Ensuring the Quality of Training

Just as organizations are emphasizing the importance of quality of products and services to being competitive, training units must attend to the quality of training. While measurements and program evaluations are ways to track quality, principles of quality must be built into the design and delivery of training. Program developers must follow principles of good training design, such as thorough front-end analysis of the job behaviors and skills to be trained, clearly written materials, and training methods that capitalize on how adults learn best. Quality improvement teams of course developers, key instructors, subject matter experts, and instructional technologists can help in improving training processes. Quality councils of training managers and directors can act to oversee and guide the direction of these quality improvement efforts.

Staffing the Training Department. One way to enhance the quality of training is to ensure that the right people are responsible for training design and delivery. Corporate training organizations usually employ training professionals, such as technical writers and editors, educational consultants, instructional technologists, computer systems and software experts, and instructors. These individuals often have advanced degrees in training design and delivery, and they consider training to be a career. These human resource development experts must learn to utilize subject matter experts in other departments to define the training content.

Sometimes subject matter experts from other departments become long-term training professionals when they transfer to the training department. In other cases, managers from line departments transfer to the training department for a rotational assignment that may last several years. Many training departments need such subject matter experts because they have experience in the major operations of the business. These subject matter experts know the client's perspective—that is, they know the field's requirements.

This enhances the ability of the training department to meet its clients' needs and therefore enhances the credibility and likely acceptance of the training.

The organization needs to decide the right mix of training professionals and company experts to maintain the department's link with the rest of the corporation. In all cases, the department must be concerned about the professional development of its training staff. Transfers to the training world need to be trained in adult learning, instructional design, and other aspects of training. Also, of course, long-term training professionals need to maintain their skills.

Meeting Customer Needs. The key determinant of a high-quality product in any industry is whether customers feel their needs have been met—whether they believe they have received their money's worth. Training departments must think of the employees they train and of the departments as clients. Therefore, training methods must recognize employees' learning capabilities. Training content must recognize the skills and knowledge the departments want their employees to have.

Training departments must also think of other departments in the organization as suppliers of the content of training. These suppliers provide the necessary information for enhancing skills and knowledge through training as well as information on future job requirements to prepare employees to meet future needs. In many cases, the same departments are customers and suppliers. Training quality is enhanced by understanding and meeting customer expectations and by developing close working relationships with the suppliers of training content and new directions for training.

Changes in Work-Force Demographics

The composition of the work force in the United States is being reshaped, becoming more diverse in age, race, ethnic group, sex, and education. Consider the changes and implications for training reviewed in Exhibit 1.

Human resource development is essential. A program of early education in elementary schools and high schools will have to

Exhibit 1. The Changing Nature of the Work Force: Implications for Corporate Training.

Age of Work-Force Members

Data: The number of new work-force entrants aged 16 to 24 years will shrink by more than half a million each year between now and the year 2000. The prime working age group, ages 25 to 44, will be 73 percent of the labor force in the twenty-first century, compared to 67 percent in 1986. Twelve percent of the U.S. population was over age 65 in 1986. By 2000 this percentage will increase to 13.6 percent of the population and to 21 percent by 2030.

Implications: A smaller pool of job-ready workers will force corporations to intensify recruitment activities, enhance job offers, and focus more on retraining valuable employees. More emphasis will be placed on continuing education for older age groups. Limited upward movement in organizations may stimulate programs for lateral development—for example, company support for release time or leaves of absence for study and retraining.

Diversity in the Work Force

Data: Ninety-two percent of the U.S. labor-force growth between 1986 and 2000 will be women, minorities, and immigrants. This can be attributed to high birthrates among minority groups and some immigrant groups, the "baby bust" (lower birthrate) among whites, and women's increased participation in the labor force. By the year 2000, about 47 percent of the work force will be women, and 61 percent of all women will be at work; the corresponding figures for men are 53 percent and 75 percent.

Implications: There will be a larger pool of talent to draw on for all sectors of the work force. Since the labor force participation rate of women with children continues to climb, the need for more flexible benefit packages, including child care, increases dramatically. Also, many women postpone childbearing until they are established in their careers, suggesting the need for flexible work schedules, compressed thirty-two-hour work weeks, job sharing, work-at-home arrangements, and part-time permanent employment. Training at home may become a way for men and women to increase their skills while they stay at home to care for young children.

Blacks in the Work Force

Data: Blacks are the largest minority in the U.S., making up 11.9 percent of the population in 1986, which should grow to a projected 12.7 percent in 2000. Blacks will account for 18 percent of the labor-force growth between 1986 and 2000. The education level for blacks is increasing. In 1985 the median years of school completed by blacks was 12.3, compared to 6.9 in 1950.

Exhibit 1. The Changing Nature of the Work Force: Implications for Corporate Training, Cont'd.

Implications: Blacks will become the largest minority group in the work force and will represent the largest number of single mothers. Training will be needed to ensure that blacks have the career opportunities available to whites. Equal employment opportunity becomes more than a social concern; it is a business necessity if job openings at entry and higher levels are to be filled by the people who are available—that is, young blacks and other minorities.

Hispanics in the Work Force

Data: In 1986 Hispanics represented 7 percent of the labor force; in 2000 it is projected to be 10 percent. Hispanics will account for 26 percent of the growth in the labor force between 1986 and 2000. Hispanics are younger than the rest of the U.S. population. In 1987 the median age was 25.1 years for Hispanics, compared to 32 years for non-Hispanics. The Hispanic high school graduation rate increased 38 percent between 1975 and 1982, while their college enrollment dropped 16 percent.

Implications: Hispanics will be a significant pool of potential candidates for entry-level jobs in the twenty-first century. However, corporations may have to provide the resources for basic skills education, remedial training, and development of needed job skills. In addition to helping Hispanics attain a solid foundation of skills and the motivation to learn, corporations will have to provide support and rewards for Hispanics to obtain college-level education. Hispanics will be a valuable resource as U.S. business expands to the Latin American countries and other global markets influenced by Spanish tradition. In addition, Hispanic cultural and language skills will be common in the workplace, suggesting the need for training to help all workers appreciate cultural differences in a more heterogeneous work force.

Asians in the Work Force

Data: Part of the increasingly diverse U.S. population, Asians include Chinese, Asian Indian, Japanese, Korean, Filipino, and Vietnamese. The U.S. Asian population grew by 142 percent between 1970 and 1980. By 2000 the number of Asian citizens in the U.S. will double to more than 8 million, becoming as large a minority by 2050 as Hispanics are now. Asians are generally highly educated. For instance, Asians comprise over 26 percent of the student body at the University of California at Berkeley, even though they total less than 4 percent of the population in California.

Implications: As with Hispanics, the increasingly global economy suggests the importance of understanding Asian cultures and languages. Asians in the United States are a critical resource that can provide firms with a competitive edge. Asians' commitment to education should continue to increase their job status and organizational level. Cultural awareness

Exhibit 1. The Changing Nature of the Work Force: Implications for Corporate Training, Cont'd.

training will be key in helping all employees understand the diversity in the workplace and in providing equal opportunities for all groups to achieve higher organizational levels. Otherwise, stereotypical thinking, especially with regard to the differences in Asian management style (which is more low key and less direct than American management), could limit U.S. corporations' full utilization of the resources Asians bring to the work force.

Educational Trends

Data: College students are in an increasingly older age group, as more minorities, immigrants, and women attend college. The number of college students aged 18 to 24 is projected to decline from 7.4 million in 1982 to 5.9 million in 1992, a 20 percent decline. 1985 was the first year women earned more college degrees than men. Almost 30 percent of Asian immigrants to the United States arrive with four years of college. The United States is a major exporter of education, in some cases educating foreign nationals on temporary visas at a higher rate than U.S. citizens. For instance, foreign citizens are earning 47 percent of the Ph.D.s in engineering, compared to 3 percent for immigrants and 42.5 percent for other U.S. citizens.

Implications: The U.S. higher education system is essentially educating future employees of foreign firms that will compete on a global basis with U.S. firms. Given a shrinking pool of entry-level workers and given the lower educational levels of some minority groups, especially Hispanics and blacks, corporations will need to work more closely with state and local boards of education to expand early learning programs and to upgrade programs through high school. In addition, corporations will be the major source of remedial education and skill development for immigrants and minorities already in the work force. Many people needed for entry-level jobs will come to the work force without the necessary skills. Their opportunities for these positions, as well as for more advanced positions throughout their careers, will depend on the education provided by the organization.

Sources: Data are based on 1987 figures from the U.S. Census and the U.S. Bureau of Labor Statistics and on material prepared by AT&T's Human Resource Forecasting and Planning Division.

be supported if young people are to bring needed skills to entry-level jobs. Recognizing this, Xerox Corporation established an independent, nonprofit research center to study how children learn.

In some cases, remedial education will be needed for current workers who do not have the basic skills required for today's jobs. Also, as technologies change, skills will have to be upgraded. Otherwise, there will be many unqualified people left unemployed even though there are many job openings. This situation already exists in many U.S. cities. In Buffalo, New York, for example, "thousands of unskilled, older, blue-collar workers have been plunged into the despairing category of permanently unemployed; they have stopped seeking work and thus have even dropped out of the unemployment statistics. Meanwhile, 'yuppies' are being imported to beef up some middle-management ranks" (Sebastian, 1988, p. 1). Factories that are hiring cannot find enough highly skilled blue-collar workers. As this situation continues, there will be a negative effect on the productivity of U.S. industry.

The diversity of the work force suggests the need for a diversity of training vehicles. For example, training may need to be provided in different languages. Corporate training will have to be broader. Recruiters will find that potential new employees do not have the basic and specific skills needed to perform entry-level jobs, and the corporation will have to provide this training. Successful completion of training may become a screening device prior to hiring. Consequently, the organization may end up investing in educating people who will never work for the organization.

As indicated in Exhibit 1, the increasing number of working parents, particularly single mothers, suggests the need for alternative work schedules and patterns, such as work at home, part-time work, and flexible work schedule alternatives. New training technologies, such as video- and computer-based training, will allow people to learn at home while taking care of their children.

Adult Learning

Employee training will be shaped by the conditions under which adults are most receptive to new learning. For instance, we know that older people learn differently than younger people. Older learners often have trouble with initial learning and subsequent recall when learning tasks are fast paced, complex, or unusual. Consequently, self-pacing and reiteration are ways to improve older adults' acquisition of new concepts (Cross, 1981). Individuals in their fifties have the same ability to learn as people in their twenties if the pace of learning is controlled and if hearing and visual deficiencies are corrected (Sonnenfeld and Ingols, 1986).

There are other learning differences between older and younger adults. Older adults typically do not perform as well on measures of formal reasoning ability. "Older adults tend to personalize such tasks, to analyze the possible ways in which a question might be interpreted, to consider affective dimensions that might be involved in a problem solution, and to suggest that several answers might be possible" (Datan, Rodeheaver, and Hughes, 1987, p. 167). Also, older adults tend to rely on intuitive and personal modes of thinking, often going beyond the information given to raise and analyze possible ambiguities and to essentially inject subjectivity into the reasoning process. This subjectivity may be viewed by educators (and corporations sponsoring retraining) as a barrier to effective learning. However, such a result may be viewed positively, as a richer, more thoughtful analytical process that could be as effective if not more so in acquiring and applying new information and concepts. The key to successful adult learning may be in designing activities, materials, procedures, and environmental conditions conducive to adult learning.

In addition, adults' more subjective approach to learning positively affects their motivation to learn. Adults have been found to be more highly motivated to learn than children and teenagers (Knowles, 1978). Adults are often more accustomed to thinking of learning as occurring in both informal and formal settings, and therefore are capable of bringing a rich variety of experiences to classroom material. While adult learners are likely to be motivated to learn, when returning to the classroom after many years they are likely to lack self-confidence and to experience much anxiety. Thus, knowledge of the adult learner suggests the type of learning environment and training methods that will maximize learning. For instance, one list of adult learning requirements (adapted from "Adult Learning Needs," 1988) indicates that adults need to

- Hear expectations and have an opportunity to express their own expectations
- Use prior experiences in learning new endeavors

- Receive feedback about their performance, principally by assessing their own learning accomplishments
- Have a relaxing environment free from anxiety
- Have the opportunity to use what they learn soon after they learn it
- Be in control of their own learning and have a sense of self-initiation
- Be aware of the objectives of instruction
- Participate in their own learning (hands-on experiences rather than being talked to)
- See the value of the information, knowledge, or skills they are learning
- Have the opportunity to work at their own speed
- Gain a sense of satisfaction and achievement from the learning.

As we will see in the next chapter, such principles of adult learning shape the design of training programs and also help explain why new educational technologies are particularly valuable. Computer-based training, for example, provides realistic simulations of on-the-job experiences, providing hands-on practice without the risks involved in actual on-the-job learning. Such techniques allow control by the learner and provide feedback on performance.

The above list of adult learning principles is based on the mainstream U.S. learner and would probably require modification for adult learners in other countries or for adult learners in the United States from other countries or cultures. As Exhibit 1 shows, there will be increasing numbers of Hispanics and Asians in the work force by the year 2000, and research will be needed on the implications of these changes in the work force for developing effective learning principles.

Toward a Continuous Learning Environment

Corporate-sponsored training has shifted from preparing entry-level workers to ensuring that all employees have the skills needed to maintain the company's competitiveness. Thus, investment in employees' education has become a strategic tool (Mandel,

1987; Work in America Institute, 1985). Also, corporations are recognizing that management training must extend beyond a select high-potential group to all managers to enhance their capabilities and preparedness for change, uncertainty, and risk.

Technological Change. Rapid advancements in technology have led to substantial organizational changes in many industries, which have affected how work is done as well as the output of work. As new technology has spread across the globe, competition has increased, with a renewed focus on the use of technology to enhance product quality and to increase a firm's competitive advantage. There has been a shift in management from concern solely about the end product (sales, inventory, and productivity) to concern about the source of quality and service (design of the product and the processes that result in the product or service) (Deming, 1987). Consider the following examples of the impact of changes in technology and the management of new technologies on job requirements and expected employee behavior:

1. Computer-aided design and "just-in-time" manufacturing have integrated automation and customization to meet more flexibly customer needs (Piore and Sabel, 1984). Such advances have changed job descriptions and skill requirements.
2. Computerized remote monitoring centers of operating systems, such as a telephone network, have lowered the skill requirements for on-site technicians and changed reporting relationships, with maintenance employees taking instructions from machines rather than supervisors (London and MacDuffie, 1987).
3. Electronic mail has changed the way people communicate by increasing the speed of communications and the number of possible contacts.
4. In selling electronic components, such as transistors, the focus in the past was on components as interchangeable commodities sold to manufacturers' purchasing agents. It is now considered an important part of such selling to develop partnership relationships with manufacturers' systems designers—for example, to demonstrate how a computer chip can be customized for use in a customer's high-technology products.

5. Branch sales managers who know their product line and how to sell now must learn sophisticated financial control and human resource management techniques in order to manage their branches as entrepreneurs/executives of a business might.
6. Technicians versed in product installation and repair must now develop project management skills in order to be part of sales teams and to work in partnership with customers.
7. Technicians who were experts in troubleshooting problems with electromechanical equipment and doing hands-on repair may have to learn software diagnosis and systems analysis in order to maintain computer-driven, solid-state machines.
8. The increased reliance on self-managing work teams requires workers and supervisors to develop new problem-solving and team-development skills (Manz and Sims, 1987).

Ten years ago technological change could be accomplished by hiring people with the required educational background and retiring long-time workers or moving them into less skilled employment. Retraining programs were thought to be expensive and to have little chance for success, given the amount of new knowledge and different skills required. Now the focus is moving toward ensuring that employees are constantly kept abreast of new developments in their fields or are retrained for new positions.

Retraining is becoming mandatory because technology is evolving continuously. Engineers must keep pace with their fields. They must be up to date about innovations in product design and be able to educate shop-floor technicians and operators in new production processes. The quality circle movement, which involves employees in improving productivity, requires employees be educated in group process skills such as conflict resolution and negotiation. Team manufacturing approaches require workers to increase their skills so team members can interchange jobs, thereby allowing flexible work schedules and maximum group efficiency. Some companies compensate workers not only for their performance but also for learning new skills that enhance their value to the firm.

Employment Security. The term *job security* is being replaced by *employment security*. Job security implies the ability to retain one's current job, whereas employment security implies that while an employee may remain employed at the same company, retraining and movement into a different job may be necessary.

The difference between job security and employment security can also be understood in the context of the *psychological contract.* This term refers to the implicit understanding between the company and the individual about what each expects of the other. In the past, especially in large organizations, the unstated psychological contract was that one could count on having a job as long as one showed up for work, performed satisfactorily, and did nothing dishonest. The new psychological contract that has evolved in American companies in recent years is one in which the employee, in return for giving top performance, can expect continued opportunities for challenge, growth, and development (Drake, Beam, Morin, Inc., 1987).

Employment security is tied to retraining, or continuous learning. While learning new skills is not a guarantee of continued employment, it becomes necessary if continued employment is to be a viable option.

At Motorola, retraining is considered part of the job and, in fact, is related to job security. While Motorola does not have a full employment policy, there is an unspoken agreement that a long and productive work history contributes to job security. In return, the company expects that employees will keep their skills current and remain productive (C. Lee, 1986). Offering retraining instead of laying off workers is an investment in the future for both the company and the workers. Advantages to the employee include an enhanced probability of continued employment with the same employer, or if that is not possible over the long term, a better chance, by having a new skill repertoire, of finding suitable employment elsewhere. Advantages to the company include lower hiring costs, the possibility of keeping employees who have a proven track record, and renewed dedication to the company.

The Work in America Institute has been carrying on a long-term study on "Training for New Technology." The fourth of five reports, entitled "The Continuous Learning/Employment Security Connection," articulates how training/retraining benefits both employer and employees (Work in America Institute, 1987; see also

Rosow and Zager, 1988, and Casner-Lotto and Associates, 1988, for publications of the Work in America Institute policy analysis and case studies). The report suggests the following conclusions, which apply to large and small companies:

- A stable, motivated, well-trained work force is critical to the long-term prosperity of an enterprise.
- Long-term prosperity enables the enterprise to fulfill its commitment to employment security.
- Employment security motivates employees to identify with the goals of the enterprise and to learn continuously.
- Continuous learning appeals to one of the most powerful drives of employees: the desire for self-development, growth, and career advancement.
- Continuous learning is feasible because employees have unexplored capacities for education, and educated employees are capable of a surprising amount of adaptation to the changing needs of the enterprise.
- Thus the continuous learning/employment security connection binds individual and company goals in a strong, resilient way.

Summary

This chapter has described the importance of employee training and education in organizations. Learning is a key to continued viability in the face of changing markets, economic conditions, demographics, and organizational structures. Also, learning stimulates individual growth and development.

Employee education may be viewed as a part of the firm's human resource system that ensures that people with the right skills are available when needed. Corporate education should be guided by adult learning principles suggesting the form and methods for training, such as practical, hands-on experiences that are clearly relevant to the needs of the organization. Finally, technological change and employees' desire for employment security create the need for a continuous learning environment—one where learning and professional growth are viewed as investments in the future and the focus is the long term, rather than meeting immediate needs.

Policy Opportunities and Recommendations

1. Training organizations should establish a clear mission and set of values. Training goals may be to support business objectives, enhance the quality of the firm's products and services, and prepare employees to make a contribution to the organization today and in the future.

2. A major goal should be customer satisfaction. End-user customers are affected by the ability of the organization's employees to deliver its products and services. For example, an installation and maintenance organization never wants to send an untrained technician to a customer's premises to repair a product. Employees are the internal customers of the training organization, and their satisfaction with training is important. They must view training as applicable to their jobs and hopefully as stimulating, interesting, and consistent with their learning abilities.

3. To ensure customer satisfaction, the training department's business plans should be made jointly with the organization's overall business plans for each year. In addition, a communications plan is needed to ensure that all training staff and clients are aware of the training department's mission and values. Goal setting and appraisals should be guided by these missions and values, and customer reactions to the training should be monitored to ensure that the managers are accomplishing their stated objectives and "walking like they talk."

4. The training department should view the other departments in the organization as customers and as suppliers. Other departments are clients or customers in that they use, and usually pay for, the training programs. In this sense, training departments should understand their customers' expectations and evaluate performance based on meeting these expectations. Other departments are suppliers in that they guide the training department's activities. Line and staff managers who comprise training boards of directors, curriculum review committees, and subject matter experts are suppliers of the training direction and content. In this sense, the training department should work closely with other departments to ensure that training programs contain the required content and are delivered in a way that enhances adult learning.

5. Training managers should be empowered by the organization to assess needs and design high-quality, cost-effective educational tools and programs. Top executives should consult with training directors along with other human resource professionals about required skills and employee capabilities. Training directors should maintain a close relationship with the functional departments served by the training department. They should know the business of the organization and be in a position to recommend needed training and other human resource investments.

6. Training should be viewed as a socialization agent that helps people understand and make a commitment to the organization's goals. Training can be used to explain organizational strategies, such as business decisions and what employees need to do to be successful in the organization. Moreover, training staff should be role models of behavior that is desired and rewarded in the organization.

7. Training should be viewed as an intervention for organizational change. For example, it can change managers' style from autocratic to participative. It can help two organizations merge by teaching group problem solving and providing team-building experiences. It can help groups and individuals understand the meaning of quality, including ways to understand the viewpoint of customers and suppliers and ways to work together to improve productivity and track its progress. Training is a flexible mechanism for change because it can be adapted as organizational requirements change.

8. Training is the heart of a continuous learning environment. Employee development is a function of work experiences and working relationships that challenge individuals and give them a chance to learn and demonstrate new skills. Training programs provide a nonthreatening environment for dealing with the discomfort of change and experimenting with new behaviors.

The decision on what training methods to use will depend on the purpose of the training, the time available for development and delivery, the resources available, and the effectiveness of the vehicle for encouraging adult learning. The next chapter offers an in-depth review of training methods by examining types of learning and their effectiveness for enhancing employees' receptivity to learning.

2

The Diversity of What and How Employees Learn

When we think of employee training, we often think of short courses, perhaps lasting one or more days up to a week. These courses may be offered in a corporate training center, at a college, or at a hotel conference center. They may be run by an internal training department or purchased from and run by a vendor outside the organization. The training may include some precourse reading, and there may be a follow-up test. The instructor may use videotapes, role-play exercises, or case examples to make points more vivid and give students the chance to practice and visualize the application of new skills or knowledge.

Development experiences are broader than training, encompassing on-the-job learning, special assignments, and university courses and degree programs, for a few examples. In addition, assessment centers and performance feedback sessions, which set the direction for future development, may be growth experiences themselves.

The purpose of this chapter is to provide training managers with a foundation for understanding the application of adult learning principles in the design and selection of training and development programs. Training managers should understand how the programs they manage influence individual and organizational change and how such change affects training and education requirements. Given the diversity of training methods available, training managers should understand how to analyze and evaluate the extent to which these methods apply to basic adult learning principles.

The chapter begins by describing the degree of change people experience in different types of training and development programs. Learning is viewed as a transition, and four transition stages are identified and used to characterize the varying degrees of change and different types of training. Different training techniques present different opportunities for trainers to apply adult learning principles. Given this as background, the chapter reviews a wide selection of more specific learning methods, with a focus on technologically based learning tools and other alternatives to instructor-led classroom training. Ways to determine when these different types of techniques are appropriate are considered. Policy issues and recommendations for the selection and design of learning techniques are raised.

Degree of Change and Learning Methods

The changes resulting from training range along a continuum from incremental change to frame-breaking change (applying the terms used by Kanter, 1983, and Tushman, Newman, and Romanelli, 1985, to describe the relationship between organizational change and individual reactions). This continuum highlights thinking about learning as a change process. The varying degrees of change along the continuum depend on the speed of change, the unfamiliarity of conditions and environment, the cost, and the risk. These characteristics can be used to describe the amount of change that takes place in various learning methods. A learning method may impose different degrees of change at different times.

Frame-Breaking Change

Frame-breaking change is rapid change, involving significant differences from prior or current conditions (for example, different ability and task requirements or new language or jargon). The environment is new and unfamiliar, having different people, facilities, work procedures and methods, and so on. Also, frame-breaking change is costly to individuals in that it absorbs energy, emotion, and financial resources. Such change entails real and perceived risk in that the new learning is difficult, and there is a high payoff if the change is successful and a high cost if it is unsuccessful.

An example of frame-breaking career change would be a sudden job change, such as a move from a laboratory R&D position to a sales support assignment requiring customer contact. Both assignments may use the same knowledge base, but the lab job entails envisioning and creating near-perfect or technically elegant products and procedures, while the sales support job requires customer responsiveness, a practical and applied orientation, and a concern for time and budget constraints. Another frame-breaking transition would be a move to a job in a foreign country given little or no advanced preparation, particularly if the new culture is unfamiliar. Other frame-breaking job moves include layoff, retirement, career change, and transferring from a line supervisory position to a staff functional expert position.

The learning method involved in transition contributes to the degree of change. One frame-breaking learning method is the "make-it-or-break-it" approach to learning in which the individual is thrust into the new position, with little or no prior training or preparation. Being successful in such a new assignment requires rapid learning. For instance, the executive who has managed a successful ongoing operation suddenly may be assigned to start a new organization. This is a make-it-or-break-it transition with high payoff for success, severe negative consequences for failure, and a relatively short time frame in which to be successful. However, supervisors and co-workers can be trained to provide a structured learning environment without make-it-or-break-it risks and anxiety. This structured approach becomes what is generally referred to as on-the-job training.

Shock learning is another frame-breaking learning method. This method may be used in a classroom or laboratory simulation but imposes strong demands on an individual. As an example of shock learning, consider a race awareness workshop that assigns people to one of two groups, the "haves" or the "have-nots." The "haves" are instructed to deride and berate the "have-nots," and the participants are intended to experience, or at least observe, what it is like to be a minority. The experience is likely to be shocking, making people feel uncomfortable as they recognize the effects of negative behaviors and consider more desirable behaviors. The longevity of the effects depends on reinforcements in the job environment and the individual's ability and willingness to incorporate the learning into his or her self-concept. Certainly, there are many race awareness programs that are effective without using shock learning. In fact, the shock component can be a barrier to learning new behavior.

Experiencing failure may be another frame-breaking change that jolts people into addressing dysfunctional aspects of their behavior that they have ignored or were unwilling to change. This assessment could occur after a negative performance appraisal or being fired. As suggested above, shock may be a barrier to learning. People may attribute the negative experience to factors beyond their control and in the future may behave in ways that prevent failure but do not necessarily lead to success.

In general, learning should not be a high-risk activity and should include the opportunity to make errors without severe penalty. Failures should be analyzed and corrected. In a classroom or simulation, learners do not have to bear the long-term impact of failure, although they should recognize the risks of not learning or of not applying new experiences on the job.

Incremental Change

Incremental change is more typical of training than of retraining. Training implies learning ways to improve performance in the current position, as opposed to retraining, which reeducates for career change. Incremental change is slow, matched to prior or current conditions, and requires fewer resources. Resource requirements may be spread out over time, thereby avoiding resource drain. Since there is little to lose, incremental change involves low risk.

Examples of incremental adult learning include acquiring

new behavior and attitudes (such as a more participative management style); a greater concern for subordinates' needs, interests, and ambitions; and an increased tolerance for individual differences. Incremental change may occur as a person acquires new knowledge. A job transfer may be an incremental change, since differences in responsibilities and requirements may become evident slowly. Another incremental change may be the shift from a tactical, day-to-day management orientation to a more strategic, long-range planning orientation.

Several learning methods apply incremental adult learning. Trial-and-error learning refers to behavioral exercises or simulations that are nonevaluative (not used as a basis for making decisions about the participants). In this sense, they are unlike make-it-or-break-it or shock learning in which the learner is required to be successful or else suffer negative consequences. A simulation or laboratory experience involving trial-and-error learning may last several hours or days, be realistic in role assignments, and involve the interaction of a number of people (Stumpf, 1988; McCall and Lombardo, 1978). Trial-and-error learning provides opportunities to experiment with new behaviors in a relatively nonthreatening setting. Feedback and follow-up development are aimed at long-term behavioral change (Graddick, 1988).

Trial-and-error learning may be built into on-the-job learning experiences in which the learner is given time to try out the methods or behaviors taught without the risk of failure. An apprenticeship program would be an example of a long-term trial-and-error experience in which the student learns by observation, instruction, and practice on progressively difficult tasks while at the same time doing productive work for the employer. However, on-the-job trial-and-error learning can also be fairly brief. For instance, in a customer service job, a new employee may listen in on customer calls answered by experienced co-workers. Students and co-workers may role play calls. Then the student may take some actual customer calls while experienced co-workers listen and assist the student in finding information and answering difficult questions.

Behavior modeling is another form of trial-and-error training. Students learn behavior principles, have an opportunity to role play, receive feedback, and then try the new behavior on the job, with trained supervisors observing and rewarding the desired responses (Goldstein and Sorcher, 1974).

Another learning method that applies to incremental change is inferential learning. This method requires the student to infer the meaning and application value of the information or knowledge learned and includes instructor-led classroom training, computer training, and other technology-based training. With this method, there is little time for practicing new behaviors and little direct transfer. This type of learning also includes observing positive and negative role models and deciding which behaviors to copy and which to avoid based on the consequences that befall the role model. Realistic job previews, which help prospective employees anticipate a job experience and develop realistic expectations, are also examples of inferential learning (Wanous, 1980).

Learning to learn is another form of incremental training. Here the focus is on teaching learning methods and helping participants understand the skills and abilities needed for development (Saljo, 1979). Study habits, writing skills, oral communication, and the value of continuous learning may be highlighted, and self-assessment procedures and suggestions for acquiring new knowledge may be offered. The goal is to establish a mind-set and, hopefully, the habit of continuous learning. Other learning-to-learn experiences include career planning workshops, which encourage participants to evaluate their career interests, set career goals, establish a training agenda, and seek job movement or career change.

A training regimen may combine several learning approaches, such as trial-and-error experiences plus inferential learning, with insight about ways to learn. For instance, a career planning workshop may help people learn about how much they value learning, how they approach learning, and new ways to learn. It might also provide some trial-and-error experiences by interviewing and giving feedback to fellow participants.

Transition Processes

Understanding the transition process that takes place during learning can help in comparing frame-breaking and incremental changes and in predicting their effects on behavior and learning outcomes. In a study of the learning process, Taylor (1986) developed a model of adult learning focused on gaining self-awareness and redirection. The model combines approaches from other models of change processes such as Lewin's concepts of unfreezing and freezing (Lewin, 1951). Taylor's model is also similar to models of learning progress such as Kolb's four-step learning cycle of concrete experience, reflective observation, abstract conceptualization, and active experimentation, which applies principally to experiential learning (what I have termed trial-and-error and inferential learning) (Kolb and Baker, n.d.; Kolb, 1976).

Taylor's approach is especially valuable to understanding retraining and career changes, which are integrally tied to a person's self-concept and understanding of his or her capabilities. The model describes critical points in the learning experience and outlines transitions between phases. The transition phases suggest what an individual must do to move from one phase to the next. Taylor recognized that people progress at different rates through the learning experience, and by using the length of the transition phases, she allowed for tracking and diagnosing of the learning progress. The model may be represented as a sequence of events forming a cycle from one state of equilibrium to another.

Equilibrium is the current steady state. People enter the learning process by observing and fitting their experiences into existing conceptual categories (Mervis and Rosch, 1981). Disorientation, the initial transition phase, is a period of intense confusion accompanied by a crisis of confidence or withdrawal from other people. Disorientation arises from the recognition of a major discrepancy between expectations and experience.

Exploration is the phase following disorientation. The phase begins with one's relaxing about an unresolved issue and entails gathering insights and evidence of self-effectiveness. This process is intuitive, collaborative, and open ended and can take different directions, depending on the sources of input and the results. A person moves from disorientation to exploration by, for example, expressing the problem without attributing blame to oneself or others.

The reorientation phase occurs when there is major insight into a new approach to the learning or career change task. This happens as one examines one's abilities, needs, interests, and opportunities for reward. Reorientation results in reequilibrium, during which the individual tests the new understanding with others. This leads to a new perspective, which is elaborated, refined, and applied to form a revised self-concept and a new sense of content.

Degree of Change and the Transition Process

The degree of change involved in retraining will affect the transition process. Frame-breaking change will require a greater disconfirmation and stronger disorientation than will incremental change. However, frame-breaking change does not allow sufficient time to work through these early transition phases. Also, with frame-breaking change, there is little time to discuss and reflect on the change, explore its implications, and experiment with new behaviors. Reorientation must occur quickly, or the individual will likely fail.

Incremental change makes for a smoother transition process. One drawback is that disconfirmation may be less obvious and thus more easily avoided; as a consequence, the training may be less effective. However, incremental change allows time for reflection and exploration of the effects of new behaviors. Nonetheless, there is less pressure to change, especially if there is little encouragement and reward in the job setting for the new behavior.

Adult Learning Principles and Learning Methods

Learning methods differ in how adult learning principles, such as those described in Chapter One, are applied. Frame-breaking change does not offer a positive learning environment. For instance, with make-it-or-break-it learning and shock learning, there is little time to formulate one's own expectations or to hear others' expectations. Objectives are likely to be uncertain or very general (for instance, "do your best" or "make this into a success"). Prior experiences are not likely to be applicable. Feedback may be delayed but is strong and direct when it occurs. There is little or no opportunity to practice newly learned skills. The individual has little sense of self-control or self-initiation. This environment provokes anxiety, for the demands of the situation prevent individuals from learning at their own speed. If the student is successful, the rewards can be high, but the probability of success is fairly low.

Incremental learning situations (trial-and-error simulations or on-the-job learning, inferential or classroom learning, and workshops on learning to learn) provide time to clarify expectations. The learning situation is likely to be similar to prior experiences, and the student has an opportunity to try out previously successful behaviors. There is relatively low anxiety, since the student can practice with little or no risk and feels in control. Flexibility in the training delivery allows students to learn at their own pace. Simulations and role plays offer hands-on experience. The ultimate value of this learning depends on opportunity for application, feedback, and reward on the job, including higher pay for the increased skills and hence increased value of the employee for the organization.

New Employee Orientation and Training

Learning a new job can be a frame-breaking change, especially if it is one's first job right after college or high school or a new job in which one hopes to make extra money after retirement. Training methods can allow for incremental learning while helping new employees experience the realism of the job and ensuring that they are productive as quickly as possible.

A combination of incremental learning methods applies during the socialization process, which occurs during the period of three to five years after a person starts to work for a new organization (Buchanan, 1974). Socialization methods include apprenticeships, mentor programs, exposure to corporate folklore, and orientation programs describing organizational procedures (Van Maanen, 1976).

The Disney World Experience. As an example, consider the Disney Corporation's operation of Walt Disney World in Orlando, Florida. (The following information was obtained from Rick Johnson of the Disney organization, personal communication, June 15, 1988.) The organization employs over 21,000 people plus an additional 2,000 during the summer in a total of over 1,100 different jobs. There are about 2,700 salaried professionals and 1,300 supervisors. The rest are hourly employees in the various divisions of the company (parks, resorts, and administration). The annual turnover rate is about 25 percent, and there is a promotion-from-within policy; everyone starts in a low-level position, even college graduates who are planning a career in resort management. Positions in the "Magic Kingdom" are called "roles" to stress the importance of the position all employees, from streetsweepers to the Disney characters, play in entertaining customers, who are called "guests." (The recruitment and hiring process is called "casting.")

Disney must attract many hourly workers, who must commute thirty minutes or longer to the park to do a job that for many is similar, if not identical, to what they could do at their neighborhood fast-food restaurant. Most of the jobs are fairly simple and repetitive, although rotation of assignments during the course of the day helps maintain employees' productivity and interest. Other "draws" are that Disney pays a slightly higher wage than other organizations in the area and that the company has the reputation for caring about its employees.

The first day of employment at Disney World involves attendance at the training center's program, which is called "Disney Traditions I." This one-day program describes the history of the organization, doing so with the pride, enthusiasm, and emotion the company hopes to generate in the recruits. The session emphasizes the four key values of the Disney culture: safety, courtesy, show, and efficiency. All employees are taught that they have a role in serving the guests and observe how employees perform this role during a tour of the facilities. The second day the program, "Disney Traditions II," outlines the support systems, policies, and procedures in the company, with an emphasis on safety and benefits.

The third day begins on-the-job, buddy training. The recruit is assigned to an experienced co-worker who, during the next two days to two weeks, exposes the new employee to a series of experiences specific to the role. These peer trainers are role models and partner with supervisors to provide the coaching, feedback, and reinforcement needed to help the neophyte learn the job and acquire the Disney spirit.

Disney has customer service down to a science. The company knows that the average guest comes in contact with seventy-three employees during a day's visit. Each employee must be attuned to meeting the guest's needs. The selection process identifies people who are likely to be responsive to Disney's expectations. The indoctrination training uses incremental steps to ensure that the goals of the organization are clear. Employees are made to feel a welcomed part of the group—almost a family. There are rules and regulations and clear expectations. Conforming to these rules leads not only to continued employment but also to the feelings of comraderie, belonging, and pride in a common identity. The on-the-job training reinforces the socialization to the corporate culture, generates a bond between new and experienced employees, and provides a chance to implement new behaviors in the job setting.

The Disney training prompts a smooth transition. The feeling of disorientation that accompanies a new experience is lessened because Disney training provides a clear focus and time for exploration and reorientation. The on-the-job learning helps the employee establish a new feeling of equilibrium, a feeling of belonging—"I enjoy being here and am proud to work for Disney." Of course this approach does not work for everyone, but the training process is aimed at enhancing the success rate while ensuring that new employees meet the company's objectives.

Awareness Training: Dealing with Diversity in the Workplace

Another important area is education to enhance employees' awareness of different cultural groups. For some new entrants to the work force, this exposure to differences is a frame-breaking change. However, sensitizing people to the diverse needs and values of those from different cultures and enhancing people's effectiveness in working together is often a slow, incremental process. Since new entrants to the work force will be primarily women, minorities, and immigrants, as mentioned in Chapter One, there will be a substantial diversity not only in talent but also in language, traditions, and behavioral expectations. This diversity is increasing just as corporations are becoming aware of the need for more collaborative behavior within and between departments. Corporations need ways to enhance the input of all employees and their unique contributions to organizational goals. If participation is going to work, differences in employees must be valued, not ignored or discouraged.

Awareness training in the form of structured classroom experiences can improve interpersonal effectiveness in multicultural work environments. Awareness training helps people consider their differences and understand their stereotypes and biases and how these influence their behavior toward others. The training might require participants to list descriptions of women, blacks, and other racial, ethnic, and sex groups. Videotapes may help people see how stereotypes prevail in our society, for instance, in television commercials. Role plays of boss-subordinate relationships or work-group situations might help people understand what it feels like to be part of different minority groups.

Of course, such awareness training alone will not be sufficient to overcome bias and unequal treatment. Organizations need to strengthen their equal employment opportunity programs. Managers should be rewarded for developing minorities, especially when such development leads to the minority employees' promotion to more responsible positions. Women, Asians, blacks, Hispanics, and other minorities should be advanced to take advantage of their increasing skills, experience, and accomplishments. In addition, work schedules and requirements should be more flexible to accommodate the needs of working parents (especially single parents) and of employees who care for elderly or disabled parents.

Team Training

For a number of jobs, people must work together as a coordinated team. Members of the team need to understand each other's roles and even be able to perform each other's jobs, as for example, do the members of flight crews, marketing account teams, manufacturing teams (such as those at Volvo), and nuclear power plant maintenance crews. For instance, at one nuclear power plant, a maintenance training program combines classroom discussion with laboratory exercises that involve hands-on experience with maintenance procedures using a full-scale mockup of the equipment (Stone, Lavender, and McAnulty, 1989). A class consists of a six-person maintenance team with two observers for quality assurance. Simulations elicit trainee involvement and enhance team building through mutual interaction. Team members rotate through the various positions during the exercise to ensure that they have a full understanding of all the tasks. The instructor initiates group discussion to define the responsibilities of interfacing team members and to review how they work with employees in other groups. The goal is for the group to become a precision team that is well prepared for routine operations and for emergencies. Team training is not a one-time event. The exercise is likely to be repeated many times, with a number of variations, so that the team will be able to respond to any situation as it arises.

Long-Term Incremental Learning

Many other learning situations involve a mix of training methods to ensure effective incremental learning and smooth transition to the job. Some training is more long term. For instance, summer internships for college students and university work-study programs are ways learners gain realistic training. Advantages for employers are that they obtain inexpensive labor and have a chance to observe, test, and ultimately select the best students for full-time employment.

Some jobs require the company to provide substantial training prior to the new employee's first day on the job. For instance, in the data systems and software programming field, a job may require the newcomer to learn the company's systems and methods and entail several months of training. Obviously, there is a risk, since the employee may not pass the training or may not enjoy or do well at the job after training. Nevertheless, the training provides a breaking-in period that improves the likelihood of successful reorientation and reequilibrium. The employee who spends the time and exerts energy in training is likely, by such personal investment, to feel a commitment to the job and the company.

Alternative Training Methods

The purpose of training should determine the method used. Sometimes, however, an organization may have no choice. Shock learning or make-it-or-break-it learning may be necessary if a rapid transition is required. An experienced manager may be needed immediately in a foreign country and may not have the time to learn the new language and culture. When most people think of training or education, they think of time and energy spent in intensive long-term classroom instruction involving textbooks and exams. However, there are many other learning methods. While some rely on traditional instructor-led training, most use a combination of methods, including sophisticated technology, to apply adult learning principles to promote rapid learning and a successful transition to a new job or environment.

There are a variety of instructional methods a company may use. *Training Magazine*'s recent survey of organizations with more than one hundred employees (referred to in Chapter One) found that 83 percent of the organizations use lectures and 71 percent use one-on-one instruction. Sixty percent report using role plays, and 49 percent use games and simulations. Videotapes are a popular training method (used by 87 percent of the organizations). Other techniques involve case studies, films, and noncomputerized self-study programs (48 percent, 41 percent, and 31 percent, respectively, as reported by the organizations) (Gordon, 1988). Computer-based training is used by 39 percent of the organizations (Feuer, 1988). Other less used techniques are teleconferencing and computer conferencing (10 percent and 4 percent, respectively).

The rest of this chapter describes some of these techniques and reviews methods for enhanced learning performance, job aids, and structured on-the-job training. Advanced technology training methods—such as computer-based training, interactive video disk, teletraining, teleconferencing, closed-circuit television, videotaped presentations, and learning laboratories—and how they relate to principles of adult learning and ways to introduce advanced technology and self-paced learning into the organization are also discussed.

Methods for Enhanced Learning Performance

There are a number of techniques for improving learning that apply the adult learning principles discussed above (Gill and

Meier, 1988). One general way is through active student involvement in the learning process. Students can be given the opportunity to learn in groups by participating in role plays, games, and team projects. Students can also be provided with a chance to select the individual learning techniques best for them. For instance, learning laboratories offer multiple ways to achieve the same goal. The student chooses his or her own learning path, using a variety of self-paced approaches perhaps in combination with group learning methods. A valuable tool is learner articulation, in which the learner repeats aloud to a partner material just learned. Articulating newly learned facts, procedures, and ideas in great detail, with demonstrations where possible, increases the pace of learning and the likelihood that it will be retained. Other learning techniques include metaphors and mnemonic devices, mental imagery exercises, and information graphs (drawing diagrams of the relationships between learned concepts).

The environment or atmosphere is important for effective learning. The enhanced learning setting should be comfortable and colorful, with soft music played throughout the day. Humor and playfulness are encouraged, with the intention of helping people eliminate or reduce fears and stresses. Time is spent preparing the students for learning, and the learning process and the learning options available are explained to the student. In some training departments, instructors are called "learning advisers" to emphasize their coaching and advising role as opposed to the one-way instruction in instructor-led settings.

Job Aids as Training Tools

A simple, relatively inexpensive training technique is to use written job aids, which reflect job methods and procedures (M&Ps), in lieu of formal training. Similar to a set of instructions, the job aid is a step-by-step description of what should be done and when, with illustrations and examples provided. A job aid may be as simple as a laminated wallet-sized card that can serve to jog the memory, or it may be a several-hundred-page binder full of information. Job aids as a learning method are relatively inexpensive, compared with instructor-led training or the use of sophisticated technologies. Job aids have the advantage of being available to the employee as the employee does the work, but they may not be sufficient as standalone training devices, since detailed instruction and observed practice are also often necessary. A job aid makes a good training supplement and is also a good way to keep employees current on changes in standard procedures.

M&Ps are the basis for job aids and are descriptions of the product and the documentation of procedures to be followed in the product's installation and maintenance. M&Ps should be written as part of product development or service design and implementation and as the product or service is being "trialed." In this way, M&Ps can include ideas for improvement and ways to counteract potential problems that arise during initial testing.

Writing an M&P should not be the responsibility of the training department but rather should be part of the service and product development function. However, often the need for training occurs during or just after the product's trial. Consequently, the training program must be designed before, or at the same time as, the M&Ps, and the training course developers will need to write the M&Ps, hopefully working with subject matter experts (engineers, designers, and so on). The advantage of this situation is that there is a close tie between training course material and the M&Ps the employees will use on the job. The disadvantage is that the work of the training developer is increased, as are cost and the time required for program development. The cost of M&P development should be absorbed into the cost of product development and should be considered a priority task, since M&Ps are critical to the proper implementation of the product and service.

Computer diagnostic systems are another type of job aid and can help employees understand and monitor job conditions and indicate areas needing action. As such, computer diagnostic systems can be training methods as well as systematic diagnostic tools. These diagnostic tools emulate or model complex decision processes (Brachman and Henig, 1988) and have been applied successfully to a number of jobs, from troubleshooting technical equipment problems to diagnosing medical problems. These systems work particularly well for remote testing and central monitoring of equipment that is deployed in remote locations. A computer diagnostic system can present employees with questions about job conditions and, depending on the answers, can branch to alternative sets of questions. Ultimately, the program leads to suggested responses. This process not only improves employees' consistency and thoroughness but teaches new employees the analytic reasoning processes necessary on the job.

Structured On-the-Job Training

The Disney Corporation example described above shows how experienced co-workers can be a valuable source of education. Called "buddy training" or "structured on-the-job training," the goal of this approach is to train employees to train others and then to make this responsibility an important part of the job. In this way, employees' jobs are enriched in interest value, and highly competent employees are rewarded with increased responsibility and pay.

The key to effective on-the-job training is a program for training the trainer. The trainer must know how to explain concepts patiently, answer questions, demonstrate procedures, and direct and maintain the trainee's attention on the task. An obvious advantage is that training is realistic and directly applicable to the job. The trainee can observe the trainer at work. Practice can be frequent and feedback immediate. Initially, the trainee can practice in a simulated environment, without the risk of direct customer contact. Later, the trainee can "trial"—that is, experiment with—the new job behavior under the watchful eye of the tutor.

Advanced Technology Training

Advanced technology has produced a number of different training alternatives. In some cases, these techniques can stand alone as sufficient ways to provide the training. In other cases, the tools are tied together to form a multimedia system for training. A single training program may rely on an instructor to present detailed material and give feedback on students' performances during practice sessions. Videotapes may be used to show standardized demonstrations. A personal computer (PC) may be a good way to simulate the task being taught, especially if the job requires using a computer. Interactive video disk, combining video and PC technology, allows students to work at their own pace, observe demonstrations, practice in response to realistic situations, and then be tested.

In general, there is an inverse relationship between the cost of developing and the cost of delivering advanced technology training methods compared with the cost of instructor-led, classroom training. Instructor-led training is generally more expensive to deliver and cheaper to develop than advanced technology methods, depending on the particular method. For instance, satellite broadcasts of an instructor-led class can reduce the cost per student in that they reach more students simultaneously. Self-paced, computer-based training, while relatively expensive to develop, can reduce the cost of delivery dramatically in that it eliminates students' travel and lodging costs. Also, because it often takes less time to obtain the same amount of learning, self-paced training decreases students' salary costs during training and makes students more productive faster. Some companies use self-paced high-technology methods for as much as 40 to 80 percent of their training. (Chapter Five provides more details on the cost-effectiveness of advanced technology methods compared to instructor-led training.) Following are some technological applications to training (with emphasis on their relative cost-effectiveness), the situations in which they are most applicable, and the steps for acculturating the organization to these new forms of training.

Computer-Based Training (CBT). U.S. Defense Department studies have shown that trainees learn about 30 percent faster using computers than in traditional instructor-led classes (Madlin, 1987). CBT enhances the quality of instruction by ensuring day-to-day consistency and by allowing trainees to repeat a section until they have mastered it. CBT is particularly useful in teaching large amounts of complex technical data—one reason why the airline industry has been a heavy user of the method in training pilots, maintenance personnel, and production employees.

Computer-based training software generally presents the student with text that supplies the information needed. Demonstrations can be provided, and the students can be asked questions and have an opportunity to trial the learning, with feedback from the computer about whether the student was correct or incorrect and whether the student needs more information. CBT programs may be linear in that the students proceed at their own pace through a preprogrammed sequence. The students may stop to go over a section one or more times, but all students progress through the same material in the same order. While such linear tutorial CBT is less expensive and easier to develop than other CBT software, it can be dull and thus no more effective than a lecture or book.

More complex CBT programs are configural, meaning that they vary the type, pace, and difficulty of the material, depending on the student's ability. For instance, students who master the first part of the training without error can be moved to a more difficult section. Slower learners can be branched to remedial sections that ensure that the student has the knowledge needed as a foundation for the training. Or a branch of the program may provide more repetition, more detailed explanation, and more opportunity to practice before going on.

Such conditional branching programs can be as challenging and fun as a video game. Computer graphics, color, and computer music can be attention grabbing and stimulating. However, these "bells and whistles" cost more money. As will be discussed in Chapter Five, the cost savings with CBT, as well as other advanced technology-based training, are not in its development but in the inexpensive delivery of the product to the student. The increased up-front development costs of CBT over traditional classroom instruction costs should be compensated for by the larger number of students who can be reached quickly. Student travel, course registration, classroom, and instructor costs are saved (unless, of course, an instructor is used to present the material).

An advantage of some computer-based training is that students can enter registration data (name, department, date), pre- and posttest responses, and answers to course evaluation questions directly into a computer system for coding. This saves in data administration costs and increases the speed of data analysis. Even when courses are on disks, as opposed to on-line systems, the disks can be collected and the data retrieved for rapid analysis.

In one example, CBT was an effective way to train customer service representatives who would receive telephone inquiries from customers ("inbound telemarketing") or make calls to potential customers to sell the firm's services ("outbound telemarketing"). These are relatively low paying, often dull and frustrating positions with high turnover. The average turnover rate in this industry is between 100 and 125 percent annually. The high turnover requires introducing new employees to the company and the job as quickly as possible.

Since the employees work with a video display terminal (VDT) to "pull up" customer accounts and place orders, the use of CBT seemed a natural way to provide the training. New employees could go through the program at their workstations. The program could present realistic examples and demonstrate possible responses. Also, the employees could practice taking orders and accessing customer accounts. In addition, colorful computer graphics were used to describe the company, its many departments, and the role of the customer service department in the firm's marketing objectives.

This computer training was used as a supplement to on-the-job training. After going through the program, a co-worker would sit with the new employee for several days. At first the employee would listen to calls handled by the co-worker. Then the co-worker would observe and coach the employee. The CBT program ensured that all new employees began with the same information, became familiar with the standard operating procedures, and understood how their performance would be measured.

The cost of developing this particular CBT program was $100,000. Given to 1,000 employees during the first year, the unit cost was $100 per employee. This saved approximately half a day of a co-worker's time, since the co-worker/trainer had been expected to cover the same material. The CBT program took about two hours to complete—less time than a co-worker took to cover the same material. The cost of this "buddy training" was estimated at $150 per half day, including the co-worker's salary, benefits, and lost productivity. However, the savings in time and money are probably less important than the assurance that all new employees received a standard and quick start.

Interactive Video Disk. This technique is a more complex form of CBT, the material being presented by videotaped demonstrations along with text and graphics. The method has the same advantages of CBT, such as branching programs to match the abilities and pace of the learner, as well as the realism of a video. Unfortunately, it is far more expensive than CBT to develop (five to ten times the cost, depending on the quality of the production, or as much as $200,000 to $300,000 for a one- to two-hour video disk program) and requires more sophisticated equipment to deliver. It has been used successfully when the cost of training is already high and realism is especially important.

One successful application of video disk training was used in training new army physicians how to handle medical emergencies during battle. Army personnel served as actors for the videos. A typical training sequence presented a medical problem, with a vivid scene of the wounded patient, a nurse describing what was done so far, and a doctor (the role being learned) questioning the patient. As students went through the program, they assumed they were in the physician's role. As the training progressed, students were requested to indicate the line of questioning they would pursue, the treatment alternatives they would consider, and the treatment they would recommend. As the student made a choice, the computer selected the sequence that demonstrated the application and outcome. At the end of the sequence, the student watched a commanding medical officer provide feedback to the new physician on the tape, thus providing feedback to the student viewing the tape.

At Digital Equipment Corporation (DEC), 80 percent of training is provided through non-instructor-led methods, including computer-based instruction and videotapes; however, the primary method is interactive video. The company has created an interactive video information system (IVIS), with terminals located at training sites. For instance, in one training site, there are sixteen IVIS terminals. One student can be at each terminal, and each student can work through a different course. An instructor, who is knowledgeable in all courses, monitors students' progress and is available for assistance. The courses visually simulate hands-on experience by showing, for instance, a product and then zooming in on a particular subsection of that product. Students can "operate" repair tools by using the terminal's keyboard. IVIS facilities include a hands-on laboratory so students can also actually work on the equipment.

PC Teletraining (Audiographics). This form of training uses a combination of technologies, with telecommunication of instructor-led presentations providing training simultaneously to many remote sites. PC teletraining rooms may be set up in local offices, with a telephone hookup to the originating location. Each room contains a conference telephone, a PC, a large screen monitor, a keyboard, and a pressure-sensitive electronic tablet. Students can hear the instructor and, using the tablet, can ask questions and answer the instructor's questions. Over the telephone hookup, the instructor and students can send written responses or drawings, which are displayed for everyone to see. The instructor's PC allows the display of text and video pictures at the student end. Using a video camera at the originating site, the instructor can send video frames (stills) over the PC so students can see the instructor on the monitor as well as hear his or her voice.

The equipment for a PC teletraining room costs about $10,000. However, the setup can become more sophisticated as technology advances. For instance, the instructor may have an overview scanner that allows transmission of realistic graphics, including photographs and small three-dimensional objects. Instructors can thus easily add or modify complex graphics as the course is delivered. Another advance is especially sensitive microphones, which make the system ideal for language training or for technical subjects requiring precise use of complex terms.

PC teletraining is relatively expensive to develop and deliver, involving, in addition to basic course development, costs for preparing software, which must be sent to each site ahead of time. However, computer development allows software and graphics to be generated fairly quickly once the course content is available, making it fairly inexpensive to redesign a standard classroom course to fit PC teletraining. The cost of delivery still must include instructor and facility costs, as with traditional classroom instruction. However, PC teletraining makes it possible to reach far more people at one time than is possible with standard classroom training.

PC teletraining is excellent for a geographically dispersed

organization. Local sites can be set up with relatively low fixed costs, and the equipment can be stored easily. Since training is on the employee's work site, travel and lodging costs are eliminated. Also, more productive time is likely, since employees can return to their jobs immediately after the training session. PC teletraining is particularly appropriate for either a short course or a sequence of classes.

Teleconferencing and Satellite Networks. This technology may use audio alone, audio combined with graphics, or video broadcast. Audio teleconferencing is essentially a conference call. Employees may dial into a "meet me" telephone number to hear announcements or updates or to participate in question-and-answer "press conferences" with top management, product designers, or workers in similar jobs. Groups of people may convene in meeting rooms and dial in on a conference telephone, or employees may be at their desks, at home, or on the road.

An audio teleconference requires some planning and coordination. Usually, one person runs the session, and a roll call of people on the conference call may be taken. When large numbers of people are on the call, questions may be taken beforehand or on another line at the time of the call and then turned over to the central speaker. This is convenient and comparatively inexpensive, given the number of people who can be reached at once, and has the advantage of being live and current, allowing many people "direct" contact with experts or top management.

Audiographic teleconferencing combines audio interaction with visual support—for instance, a pressure-sensitive blackboard that electronically transmits whatever is written to the remote locations. This technology is well suited to presentations, briefings, project status reviews, and classroom training, and some universities use it to simultaneously teach classes in several remote locations. Students at remote sites have special microphones for signaling the instructor when they want to ask a question or respond to the instructor.

Video teleconferencing requires satellite hookups and rooms especially equipped with cameras, monitors, appropriate lighting, and so on. This technology allows full-motion, face-to-face interaction for participants in remote locations and combines real-time communication with a full array of graphic support. Telephone companies in large cities rent video teleconferencing rooms for meetings or special presentations. However, the expensive equipment and facilities may make this technique impractical for routine training.

Increasingly, large companies have been developing their own satellite television networks for training. For instance, Tandem Corporation has a corporate teleconferencing network with eighty-five "downlinks" (reception locations) and the capability of adding additional downlinks as needed. Courses are announced to employees by electronic mail, and employees who register are sent precourse materials. A training session might run for three consecutive half days and is done live, with students being able to phone in questions. Also, sessions are videotaped for others who wish to view them later. As many as 1,900 employees have enrolled in a class, with the average cost per student hour being only $2.50, including the costs of production and delivery. This figure is only about 10 percent of the cost of traditional classroom instruction. The advantage of a satellite network course is that it can quickly reach a wide audience and can act as an intervention for the entire organization, allowing the firm to be prepared to deliver new products quickly. (See the description of IBM's satellite network in Resource B. Also, Chapter Nine describes how university and business consortia deliver courses via satellite.)

Closed-Circuit Television. This technology is a good way to present product and service updates and to make announcements, while also being an effective training tool. Two-way audio communication may be possible via separate telephone connections, just as a television talk show host might take on-air calls from viewers. Some large nationwide firms have closed-circuit networks that use satellite and private-line telephone network transmissions. Closed-circuit television provides a good way for employees to see a live broadcast of the company's annual meeting or some other important event.

Videotapes. An extension of the familiar "twenty-one-inch classroom" and an outgrowth of the industrial movie, videos are widely used as training tools and often supplement classroom learning. Videos vary extensively in price and quality. Using a home video camera, a manager can make a video on product improvement and can provide excellent demonstrations of installation, close-ups of parts, and interviews with product designers and users. A local department may produce its own videotape and then send it to other similar departments. (See the description in Chapter Three of locally developed training.) Videotapes can be stand-alone, used in conjunction with in-person explanation from experts ("tutored video"), or used as part of an instructor-led course.

A twenty-minute to one-hour videotape can be produced internally for as little as $3,000; however, a one-hour professionally produced tape can cost $30,000 or more. The expense incurred and the quality of the tape required depend on the amount of use the tape will receive, the audience, and, of course, the money available. A brief announcement or demonstration can be communicated effectively in a short tape, which then can be duplicated and sent to each site for viewing at employees' convenience.

A major production is worthwhile if the tape will be used to convey a corporate image or if it will be seen by many people. For example, a high-quality tape was recently produced by a union-management cooperative team to inform employees of available retraining options. Aimed at a wide audience (more than 50,000 potential viewers), the tape needed to highlight the value of the program in an attractive way. Produced as a documentary, the tape included interviews with midcareer employees who were going back to school and showed students in the classroom describing their fears and successes.

Digital Equipment Corporation uses videos to archive discontinued instructor-led courses. As the need for a course diminishes, a videotape of the course is produced using instructor notes and other pertinent material. If it becomes necessary to offer the course again, the course is "dearchived" by an instructor who uses the instructor notes and video to reproduce the course.

Advanced Technology Classrooms. Standard classrooms may be upgraded for easy use of graphics, video disk material, videos, computer-learning sequences, and other advanced technology supplements to instructor-led training. Student response units allow students to answer the instructor's questions and then view the average and distribution of responses on a PC monitor. IBM has found that this type of classroom increases learning in that the attention of all students is enhanced. In particular, response units require all students to answer questions, not just observe an interaction between one student and the instructor. These techniques can also be used in satellite networks of classrooms. (See Resource B for a description of IBM's satellite network and advanced technology classroom.)

Learning Laboratories. Another form of training simulates the job environment in a laboratory setting, using actual equipment to give students ample hands-on experience. Computers may be used to activate the equipment, demonstrate principles of operation, and show what problems may arise. Students experiment by using the equipment, just as they will be doing on the job. The laboratory may be instructor-led or self-paced; an instructor can provide advice or help demonstrate methods and procedures of operation.

Learning labs are generally an expensive venture for the organization, especially when the equipment is costly and when the technology changes frequently. Nevertheless, the lab offers a safe environment for new employees to experiment with new learning and for experienced employees to try out new ideas for more effective operations.

Guided Learning Centers. One way to take advantage of multiple training media is to establish a guided learning center. Such a center includes facilities for CBT (PCs, video disk equipment, and on-line terminals) and video (videotape players and monitors). Instructional experts operate a materials library, provide guidance in using the equipment, and offer information on subject matter areas. An instructor may guide students involved in a self-paced course using PCs, answering questions or providing direction on where to find additional information. Guided learning centers can be built into existing sites (manufacturing plants, laboratories, office buildings) or be part of training centers that also have standard classrooms and broadcasting facilities. Such a center can be an ideal way for a small company to offer employees the latest techniques in instructional technology while avoiding the costs of setting up large classrooms with multiple computer terminals and other sophisticated equipment.

Applying Advanced Technology

The advanced technologies described above vary considerably in cost and value but all provide a way to communicate information in a standard way. Interactive techniques, including computer-based and instructor-led training, provide opportunities for clarification, performance feedback, and pacing to meet student need. Indeed CBT is more flexible in being able to match each student's abilities than is an instructor, who must meet the needs of everyone in the class. While some individual attention is possible in the classroom, instructors often have to teach to the "lowest common denominator"—the student with the least abilities or background—thus wasting the time and losing the attention of more experienced or able students. However, CBT is only as good as the programmer, and flexibility and adaptation may be limited.

Advantages of self-paced technology are that the student is in control of the learning, realistic demonstrations are possible, and simulations allow hands-on experience. Advanced technologies can be valuable adjuncts to standard instructor-led courses. Videos or CBT programs can be sent out in advance of group training so that employees arrive in class with a fair degree of preparation. This saves classroom time and expense and also ensures that all students are fairly equal in knowledge.

Training methods that use advanced technology are generally more efficient in the speed and amount of learning that can take place, compared to instructor-led training. For instance, a one-hour video or a one-hour CBT disk can provide as much training as three hours of instructor-led training. PC teletraining is generally one and a half times as efficient as standard instructor-led training. (See Chapter Five on cost comparisons of training alternatives.)

A video or a self-paced learning tool is particularly good for conveying information and concepts, and computer simulations allow some hands-on trial-and-error training. Combinations of methods should be used to encourage learners to practice and test their knowledge. An example of such a multimedia approach to self-paced training was applied to train technicians on a new computer system for scheduling maintenance on company equipment. A written job aid was produced, but tests showed it did not provide a good overview of the product. The solution was to produce a videotape providing an overview and introduction to the new terminology. Also, a simulation of the system was produced on a floppy disk to provide the trainee with hands-on practice with the entire system. The original job aid was included in the training package to provide the user with a reference manual. Regional field training coordinators were available to handle trainees' questions and provide administrative assistance (such as how to gain access to the computer system). This entire training package took longer to develop than a traditional instructor-led course, but the firm's training experts believed the package was just as effective in delivering the information and far more economical in that it reached a large, dispersed student audience.

Studies have been done to compare modes of training delivery and student achievement outcomes. For instance, one study presented two groups of students with either traditional, face-to-face classroom instruction or remote teletraining using state-of-the-art equipment (Chute, Bruning, and Hulick, 1984). The course content and the amount of instruction were the same for both groups. The results showed that pretest scores between the two groups on amount learned were not significantly different, but the posttest scores were significantly higher for the teletrained group than for the classroom group. Data from a related study by the same researchers showed that students perceive courses delivered via teletraining and classroom training to be equally effective.

Another study of user acceptance found a high level of satisfaction with teletraining courses (90 percent of the students were highly satisfied with the mode of delivery and the content of each course) (Youngblood, Tanner, Poston, and Chute, 1987). The researchers reported that student satisfaction was higher when the content of the teletraining course was relevant to their jobs, challenging enough for their level of expertise, cost less than the classroom course, used high-quality visuals, and allowed interaction with an instructor and other students similar to that in traditional face-to-face classroom instruction. Also, short teletraining sessions (one-half to one full day) using full-motion video at a site near the office were rated as very appealing.

In general employees should be offered multiple learning

options. An organization should not adopt just one training technology but should use all of them. Motorola, for example, provides at least three learning format options for every course. Xerox writes all its courses on computer disks so that the material can be tailored easily to suit local needs.

Translating an Instructor-Led Course to Advanced Delivery

Consider a three-day, instructor-led course intended to provide an overview of a technical system. The goal of the course is to introduce the technology to newcomers and employees who are not in technical positions. Such employees can benefit from knowing more about the technology by helping them understand and support the company's strategies and objectives in their own jobs. Such knowledge can also help in how employees represent the company to outsiders and can enhance employees' abilities to adapt as technology changes and new products and services are introduced.

Such a broad objective for this course presupposes a broad audience. Employees' technical knowledge will vary considerably, and, consequently, it is difficult to please everyone. Disadvantages of a three-day, instructor-led course are that it can reach only a limited number of people—optimally fifteen to twenty—and is expensive and time consuming to teach.

Thus, to reach a large audience and to reduce costs, the course was converted to a PC-based presentation. The package included several disks, which comprised eight hours of intense self-paced training. The material was split into stand-alone modules. Pre- and postmodule tests on the disks helped students identify modules that needed to be mastered or could be bypassed. The posttest was scored by the computer to provide immediate feedback. The student completed the tests and filled out a course evaluation questionnaire, also on disk, to receive credit for the course. The training disk was then sent back to the training center for processing student credit and reviewing student performance.

This computer-based course can be distributed easily to any employee who requests the course. Most employees have access to a PC and know how to use one. The modularization of the course allows employees with sufficient background to skip areas they already know. The tests provide guidance to students about which modules they need to review carefully. In addition to the PC-based course, an instructor-led program was continued in an enhanced form for employees with more technical sophistication who could benefit from classroom discussion with other employees and the expert instructor.

One advantage of advanced technology training methods is that they are flexible; information and materials from one media can be adapted and used in another. For example, program content can be developed once and then integrated into computer-based, self-paced learning or used in classroom instruction. In fact, the computer disk, or on-line, system can be used in the classroom as a demonstration technique. Moreover, the demonstration can be broadcast via satellite network to remotely located students.

Introducing High-Technology and Self-Paced Learning

Many company training units are increasing self-paced training programs and decreasing reliance on classroom instruction. This approach is proving to be a more cost-effective, flexible way to meet the organization's training requirements. However, making the change is not easy for students who are used to standard instructor-led training and to courses involving written text, student guides, and instructor manuals.

In an effort to increase the amount of technologically advanced, self-paced training methods, one organization established a unit responsible for helping course developers and instructional technologists identify existing high-attendance courses that could be converted to self-paced methods. Also, as subject matter experts and curriculum review committees identified new areas for training, the unit helped developers determine how self-paced methods could be applied. This advanced delivery training unit consisted of experts who could not only advise course developers but could also directly work on the conversion or assign the project to a vendor outside the firm. The unit designed special announcements to highlight the availability of self-paced courses and established a PC teletraining department to convert courses, set up a network of six teletraining sites, and train instructors in how to use teletraining technology. Every curriculum development team in the training department had a contact in the advanced delivery training unit—a media specialist who could assist from the earliest stages of project development, suggest appropriate media, and do cost-benefit analyses to compare the price and outcomes of alternative learning methods.

The introduction of more self-paced training and more advanced training technologies in this organization required not only changing how courses are developed and delivered but also changing the expectations of the organization's employees about the nature of training. Employees were accustomed to instructor-led classroom training, and self-paced learning put more of the burden and responsibility for learning on employees. They had to work with their supervisors and peers to schedule time during the work day for training. Supervisors could schedule an instructional videotape and play it several times during the day to ensure that everyone saw it. As a result, training became part of the work that had to be managed, not a separate event that required a person to be away from the work group. Also, since more training was localized in this way, there was more opportunity to discuss how the new information or techniques in the course could be applied on the job.

Summary

This chapter distinguished between frame-breaking and incremental learning. The learning process was considered as a series of transitions, encompassing the stages of disorientation, exploration, reorientation, and reequilibrium. Frame-breaking change entails more difficult transitions because it is sudden and provides little support or structure for learning. These changes are make-it-or-break-it situations and may entail shock learning. Incremental changes include simulation training (trial-and-error learning), classroom training (inferential learning), and instruction on how to learn (learning to learn). Self-paced and advanced technology training methods are generally incremental in nature and lend themselves to applying principles of adult learning, such as self-direction and feedback, which enhance receptivity to learning. On-the-job-training and job aids are other ways to learn and perform better.

A diversity of learning tools is available. The choices will depend on applicability to the subject matter, cost, and speed required to deliver the training. Decision criteria to make these choices will become clearer in later chapters, which include sections on cost-benefit analysis (Chapter Five) and program evaluation (Chapter Six).

Policy Opportunities and Recommendations

1. Understanding career changes and learning experiences as a series of transitions suggests the important role of training in supporting the transition process. People are most receptive to learning when they are confronted with a new, ambiguous situation, as they are when they start their first job or when they change jobs, especially if the switch is part of a major career change. Organizations should take advantage of this receptivity by providing orientation training, which may include orientation to the organization's policies, practices, and values; an introduction to management responsibilities for new supervisors; and overviews of corporate strategies for mid- and top-level managers. IBM uses such a sequence of introductions for people promoted to higher organizational levels. The training becomes a rite of passage, a way to smooth the transition by enhancing self-confidence, making the employee feel part of the team, and reducing the shock of what might have been a make-it-or-break-it learning experience.

2. The organization's training programs should take advantage of adult learning principles. This chapter described how accelerated group learning, self-paced training, and advanced technology training tools can enhance the learner's control over learning, provide realistic opportunities for practice and feedback, and offer rewards for successful learning. Multiple techniques can be used together to form an exciting, effective learning experience.

3. Organizations should realize that clear methods and procedures (M&Ps) and job aids can be excellent guides and learning devices. They are inexpensive to develop, do not necessarily require sophisticated equipment (except for artificial intelli-

gence computer applications), and are easy to distribute and update. Preparing M&Ps should be the responsibility of subject matter experts in the product and service development departments. The training department can play a critical role in this process by providing the structure, format, and needed program support (for instance, simulations, classroom instruction, job aids, and so on) required to explain the M&Ps.

4. Alternative training methods offer flexibility in the intensity and depth of knowledge required, and the training method used should match the need for training. For instance, job aids and videos should be used to demonstrate updates and enhancements, there being no need for expensive in-depth courses. More intensive training methods should be used to provide employees with the fundamental concepts underlying major clusters of the organization's products and services. Then, as advanced products and services are introduced, employees can absorb these changes easily through easy-to-administer and relatively inexpensive communications and training methods.

While these recommendations seem obvious, what often happens is that courses are developed on each product and service even though there are substantial similarity and repetition in the courses. Because the organization does not train every technician, sales representative, or technical consultant in all products and services, the assumption is that each course must cover every detail. However, if all employees had the same solid foundation of underlying technologies, cross-training would be easier, and employees would not have to specialize in narrow product or service areas. This would provide more flexibility, as market and economic changes require shifting employees from one product or service to another.

5. The use of self-paced learning and advanced technologies can be a cultural change for organizations that previously relied on traditional classroom instruction. These organizations should develop mechanisms to support the use of this training. Examples of such support include rewarding supervisors for allowing time for subordinates to use self-paced training programs and for designing and applying local training programs that utilize videos, CBT, and other materials developed by the training department. The next

chapter describes the value of locally administered training and ways to give employees credit for the skills and knowledge acquired in local programs.

The major goal of the next chapter is to describe the roles and responsibilities of different training professionals and alternative ways of structuring training functions. A critical point is that the training department supplies the resources for learning. However, accountability for learning rests with local supervisors and with employees themselves. That is, all supervisors should support the development of subordinates to meet the organization's current needs and to be prepared to meet future needs. Also, employees should be responsible for their own education and development.

3

Building the Professional Staff for Effective In-House Programs

This chapter describes the functions, roles, and structures for providing employee training in an organization and considers alternative organizational structures and options for in-house employee training. Policy issues and decision criteria are examined to help managers determine whether to establish internal structures or to go outside for needed training. The chapter also outlines training managers' and professionals' roles in relationship to their customers (students and departments) and their linkages to suppliers (subject matter experts).

In-House Training Organizations

Many organizations have their own training units—for instance, McDonald's has its Hamburger College. The Carnegie Foundation estimates the 60 to 80 percent of all company-sponsored training is provided by in-house training departments (Chmura, Henton, and Melville, 1987). In-house training gives the organization control over program quality and content and allows programs to address subtle issues of corporate culture. Large organizations often have a variety of training departments.

In many companies, management training is organizationally separate from technical or functional training, often even operating from different departments in different parts of the company. Management training is usually housed in the human resources department, and technical training may be located in the research center, the engineering group, or a corporate-level general technical training center serving several different departments. Another possibility is that each functional department have its own training unit, with training programs in the department's specialty. A large organization may have a variety of training departments. Consider the following examples of Ford and Motorola.

Training at Ford Motor Company. At Ford, education and training is conducted by specific organizations, functions, plants, and offices. In addition, to help manage and coordinate efforts, Ford has several distinct institutions dedicated to specific programs and specialized training requirements, including the following:

- *Ford Executive Development Center*—designs and delivers executive development programs.
- *Ford North American Human Resources Development Center*—creates and administers education programs and courses for salaried employees and technical training for many blue-collar employees.
- *Quality Education and Training Center*—develops and delivers courses aimed at improving product quality.
- *Finance and Insurance Training Center*—develops and administers courses on financial services.
- *Ford Marketing Institute*—provides courses for dealership and company personnel and runs a special development program for new field managers.
- *Robotics and Automation Applications Counseling Center*—trains and retrains employees who are using the firm's newest high-technology machines and systems.
- *Service Training Center*—teaches both company and dealership employees the maintenance and repair of the company's products.

- *Local Learning Centers*—are dedicated learning centers located in most plants and offices.
- *United Auto Workers/Ford National Education, Development, and Training Center*—monitors the company-union joint programs in worker development and labor-management relations.

Motorola's Training and Education Center. Many large organizations have a number of different specialized training organizations, as does Ford, and may also have a corporate unit to support these various training departments. An example is Motorola's Training and Education Center (Wiggenhorn, 1988). The center's mission is to improve individual and organizational performance and productivity in Motorola's facilities across the globe, and it markets training and education-related products and services to Motorola employees and subsidiaries. The products and services are designed to address key initiatives and goals of the corporation. Functions include consultation in training planning and design, information services (such as a computerized catalog), management and executive education programs, and the design and delivery of special seminars.

The services of Motorola's Training and Education Center may be used by the company's local training units in manufacturing, engineering, sales, and other major functions in each of its subsidiaries. Within the company's business units, site training organizations are included in the personnel departments at each major site. These small training units generally have between three to six people, including a training manager, a clerk/coordinator, a person in charge of manufacturing training, and a person in charge of engineering training. The sites communicate regularly with the central Training and Education Center. Also, the center's manager of planning and evaluation brings representatives together quarterly from each site to participate in a training managers' council meeting. Line operators in assembly maintenance and machine operation are taught to be trainers and are temporarily pulled off the line to train new employees. Sales training is conducted by full-time training personnel in the sales organizations. Each sales unit conducts its own customized training, drawing on the center for courses and services as needed. (See Resource B for more information on Motorola.)

Training Department Size. The size of training departments varies, depending on several factors: (1) the number of employees, (2) the number of functions, (3) the diversity of training, (4) the specialization of training, (5) the frequency of training changes (as the firm's technology changes), (6) the centrality of the training function in the organization (that is, the more it serves the needs of the entire organization), and (7) the availability of training programs for purchase outside the firm.

In addition to major centralized training institutes that serve an entire corporation and send employees to outside courses, a department within an organization may establish its own training function. This function may be a sizeable operation, providing specialized training needed by the department, or it may be a highly localized operation, with individual managers setting up special training programs to meet particular needs.

Many small firms (companies with five hundred or fewer employees) have their own human resource development (HRD) operations but are likely to purchase many of their programs from outside vendors. Actually, companies of all sizes use both inside and outside sources for training (Gordon, 1988). Universities, professional associations, and consulting firms offer programs in general management or in specialized technical disciplines. Also, training services are available for program design and development for firms that want to run the programs themselves.

Training Functions

Whether training programs are purchased from outside training firms and possibly delivered by these firms as well or whether training programs are developed and delivered in house, similar functions are involved. This section provides a description of the different roles and functions often needed to provide training and education. Though job titles may vary from organization to organization and functions are combined in different ways in different training departments, there are three major types of jobs: administration, development, and delivery.

Administration. Training directors are the top managers and oversee the entire training department. The head of training in an organization is likely to be a vice-president and officer, which status reflects the critical role of training and education in meeting the organization's objectives.

Development. Development personnel have the following roles:

- *Development and project managers* supervise program and course developers.
- *Instructional technologists* advise program developers on the design of training materials to enhance adult learning and also may develop measurement instruments and methods for evaluating training success.
- *Professional writers and editors* produce documentation and student guides.
- *Educational consultants* in the training organization may be available to help field managers evaluate employee skill needs and develop training plans for individual employees or for groups of employees.
- *Systems designers and computer experts* develop computer-based training materials.
- *Artists, actors, film crews, video technicians, and other production experts* may be involved in various stages of the development process.
- *Program and course developers (or project managers)* interface with subject matter experts, write materials, coordinate production with internal departments (such as video production crews) or external vendors, and deliver the training or work with those responsible for delivering the training.

Delivery. Staff responsible for delivery perform the following functions:

- *Delivery managers* supervise instructors.
- *Site managers* oversee training facilities (classrooms, materials, equipment, and so on).

- *Registration clerks* provide information about available training and schedule students for classes or arrange for students to receive self-paced training materials.
- *Instructors and "learning advisers"* present training in a training facility (classroom or conference room), and may be course developers, employees assigned and taught to be on-the-job coaches or classroom instructors, or professional teachers.
- *Trainer/consultants* are responsible for helping field departments analyze performance problems and determine training needs and are able not only to suggest training alternatives but also to design and deliver programs.

Alternative Organization Structures

A full-service training organization provides most, if not all, of the functions listed above. Figure 1 is an example of a centralized organizational structure that separates the development and delivery functions and administers the delivery of training geographically. This format is likely to be used in a large department because it includes most of the major functions and the training for each product and service offered by the organization. This structure provides delivery of training in each geographical region served by the firm and, perhaps, to customers and suppliers as well as employees. There is a specialized unit providing management development programs and an administrative and training support services division that can aid in tracking expenses, developing new data systems for monitoring the amount and quality of training, designing training evaluations, and publishing course announcements and a catalog of courses. (Such administrative functions are described in Chapter Four.)

The organizational stucture depicted in Figure 1 may employ from fifty to two or three hundred people, or even more. The annual budget may run from several million dollars to tens of millions of dollars. A very large corporation, as we have seen with Ford Motor Company, may have several large training departments and perhaps several small ones, with the total annual training bill in the hundreds of millions and the total number of training personnel in the thousands.

Figure 1. The Structure of a Full-Service Training Organization.

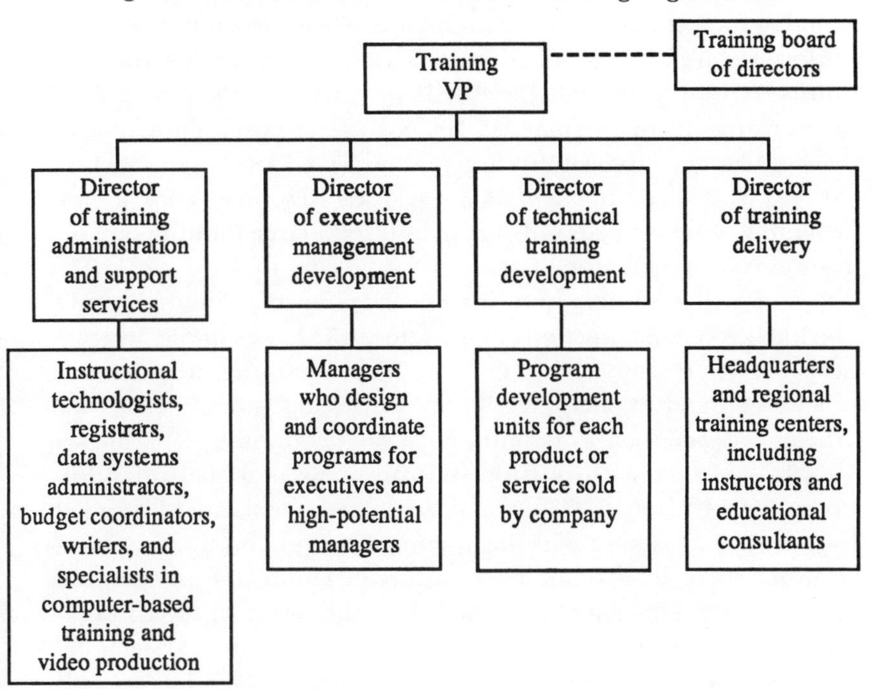

An alternative organizational structure would be one that organizes training development and delivery by product or service line and operates separate training centers for each product or service. The center would develop and deliver all courses and self-paced training for particular products or services, and all employees connected with that product or service would go to the center for classes or order self-paced or locally administered training products from the center.

Running a large training department requires considerable administrative support, which includes developing the budget; tracking expenses; ordering equipment; doing the paperwork for staffing (moving people in and out of the department); coordinating other personnel activities such as appraisals, salary administration, and career planning; developing business plans for the department; designing and administering data systems for student registration and tracking student participation in training; publishing a catalog of programs and materials (perhaps maintaining the catalog on a computer for easy client access of up-to-date training information). Similar functions are necessary in smaller training units as well, although there will be fewer numbers of people performing them (perhaps as few as one or two administrative clerks having responsibility for planning and tracking, which is shared with department managers). (See Resource A for a case example of how an administrative unit for a large training organization is organized and directed.)

Smaller training units than the one shown in Figure 1 would be likely to merge functions in the same role. For example, instructors may be responsible for developing and refining the programs they teach and for helping employees develop training plans for themselves and their work units. Even smaller training departments might contract with outside training experts to help develop programs. University faculty and graduate students are often good sources for assistance with instructional design and training evaluation. Also, in a small training organization, the budget and systems functions may be provided by other units in the corporation, such as the finance department or the information systems department. Figure 2 depicts a possible structure for a fairly small training department.

In this example, the manager of leadership development programs may have a staff of one or two high-potential managers that works with corporate officers to establish policy for fast-track advancement programs. The policy would include criteria for selecting candidates and suggested guidelines for training courses and job experiences. The staff may try to promote interdepartmental transfers of fast trackers and may contract with vendors (universities and consulting firms) to run leadership courses for fast-track managers and management development courses for those managers on a more standard career track. The programs may be given at the company's training center or at hotels close to student locations.

The manager of technical training coordination may have a staff of supervisors, each with several clerks, that is responsible for running the firm's single training facility, registering students, and distributing self-paced training materials. Several training experts reporting to the manager would assist line departments in selecting

Figure 2. The Structure of a Small Training Department.

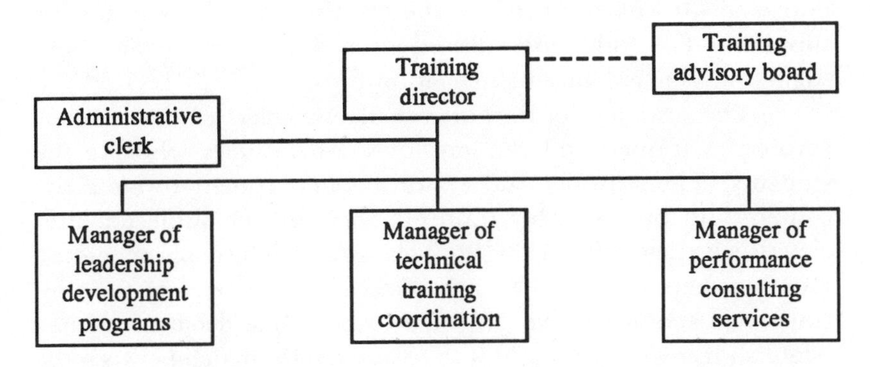

courses and self-paced programs. These programs may be developed jointly by outside vendors and subject matter experts in the firm, with training experts indentifying vendors and facilitating the arrangement.

The manager of performance consulting services might have a staff of two or three organization development consultants that conducts performance analyses for client departments and recommends and helps implement improvements, which may include training.

In small line departments or in small organizations (which may have a number of line departments), training may be the responsibility of one or two people, or the training function may be only part of one individual's responsibilities. In such firms, the training manager is basically a training coordinator who monitors employees' training needs and contracts with training firms to provide the training. Still, the coordinator will have to know how to evaluate the quality of training programs, work with vendors and contractors to design programs that match the organization's requirements, and interface with the organization's managers and employees to be sure training needs are well understood.

Critical Linkages

Whether a training department is large or small, there are three vital linkages to consider: (1) linkages between customers and the training organization, (2) linkages within the training organization, and (3) linkages between the training organization and its suppliers. The following subsections review these linkages and suggest ways to enhance these relationships.

The customers of training are the managers who want their employees trained and the employees themselves who are the students. The suppliers of a training department provide the content and processes for training; they are the subject matter experts who determine what should be taught. The departments are also suppliers in that they help determine the type of training employees should receive. In some cases, a line department may establish its own training unit to ensure a tight match between the department's needs and the training provided. In other cases, the training department is a separate unit that services a variety of internal customers. (Alternative organizational structures for training are discussed later in this chapter.)

These customers and suppliers "call the shots" in deciding what training is needed and who needs the training. In addition, the customers have input on the format for the training, since they "pay the bill." The ultimate criterion for training effectiveness is whether the customer is satisfied with the knowledge and skills that employees acquire. However, the customer does not have the expertise or responsibility for making and implementing these decisions. The role of the training organization is to help the client departments determine job requirements and employee skill deficiencies, develop training plans, identify cost-effective training methods that match the material to be learned, schedule students, and develop evaluation criteria.

In many organizations, the elevation of the training director to a corporate vice-president and officer position signifies the importance of training. The training department becomes an equal partner with other major organizational functions in accomplishing the firm's objectives. The vice-president (VP) of training may be a senior VP or may report to a senior VP of human resources. The training VP may be responsible for all technical and management training in the organization, with all training units directly under his or her control. Or the training VP may be responsible for a centralized training support unit that provides guidance and general programs used by training units in each functional department. In any case, the training VP's role is to represent human resource development needs to other corporate officers to determine whether employees have the skills and knowledge needed to carry out corporate plans and objectives.

Curriculum Review Committees. One vehicle for building customer relationships is the curriculum review committee. This is a group of field managers and training program developers responsible for a particular discipline. The group reviews existing courses and self-paced programs, considers employee skills and knowledge in relation to organizational needs, and suggests areas for revision and requirements for new training programs. Department needs may require that a program be shortened to concentrate on a particularly needed aspect or to provide training faster.

Early Warning Mechanism. Another linkage is between the training department and the departments responsible for new product or service development. A key to product rollout is having service representatives who can install and maintain the products. Obviously, these representatives must be kept informed about changes in products and about new products. This linkage may be strengthened by having product and service managers represented on the curriculum review committee or by having a member of the training department's development staff regularly sit in on product planning and product management meetings. This individual's responsibility is to act as an "early warning mechanism"—bringing planned changes and likely changes in products and services to the attention of training program developers.

Service Agreements. One way to strengthen the link between the training department and its clients is to establish service or partnership agreements. These are statements of need and what the client and the training department will do to meet that need. The written document is signed jointly by a training manager and a key manager in the client department. For instance, the agreement might specify that the training and client departments will work together to develop a skills inventory that lists employees and their current skills and to establish a twelve-month training plan for every employee.

The client department might commit to recruiting subject matter experts for training programs being developed; to supplying the latest technical documentation for use in program development; to offering timely feedback on program design and instructional materials; to facilitating needs analyses prior to program development to ensure the right programs are being developed; to providing subject matter experts to serve as students during tests and field trials of new programs; and to assisting in acquiring hardware and software to support instructional labs.

The training department might commit to developing and delivering high-quality, job-relevant, and cost-effective training; to examining alternative strategies for nontraining solutions to performance problems; to providing periodic updates on the status of programs under development or revision; to requesting needed technical documentation in a timely manner (giving the client time to respond); to presenting timely requests for students to test new programs; and to offering advisory services in state-of-the-art performance technology and training methods.

Training Department Boards of Directors. A training department board of directors is another mechanism for developing a linkage between the training department and its customers. A board of directors may consist of high-potential managers in client departments, such as the board at Xerox Corporation. Or the board may be composed of the training director and directors of client departments. The board may meet semiannually or as often as necessary to

- Review and advise on key training directions
- Set key training policies and practices
- Advise on funding strategies, resource levels, and measurement criteria
- Represent and communicate special regional or department training needs
- Review training results to ensure that training is supporting the goals of the organization and the departments it serves
- Initiate special educational efforts and evaluations of training programs.

Motorola's Training and Education center is guided by an executive advisory board consisting of senior managers representing the company's major businesses and departments. Meeting two or three times a year, the board focuses on the needs of the corporation as a whole, prioritizes the training to be developed during the next year, and addresses the key corporate business issues and budget constraints. The center also has five functional advisory councils for engineering, manufacturing/materials, marketing, sales, and personnel. Each council meets two to four times a year to review training development for all the populations within the function, to review existing curricula, and to help develop requirements for curricula. Each council articulates key business issues for its function, helps decide the best strategy for implementing a training program, and selects project committees and subject matter experts to assist in program development.

The board of directors should formulate a written charter outlining the board's functions. Throughout the year, board members should receive regular training reports indicating the numbers and functions of employees completing different training programs and the numbers and types of programs developed so board members can stay abreast of the training department's progress.

A board of directors or council is one way for the training director to mantain contact with, and to be guided by, the department's clients. Also, the board can be helpful in implementing the training department's policies. For example, one training department was concerned about the rising number of student cancellations and no-shows for its classes. The board of directors agreed to a penalty process whereby the departments sending students would pay extra fees when students did not show up for a class or when students cancelled too late to assign the seat to another student. In this case, the board members understood how the departments under their control were hampering the training organization, and they agreed to a control mechanism (a financial penalty) that would emphasize the importance of training.

The members of the training department's board of directors can collect information from all departments about training needs and can then represent these needs to the board and the training department. At AT&T's Bell Laboratories, for instance, the Committee on Education (the training center's board of directors) is comprised of the directors of major research laboratories. Each committee member is responsible for a particular curriculum and chairs a curriculum review committee comprised of department managers. To review progress and set policy, the committee meets as a whole once a month and each member is involved directly in guiding a particular curriculum.

In addition to meeting with the board of directors, the training director should meet, as necessary, with other directors and clients to review training plans and customer needs. Training program developers should meet regularly with product and service developers and with field supervisors whose employees attend training.

Maintaining Quality and Control

The training department must understand its clients' needs and must work closely with suppliers of training materials to ensure that quality requirements are met. Methods of performance analysis and quality improvement are discussed below.

Performance Analysis. The training organization must be sensitive and responsive to customer needs. This suggests that training managers must be aware not only of how well employees do in training but how well they do on the job. While lack of training is certainly not the only possible explanation for performance problems (poor management, scheduling difficulties, and lack of equipment are others), training may be needed to address a deficiency. Performance analysis is critical for analyzing work flows and breakdowns. If the source of a problem is lack of skills or knowledge, training in these skills may be required. Job aids and clearer methods and procedures documentation are other possible solutions, and several such solutions may be used together.

In the example of a small training department shown in Figure 2, one of the units in the training organization was responsible for performance analysis consulting. This group should work with managers in client departments to examine performance problems and determine whether a training or nontraining solution, or combination of solutions, is appropriate. While the example above shows the group as part of a fairly small training organization, such a group may be found in large training departments as well. When the training department does not have a performance analysis group, there may be an organizational development (OD) unit in the firm, perhaps in the human resource department, which is responsible for helping managers enhance the performance of their units and handle organizational change. There should be a close working relationship between the training and OD departments that allows them to work together, recommending each other's services when appropriate and combining forces on organizational development interventions that require training.

Quality Improvement Teams. Some organizations use quality improvement teams (QITs) to examine work flows and identify areas for improvement. (See the overview in Chapter Eight of quality processes and programs in training departments.) For instance, a customer service department may analyze the work flow from the time a client calls with a problem to the time the problem is resolved. A trainer/consultant or training program developer should be a member of such a quality improvement team and should suggest training solutions when appropriate.

Applying Training Solutions to Training Problems. Often trainers may likely suggest a training solution to a performance problem that is not necessarily the best solution. Some types of consultants (such as experts in organizational development and human factors) are likely to be biased in favor of solutions they can implement (such as team building, better job design, and so on). The goal should be to keep an open mind about the source of the problem until the analysis is complete and then to maintain a broad view about possible solutions. Training professionals should be trained in performance analysis methods and should know when to recommend calling in other experts for help.

Recall the example described in Chapter One of a problem that arose when service technicians did not have the knowledge to install or maintain some of the company's products. The company became aware of this problem from a key customer who threatened to cancel a lucrative sale because the products were not being installed adequately. The head of the company invited the customer to a service review meeting. One of the issues that arose from the meeting was that technicians who had certain product knowledge were not being assigned to work on the product. Thus, part of the problem was that first-line supervisors were not taking technicians' skills into account when making daily work assignments. One solution was to provide supervisors with better records of subordinates' capabilities and to develop a job aid to assist supervisors in making assignments.

In this case, there was no need to have all technicians trained in every product. However, there was a need for more training, since too few technicians had the skills they needed. Therefore, training plans were developed for each field unit, and the training department initiated a set of crash training programs. Courses were redesigned to be more concise, classes were scheduled in the evenings and on weekends, and trainers and students received overtime pay. The number of technicians trained was tracked, and weekly conference calls were held with top management to review progress. As a result, the company was able to ensure that an untrained technician was never sent on a customer service call.

Training for Mastery. Training can be designed to emphasize quality and encourage employee commitment to high performance standards. It is important that training curricula are related to the goals of the department, and a curriculum review committee (as described earlier) may be the means for communicating these objectives and designing needed training programs.

In one case, a department wanted to ensure that all its employees achieved a high level of professional development. Employees worked in teams to develop mastery paths for each discipline. A mastery path consisted of the skills and job experiences required to do an excellent job. The department worked with the corporate training organization to develop training programs that would help an employee "achieve mastery" (that is, to certify; the term *certify* was avoided because it connoted a make-it-or-break-it objective). Mastery was intended to be a progressive set of accomplishments that all employees would work toward at their own speed, although time guidelines were established as benchmarks for evaluating progress.

Training was just one part of the mastery path. Supervisors were trained to evaluate subordinates' accomplishments on the path to mastery and to assign them to progressively more difficult tasks. Ultimately the supervisor determined when an employee could be designated a master of the discipline. For some jobs, the reward was higher pay. In other cases, the reward was a certificate that acknowledged to others that the individual had achieved mastery. Individuals who wanted to be considered for promotion had to achieve mastery in their current assignments.

Vendor Relationships. Training departments obtain materials and programs from many sources outside the organization. These supplier relationships need to be managed just as internal supplier relationships. External suppliers may be consultants who write courses or production firms that sell "off-the-shelf" video programs and CBT or that produce customized programs. A training department project manager will be responsible for overseeing programs developed or delivered by outside firms and ensuring that these programs meet the organization's and the departments' quality needs and objectives.

There are many training consulting firms, and choosing such a firm is no different from choosing any other consultant or purchasing any other product. When an off-the-shelf program is being considered, the program can be trialed by sending employees through it. The content and cost of the program should be compared to alternatives, such as programs sold by other vendors or programs that might be developed by the training department.

Selecting a vendor is more difficult when an existing product needs to be customized to meet the organization's specifications, or when a new product needs to be developed. Here the vendor's reputation and the organization's previous experience with the vendor are key in making the decision. In all cases, the motto should be "Let the buyer beware."

As noted at the outset of this chapter, organizations form their own training departments to maintain quality and control. Another reason for this is to guard proprietary technical information and reserve general corporate strategies for the types of leaders and managers the organization wants to develop. If employees' skills and knowledge are the determining factors in the organization's competitive edge in the marketplace, then high-quality training becomes a strategic advantage to maintaining that competitive edge. Vendors and consultants should be required to sign nondisclosure agreements as a condition of the contract.

Internal training organizations have another advantage over vendors in that the internal departments "know" the organization. The training director, training managers, and the instructors and program developers develop close working relationships with their clients, perhaps even having worked in clients' departments at one time. The training staff should have experience in the firm that will give them credibility with customers of training. Thus, they will be able to relate to the technician's job because "they have been there."

Relationships Within the Training Department

A list of training roles and functions was provided earlier in this chapter. Clearly, many people have to work together to develop and deliver training, and these relationships need to be nurtured in the same way that customer-supplier relationships need to be developed. In fact, training department professionals are, in a real sense, one another's customers and suppliers. Program development feeds into delivery, and both are supported by training technologists and other production and delivery experts. A brief outline of the development process will aid an understanding of the training process and areas for potential breakdown.

The Development Process. Program development includes the following stages:

1. *Project planning.* Curriculum review committees and other meetings with clients help in establishing customer needs and in developing agreed-on plans for needed training.
2. *Design.* Program developers should work with instructional technologists and instructors to identify and evaluate program alternatives.
   - *Front-end analysis.* Front-end analysis involves analyzing the target population's skills and knowledge; analyzing the requirements of the job; and determining available resources, facilities, and equipment. Alternative training media should be considered in relation to the training goals, and the analysis should conclude with a cost-benefit comparison of two or more training alternatives.
   - *Coordination with program registration.* The group re-

sponsible for course announcements and registration should be involved as early as possible so it can help coordinate trials and schedule employees for training.

3. *Development.* Student and instructor guides, video scripts, computer software, and other materials must be written and produced. Subject matter experts should provide the content and review training materials for accuracy. Instructional technologists can offer ideas for applying adult learning principles to the content and the chosen media. Development is an iterative process, requiring continuous revision and polishing.
4. *Trial.* Pilot tests are needed to assess the training materials. Developers can obtain feedback from the target audience for the training as well as from the people who will be delivering it.
5. *Training trainers.* Instructors or learning advisers should be trained to deliver the program.
6. *Equiping facilities.* Classrooms or local workrooms need to have the equipment necessary for training. (See the description in Chapter Two of alternative training media.)
7. *Program rollout.*The training program must be announced to the target audience in company bulletins, curriculum brochures (training "maps"), and course catalogs. Supervisors and employees must know the purpose of the training, the time required, the cost to the department, and the expected output. Special sessions or written bulletins should brief supervisors on the training goals and how they should support the new learning once the employee returns to the job.
8. *Tracking and review.* Program developers and the curriculum review committee should examine regularly data on the number of students participating in and completing the training, their satisfaction with the program, their performance during the training, and their improvement on the job. This information should be used for program maintenance—for example, updates, refinements, and customization to meet local needs.

These are very general steps. The time required for program development, the people and other resources involved, and the costs will depend on the complexity of the content and the media chosen.

Nevertheless, the steps and the flow of the process suggest critical relationships within the training department as well as potential barriers.

Development-Delivery Interaction. In many cases, those who write the courses are not the same as those who deliver the courses. Program developers are concerned that the program or course be delivered exactly as it was intended, thereby maintaining consistency in content and quality. However, instructors may want to vary their delivery, depending on the experience level of the audience. Or they may want to embellish the training material by providing their own examples or describing their own experiences with applications.

One way to enhance the development-delivery relationship is to involve one or more representatives of the delivery arm in program development. The key instructor, an instructor assigned to work with the program development team to design and test the training program, is a critical part of this interaction. The key instructor should maintain continual communication with the other instructors about the progress of the program and bring to bear his or her experience with program delivery. Other members of the team (instructional technologists, technical writers and editors, software designers, and subject matter experts) can benefit from such input, perhaps not having had such direct experience themselves.

The key instructor can help determine the prerequisites students should have, since instructors are familiar with the contents of other classes and the backgrounds of those employees likely to participate in the training. (This assessment should be corroborated by a thorough front-end analysis that includes determining task requirements and assessing employees' skills and knowledge.) In addition, the key instructor can be especially helpful in writing the instructor guidelines, which provide instructors with information on how to present the material and express the standards to be followed in administering the program. The clearer and more practical these guidelines are, the more likely it is that they will be followed consistently.

Technologist-Developer Interaction. Instructional technologists have technical expertise in adult learning, training media, performance testing, and feedback methods, to name a few areas important to instructional design. Program developers, subject matter experts, and instructors bring their own individual experiences to the development process, and thus conflicts may arise. Some center on quality and practicality; others may concern instructional technology or adult learning theory versus what instructors believe will work.

One way to overcome such conflicts is to cross-train training professionals and assign them different roles at different times. For example, program developers and managers should have some training in adult learning theory and methods and in instructional design procedures. They do not need a master's or Ph.D. degree in the field to grasp basic principles and the role instructional technologists play in the design process. Instructional technologists should be assigned on occasion to write material, oversee projects, and teach courses so they understand the various perspectives that may emerge during program development.

Relationships among developers, instructional technologists, and instructors can be enhanced further by periodic program reviews. Data on students' performance in the course, reactions to the material, and later on-the-job performance should be examined and the program refined. Discussing the data in a group session that encourages open analysis and discourages attributing blame can strengthen the development team. The group might observe training sessions as a basis for discussion. The goal is to develop a shared, common experience on which training developers can draw as they work together in the future. This common background can also be helpful in working with other development teams.

Centralization Versus Decentralization of Training

One way organizations structure training is to form training departments within each organizational unit. Such training units arise because departments want control over their own training. However, a centralized training organization offers a number of advantages. Centralized training can result in economies of scale, since there is a single training facility and staff. Centralized training works well for training that is generically applicable to different parts of the company, such as new employee orientation, supervisory skills training, and management development of various sorts.

Companies such as Disney, Exxon, AT&T, and IBM have central training departments as well as local training units. The central departments provide general training consistent with overall corporate goals. In some cases, departments are charged back for the costs of sending employees to courses at the company "university." In other cases, the firm's corporate headquarters absorbs the costs, which are paid for, in any case, by general cost allocations to the different company divisions.

Training that is specific to the functions and disciplines of a given department may be offered by a training unit within the department, perhaps using the facilities of the centralized training organization. Another model is to have the centralized training department contract with individual departments for specific courses or entire curricula. In such cases, the central training department should be as competitive as an outside training vendor in terms of cost and quality of service. A curriculum designed for a given department can incorporate the general courses offered by the central training department. In this way, the department becomes the marketing arm for the central training unit and can ensure that courses available to employees are consistent with the department's objectives and strategies.

Relationships Between Training Units

When an organization has multiple training units in individual departments, the organization as a whole can benefit from a council of training directors. The council can monitor the costs and benefits of training to ensure the best use of the firm's educational resources. For instance, it can try to prevent redundant courses, define specific roles for each training organization, encourage sharing resources and offering courses to one another's employees, and relate training programs to organizational strategies. The council also can facilitate career development for training professionals by encouraging transfers between training departments and supporting joint educational programs for trainers.

(Professional development for training staff is covered in Chapter Seven.)

A corporate training support group can be established to reduce the cost of training by consolidating training facilities, forming a single unit of instructional technologists to consult with the different training departments, and developing and administering a common registration system and training record data base. In addition, a central support group can negotiate corporate contracts with external vendors rather that have individual departments negotiate separate contracts for the same services. Moreover, the central group can publish a single organizationwide catalog of training programs in which employees from any department can enroll.

Local Training

In addition to departments having their own training units, considerable training occurs at the local level—that is, training arranged by supervisors for their own work groups. The balance of the chapter examines how much local training may occur in an organization, demonstrates the value of local training, describes different types of local training, and suggests resources and methods for enhancing local training.

Definition of Local Training

Local training is any training that is developed by or for local personnel and delivered within the department or region. It is not part of a course designed and delivered by the headquarters or departmental training organization. Some local training may use materials developed by the training department, or materials may be developed by an external consultant or by local experts (such as experienced employees). The training may be organized and delivered within a field office or within a regional or district group for all relevant personnel in the region or district.

Local training does not take the place of formally scheduled training but rather supplements formal training by meeting local training needs that may not be applicable more broadly. Moreover, local training may be a faster way to meet a training need than waiting for the training department to design a generically applicable program.

The Training Gap. Local training is important because it contributes to reducing a department's training gap. The gap is the difference between the training planned by the training department and the total amount of training needed by fieldwork groups. (Methods for evaluating the training gap are described in Chapter Four.)

Amount of Local Training. One way to estimate the amount of local training is to survey a random sample of departments about the types of training they provide on their own and how much of that training they plan to provide during a given period of time. One organization projected the total amount of local training to be equal to about half the formal training in the company. If informal explanations and demonstrations given by co-workers were included, the amount of local training would be far greater. Indeed, almost everybody is involved in this type of training every day.

While some local training may take the place of formal training or provide enough knowledge and skills to eliminate the need for employees participating in local training to take a course, other local training may be needed anyway to prepare the employee for a course (that is, to provide the prerequisites) or to meet a need that is not met by the training department's curriculum.

Changes in the Gap and Local Training Needs. The size of the training gap and the need for local training will change as business conditions change. The training department's resources may be increased to lessen the training gap in a particular department. Also, the gap will change as new products and services are introduced. New production technology may require fewer people, which may mean less training, or it may mean more training because fewer people must now handle more diverse functions. The gap continues until the employees who need the new knowledge and skills are trained. Local training is often a way to reduce a particular training gap quickly.

Reasons for Local Training

Local training is needed when:

- *Customized training is necessary to meet an immediate local need,* and available courses do not provide all the needed knowledge or skills.
- *New technology* documentation is not yet available, and a new installation is planned or already initiated.
- *Technical enhancements and software updates* cannot wait for the training department to develop a general course.
- *New employees need initial knowledge and skills to begin being productive* and before they can be scheduled for courses.
- *Knowledge of old equipment* may be required but the training department no longer has training courses on the equipment.
- *Cross-training* of employees is desirable so they can fill in during overflow periods. Owing to time or resource constraints, the supervisor may not be able to train all employees in the work group; however, employees can train each other.
- *Hands-on training* is needed for technicians who need more direct experience with equipment, software, and procedures than is given in classes or who need to refresh hands-on skills.
- *Course availability* is reduced so that employees cannot be scheduled into formal classes soon enough to meet the work group's need. This may happen because classes are filled, local classes are not available, or the entirety of a formal class is not required.

Local Training Solutions

Some of the resources and methods of local training include:

- *Temporary minitraining centers.* When a new technology is introduced, a temporary training center is set up where technicians who will be working on the new equipment can learn firsthand from the experts and work with equipment before it goes on line.
- *Sending employees to other sites.* Employees needing training

may be sent to offices where there are more experienced people who can help educate employees on technical issues or on improving mutual understanding and enhancing working relationships among departments.

- *Local experts as instructors.* Experienced technicians may develop their own training materials or borrow existing course materials and then hold a class in their home offices or perhaps in other offices in the region or district.
- *Retired experts as instructors.* Retired technicians or managers may be hired to develop and/or deliver local training.
- *Adapting training department materials.* Materials designed for formal training classes may be used as is or adapted to meet local needs. These materials may include student and instructor guides, PC disks, and videos.
- *Locally designed training materials.* Local resources can be used to develop inexpensive job aids, videos, and other training materials. For instance, home video recorders can be used to record a new installation procedure, and the videotape can then be duplicated and shown in other offices.
- *Local equipment for hands-on experience.* Local experts can use on-site equipment to demonstrate techniques and procedures to give employees hands-on experience.
- *Buddy training.* Since much training results from one co-worker imparting job skills to another co-worker, employees should be better trained to be buddy trainers, and supervisors should be trained to value and encourage such training.
- *On-the-job training.* With this method, employees work at the job to develop necessary knowledge and skills. On-the-job training employs a combination of local training solutions.
- *Regional and local training coordinators.* Departmental coordinators in the local department can coordinate the development and delivery of a local training effort. The coordinator arranges for people to work on the training design, sets up the class times, and registers students for the classes.
- *Having supervisors arrange on-site training.* A local first- or second-level supervisor may perform the same functions as a regional training coordinator in perceiving the need for local

training and arranging for its development and delivery to the local group.

- *Local training as a one-time event.* A specific training need may arise that makes the training a self-limited event for a particular one-time need.
- *"Suitcased" courses.* While some local training occurs just once, other local training can be shared with other local offices by having the local expert hold the training at other offices or by sharing video presentations within a region or between regions.
- *Training local supervisors as instructors.* A local supervisor may take courses to learn how to be an instructor and how to deliver one or more courses. The instructor can then provide the course locally or can be loaned to the training department to deliver the course when needed.
- *Customized seminars combining selected training course material.* Local management may ask the training department to design a special seminar or course to meet local needs. For example, there may be a need to adapt an in-depth course reviewing a new technology to a half-day overview.

Examples of Local Training

The following are examples of local training that demonstrate the creativity and ingenuity of local personnel in recognizing a need and utilizing available resources to meet the need quickly. The examples show how some of the above local training solutions are applied.

Minitraining Center. In this example, a company developed a "facilities" work group that was responsible for the repair of equipment and machinery used in the company's operations. The group was faced with a changing situation—new technology, several new and inexperienced employees and supervisors, new testing systems and tools, no formal training available for old technology, and increased customer needs for improved operations. Temporary training centers were set up at various field sites. Experienced "buddies" were assigned to give inexperienced coworkers on-the-job training, experienced technicians were promoted temporarily to instructor positions to deliver on-site classes, and outside subject matter experts were brought in to deliver special training on the new technology. New equipment not yet in service was available to give technicians hands-on experience, and videotaped presentations were produced locally to describe and demonstrate the new test equipment.

The technicians trained in this temporary training center were sent to other facilities work groups that were also implementing the new technology. In some cases, the technicians were transferred to these groups on permanent assignments so the groups would be staffed with experienced people who could then train others. In other cases, some experienced technicians from the initial temporary training center were loaned to other work groups to help as the new technology was brought on line. In addition, the training materials from the first work group application, such as the videotapes, were shared with other offices.

Cross-Training. In another facilities work group situation, an auxiliary work group, which was responsible for monitoring equipment conditions and reporting trouble and breakdowns, needed more experienced people to work in the different functions of the facilities work group. In this case, people experienced in working on the equipment were needed to do equipment monitoring. Since the monitoring group gave directions and set priorities on what to repair, it helped to have these people understand the problems encountered in equipment repair. Unfortunately, no experienced people from the facilities work group were available for transfer to the monitoring group.

To resolve this problem, an apprenticeship program was established to temporarily transfer several employees from the monitoring group to the facilities work group. The apprenticeship consisted of an eighteen-month series of job assignments and training courses. The series of work assignments were established to cover important and complex activities in facilities installation and maintenance. Since the intensive nature of the experience meant that only a few people (three to five) could start the program together, a new group was added every four to six months until the required number of people was trained. Instructor salaries and program expenses were charged to the monitoring group, which thus made a long-term investment by sending technicians through the program.

Service Technicians Observe Engineers. A similar, but less intensive, on-the-job training experience was designed for technicians who service equipment sold to customers. Service technicians were sent to field engineering offices to spend several days observing and working alongside engineers. The goal was to improve the interface between the engineers and the technicians and to enhance the technicians' knowledge of the equipment.

Service Technicians Learn Computer Software. In this example, local management felt that field service technicians needed MS-DOS knowledge to help them deal with software problems that could arise in the computers used in the firm's products. Since the technicians did not need the in-depth MS-DOS course offered by the company's training department (which was, in addition, offered in another city and would involve travel expense and time away from the job), a local technician who was well versed in MS-DOS revised the training material and split the course into several short sessions to be delivered by him once a week.

Seminars Emphasize the Importance of Training. The director of a regional data service organization, the unit of technicians servicing customers' computer equipment, recognized the need for first- and second-line managers to support and encourage the training of their technicians. The director's staff designed a half-day seminar for managers in each unit, which began with the director discussing her expectations. The educational consultant from the company's training organization described the support available for constructing training plans as well as the headquarter's career planning and development programs. The unit supervisor (a third-level manager) concluded the session, outlining training and development expectations for the unit. The managers then directed separate seminars for each of their units.

Materials Libraries. An administrative support group responsible for assisting supervisors of technicians in scheduling work assignments and introducing new equipment needed to ensure that equipment documentation was readily available to the technicians. (Recall from the discussion in Chapter Two that such documentation and job aids can supplement training and sometimes replace the need for training.) The support group established centrally located libraries of reference material, including methods and procedures, job aids, and other technical information and data to help technicians and their supervisors. This saved training costs and also the cost of individually distributing the lengthy methods and procedures.

Training on Performance Analysis. As a way to analyze and deal with a potential training gap in one department, a program was devised to ensure that managers had a good grasp of their groups' need for training. First, a needs analysis was conducted, and the training needs were compared to the amount of training planned. Next, managers attended a performance analysis workshop delivered by an external consulting firm. The workshop provided a way to analyze performance problems in the group and to determine which problems were due to the need for training and which problems could be solved better in other ways (for instance, through better scheduling or through performance feedback and improvement methods). Another training needs analysis was conducted shortly after the training and again several months later to see if the initial training needs were still present. The staff planned to develop artificial intelligence diagnostic and computer-based training techniques to meet the remaining training needs.

Employees Complete the Company's Professional Development Program. In this case, the firm's professional development program invited employees to assess their skills, attend relevant training classes, and experience developmental job assignments related to technology, people, quality, and customer satisfaction. Members of one work group agreed to work together on the people module, commissioning an outside consultant to present a workshop on interpersonal relationships. The workshop was held on a Saturday, and interested employees came in on their own time. By participating as a group to choose, develop, and experience the training, these employees enhanced their working relationships while satisfying requirements of the professional development program.

Employees Develop Customer Interface Skills. Similar to the above example of group training, a work group with the principal function of dealing with customers held a voluntary Saturday session conducted by an external consultant to learn about better ways to deal with customer problems.

Credit for Local Training

The purpose of a training record is to help current and future supervisors make assignments and understand the overall skills and knowledge of the work group. Thus, training records should be complete and meaningful, and the organization's training records data base should provide a way to credit employees for participation in local training. Just as employees may be credited for formal training, locally developed and administered training can be given a course title and description and this can be recorded on the employee's permanent record.

However, not all local training should be credited. Training that is appropriate for credit should satisfy a requirement or a prerequisite associated with a training curriculum. Therefore, the appropriate course developer or curriculum manager in the training department should review the proposed training and, if needed, make suggestions to improve its applicability for credit. In general, the training department should recognize that local training is desirable because it meets a local need and contributes to the effectiveness of the organization while possibly reducing the training gap. The training department should support local training as long as it is adequate and sufficient.

Summary

This chapter reviewed training functions and processes, describing critical linkages between functions within the training department and among the departments, the customers of training, and the suppliers of training content. Several mechanisms were suggested for enhancing these relationships, such as curriculum review committees, training boards, and quality improvement teams. The description of the training development process considered ways to improve internal relationships among program developers, instructors, and instructional technologists. The pros and cons of centralized training deparments were reviewed, and training councils were described as a way to tie together training goals and products within the organization.

In addition to training department functions, the chapter highlighted the importance of local training. Supervisors and their employees often assume responsibility for their own training needs. Local training is a way to generate and provide a timely, customized program.

Policy Opportunities and Recommendations

1. The discussion of local training suggests the importance of empowering employees to assume responsibility for their own education. Training organizations should encourage local training efforts by developing special materials, revising and customizing programs for local needs, and delivering programs at local sites (suitcasing). In addition, line supervisors should be rewarded for generating development plans for their departments and for generating their own training. Employees should be encouraged to participate in the design and delivery of their own training, using the resources and advice of training experts.

2. Customer responsiveness is critical to ensure that the training department meets organizational needs. Training departments should establish curriculum review committees, and line supervisors should be encouraged to participate.

3. Training directors must be linked to clients at higher levels of the organization, working with directors of other departments to encourage training plan development and to monitor progress. Training directors should realize that training program developers and instructors are close to the customer in understanding their needs and reactions to training programs. Training professionals should be empowered to revise and develop training programs in response to customer requirements.

4. While the training department must be responsive to the departments and individuals it serves, it also must be responsive to the needs of the organization as a whole. As described in earlier chapters, training is a way to communicate and engender commitment to organizational goals. Therefore, interfaces among training units and among training and organizational planners and human

resource officials should identify the need for training programs to explain organizational strategies and to prepare employees to make a contribution to the organization.

5. Training professionals should be aware of the flow of the training process (how ideas for programs arise, how the programs are developed and delivered, how they are received, and how they are updated). Quality improvement teams are one means for examining this process, identifying areas for improvement, and implementing these improvements. These teams should include representatives of customer groups, subject matter experts who guide the content of training, as well as training personnel involved in the processes under review. The committees should be empowered to invest organizational resources and to implement improvements.

The underlying message of the above recommendations is that managers of training functions should be responsive to customer needs and should do so by empowering those subordinates close to customers to act in whatever ways necessary to satisfy the customer. This puts the training manager in a predicament. The environment in many organizations today is one of tight resources, with all managers held accountable for making expenditures to the maximum advantage of the organization. This is why training, along with all other functions, must contribute to the organization's objectives.

When strong demands are placed on the training organization to meet the many, and possibly conflicting, needs of multiple clients, the tendency is often for training managers to exert control, monitor progress closely, and provide direction. Yet this is the time to do just the opposite. In times of change, conflict, and pressure to produce, the training manager must trust subordinates to do what is needed for the organization as a whole and for individual client departments. Just as parents must relinquish the natural tendency to be all-knowing experts and to protect and control children as they grow older, organization leaders and managers must do the same with their work groups once they have selected competent professionals and developed their competence through increasingly more responsible work. The training manager's objective should be to develop an environment of trust, openness, and freedom for responsible action and to hold subordinates accountable for the outputs of their work.

How can training directors and managers empower subordinates in this way, particularly when the environment is increasingly difficult to predict and manage? In some cases, the organization must suffer a trauma before managers recognize the need for change. Ford Motor Company is a good example of a firm that came close to bankruptcy before its leaders realized that the skills and capabilities of employees at all levels were needed to solve problems and that cooperation and joint action were necessary to develop products that met the demands of the marketplace. Employee training and retraining efforts were part of this organizational change. The trauma suffered by the company enabled its managers to overcome rigid, limiting organizational structures and to empower employees closest to the customers to make suggestions and take action.

Hopefully, organizational trauma is not necessary to create a participative, trusting environment. The next three chapters on training administration and business planning, budgeting and cost control, and measurement and evaluation pose food for thought on how these processes can be utilized in ways that encourage employees to enhance the responsiveness of training to organizational needs and to assume responsibility for their own education.

4

Managing and Supporting Training Programs

Planning is an important part of any function. In a training department, plans are needed for the types of projects and products to be produced and the time frames for delivery. The linkages between the department and its clients and suppliers are critical to the planning process, since plans must be based on clients' needs and the availability of material and information from suppliers. This chapter examines the role of strategic and operations planning in a training department and also describes a process for establishing training needs (that is, gap analysis) as input for planning.

Strategic Planning

Strategic planning means determining a desired future and what is necessary to achieve it. Ackoff (1981) argues that organizations should use control, responsiveness, and employee participation to create the futures they want. Owing to unanticipated events and to changes in the values and assumptions underlying goals and actions, planning should be a continuous process. Ackoff distinguishes among four types of planning: inactive, reactive, preactive, and interactive.

Inactive planning ignores the need to plan: the status quo is the ideal, and the main goal is to not "rock the boat." This type of planning fits nicely into bureacratic organizations that operate on the principle that "if it isn't broken, don't fix it." The danger is that the training department can find itself adrift in a rapidly changing environment.

Reactive planning involves taking opportunities as they come: choices are based on what is needed now. While training departments must often react to the immediate needs of the field, reactive response can, unfortunately, be at the long-term expense of the organization—for instance, if the firm unnecessarily trains too many people in skills that will not be required later.

Preactive planning accelerates the rate of change and attempts to exploit change, having as a goal to predict and prepare for the future. A difficulty with establishing a set of objectives is that the focus tends to be only on accomplishing those objectives and other aspects of the work or changes are not recognized until it is too late. Generally, whenever it is assumed that things will go smoothly or continue as they are, something changes or goes wrong (Murphy's Law).

Interactive planning is the process Ackoff believes organizations should follow. He recommends that organizations create their desired future by doing the following: (1) appreciate the current situation, (2) determine the desired state for the organization, (3) identify ways to get to that state, (4) develop needed resources, and (5) implement a plan for creating this future. The organization should not assume that something cannot be accomplished just because the required resources are not currently available. This is not to say that reality should be ignored but rather that the organization should take control of it.

To be more specific, Ackoff believes that the most effective means of control is responsiveness, which suggests the value of contingency plans. Instead of predicting what will happen, contingency planning (another term for interactive planning) identifies likely occurrences and outcomes. Contingency plans help us respond to events rapidly and effectively, in contrast to reactive plans, which require us to wait for something to happen before responding. Contingency, or interactive, planning means designing and controlling the future by minimizing the effects of events beyond our control but still being willing to change course when necessary.

Designing and creating the future and planning for contingencies require comparing assumptions with relevant others—especially with customers and suppliers in the case of a training organization that is in the business of serving others. The goals of the training department must match—that is, contribute to—the goals of its clients. Checking assumptions should help in identifying the needs underlying the training department's goals and possibly in discovering other ways to meet those needs. For instance, a goal might be to train more employees. However, the client's goal may be to improve performance. Focusing on the underlying need (performance improvement) may suggest other ways than existing instructor-led courses to meet the need.

Planning is a continuous process. It is not enough to come up with a plan one day and then let it guide the department for the next year. Department managers do the guiding. The theme or basic objective (for instance, customer satisfaction) may remain constant, but the specific methods and actions may change. Organizations use all four modes of planning to different degrees. Training departments are more likely to be reactive planners than contingency planners. While there may be a vague idea of what the department should accomplish, each manager is operationally focused—that is, focused on the tactics of current projects and on responding quickly to the needs of clients. While this is important, all training managers, led by the director, should discuss and agree on an overall strategy that should be a clear motivator of behavior, not a set of platitudes without effect on action.

Statement of Mission. The process of developing a departmental strategy should begin with a concept of organizational mission, or a vision for the future. Arriving at this mission should be a participative process involving department managers and client representatives. The training director, along with other training managers, should communicate and discuss the strategy with their colleagues in client departments as they hold training review meetings and speak at client group meetings. Also, clients should be brought in to speak at training department meetings so that instructors, program developers, and instructional technologists can keep in touch with client objectives.

The company's vision of the future should be formalized in a mission statement, which may be very general or quite specific, as the following examples illustrate:

- All managers will recognize training as an integral part of their development.
- Every employee has training plans, and these plans guide the training department's work.
- Assignments in training are seen as key to employee development and as contributing to upward movement in the organization.
- We will fulfill every promise, meet every requirement, have the courage to say no, act as partners with our customers, and treat ourselves, and our suppliers and our customers with honesty, integrity, courtesy, and openness.

All these statements are very general. The first two focus directly on the client. The third establishes a goal that is internal to the training department. The fourth focuses on how training department personnel will work with one another and with clients.

While the training department may have a general major mission, such as to enhance customer satisfaction, there may be a number of more specific supporting statements. Moreover, each group within the training department should have a mission statement to guide each individual's general commitment and specific objectives, on which are based the operational (tactical) plans for the department.

Some mission statements are established top down. That is, the training director puts forward a guiding statement, such as the first mission statement above. In other cases, the mission comes from the input of employees made at group meetings. As an exercise, each training manager can be asked to assume that it is three years later and that "you are the training director and have been asked to write a summary of your diary that highlights your accomplishments." The accomplishment statement then becomes a basis for discussing the department's mission. Mission statements should be reevaluated periodically by discussing them at client meetings or by using them to evaluate accomplishments, for example, during performance appraisals.

Tying Organizational Plans to Training Department Plans. As emphasized in Chapter One, the training department's plans should be tightly connected to the goals of the clients it serves, being guided by the clients' training plans. Clients' training plans may be at the aggregate department level—for example, "to ensure that all employees are fully trained on the curriculum associated with their function." The aggregate plans should be made known at the individual employee level, so that each employee knows how much training is needed for departmental and personal success.

Training plans for employees should be consistent with and supportive of the client department's goals, and the training department's objectives should support these individual and departmental goals. This requires that training plans be constructed in the same context and by the same process as the organization's business plan and should be viewed in direct relationship to it. Moreover, the training goals should be monitored regularly and subjected to a thorough annual review alongside the business plan (Latham, 1988).

A difficulty with matching training goals to organizational goals is that the organization's goals may not be well formed or may be changing. Consider the remarks of Charlotte Siegfried, the manager of training for Lincoln, a St. Louis, Missouri, firm that has made many structural changes since 1986, including increasing its use of outside consultants and making a work-force reduction that eliminated half of the company's top management positions.

> Looking at things from a training perspective, we don't really know where we are going long range. I don't think we can accomplish the long-term results training is capable of if we're always just putting out fires, but we don't really have the direction as to where the company wants training to go yet. So we have to address the problems that are perceived as real, the critical issues for the organization in terms of meeting customer needs or dealing with products. We have to

> step in and do whatever is needed. But at the same time we have to pull together the information needed so we can eventually sit down with management and ask, "Are we in a position now to lay out some plans and link things together or to develop a new strategic plan?" ["Quick Fixes . . . ," 1988, p. 2]

The value of long-term plans, especially when they include contingency plans, is that they have a good chance of eliminating unexpected, short-term training crises. Clients' requirements for training will change as new people are hired, employees are moved to new assignments, and new products and services are introduced. However, these changes can be anticipated. Clients will be confident that their needs are attended to when they participate in setting priorities with the training department.

Jeff Murphy, staff director of human resources for Nynex Enterprises, is trying to match long-term business plans with training plans by involving line managers in the process ("Quick Fixes . . . ," 1988). He is working on five-year plans with company vice-presidents to find out what skills employees will need in different areas so appropriate programs can be designed. Murphy involves managers in the selection of courses, using as a basis their vision for the future and the kinds of workers they will need. Thus, he can involve top managers as well as lower-level managers in the planning process.

Ideally, training and education programs should give employees the feeling that they can simultaneously fulfill their own personal needs and the needs of the organization. The organization should support this approach by adopting the philosophy that people should be developed to meet current needs as well as anticipated future needs of the organization. In an environment of tight resources, this means that preparing employees to make a contribution to the organization in the future should be considered a necessity, not just a nicety. Such preparation, of course, will be guided by future directions, not just by what employees think would be interesting. (Chapter Eight's discussion of retraining describes a number of programs that can help employees maintain employment security through education that meets future organizational skill and knowledge requirements.)

Strategic Planning Processes

The strategic plan for the training department should be formulated in concert with the strategic plans of the departments it serves and the overall organizational plan. Training should be part of the human resource plans of the organization. Following are several suggested steps for developing a set of coordinated plans (a process usually done annually, with the proviso that updates can be made as circumstances change):

1. Training department managers should meet with client managers to formulate training objectives for the coming year, including training programs to be developed, existing programs to be continued, and the volume of use (approximate numbers of employees using the programs at different locations during each quarter of the year).
2. The "bottom-up" views developed in Step 1 should then be aggregated to form an overall plan for the training department to serve all its clients. (The budget process, discussed in Chapter Five must parallel the planning process, because agreed-upon levels of training should be accompanied by agreements for funding—whether costs are charged back to clients depending on usage or whether costs are allocated to departments on an aggregate level.)
3. The training department should work with top management groups and possibly with corporate headquarters groups, including the personnel or human resources department (of which the training department may be a part), to develop overall corporate objectives. For instance, generic management training may be applicable to all departments. On the one hand, the strategy for generic training may be to provide a menu of courses and programs on major topics of management. On the other hand, the strategy for management development may be driven by a corporate philosophy of what constitutes excellent management and leadership. This model

of desired management behavior should be the basis for training programs as well as other support mechanisms, such as appraisals, compensation, and promotions.

4. The training department's plans should be written and communicated to clients and to members of the training department. Meetings should be held with the director and training staff to explain the plan so that all training professionals will understand how they contribute to its fulfillment. The strategic plan should be the basis for each employee's annual commitments and specific objectives.

These four steps appear to be logical and simple, but, in fact, they are likely to take substantial patience and perseverance to accomplish. Client relationships must be clear and well established. Each client department should have training coordinators responsible for negotiating training agreements; training department managers should act as liaisons for client coordinators, and all involved must be empowered to reach accords after appropriate input from relevant managers.

Developing an overall management or leadership model applicable to the entire organization is likely to take months of meetings with the CEO, department officers, and other managers, and a task force may need to be commissioned to generate and review alternative approaches. Once a model is established, all must agree on the approach to training (the types of programs and their cost).

Despite these difficulties, the planning process is worth it. The process will engender a sense of mutual support among departments. The training department will be a clear partner in the enterprise of the organization, and training professionals will feel they have a critical role in helping the organization accomplish its goals. Furthermore, employees in the organization will feel that education is an important part of their jobs, which will, in the long run, enhance the viability of the organization and the employment security of its members.

The Plan Format

The format for the written plan is not critical. It may be a single document, or it may be a series of documents for each curriculum area or each client served. The following components might be included in a comprehensive strategic plan:

1. *Mission statement.* As suggested above, the training department should have a written mission statement. This might be one general statement, such as "to be a key partner in the evolution of the organization by designing and delivering training that meets clients needs." The mission statement should also include more specific goals regarding client service and the evaluation, reward, and development of the employees in the training department.
2. *Key initiatives and imperatives.* The plan should include a list of key initiatives and imperatives, which consist of general approaches to the operations of the training department (such as the commitment to be driven by client needs, to optimize the organization's investment in training, and to meet client training needs effectively and efficiently). Clarifying statements should accompany each imperative, explaining how it will be accomplished. For instance, the training department's commitment to effective and efficient training delivery could be accomplished by (1) serving as a consultant for all organizational managers to ensure that training is available to meet their needs, whether that training is provided by the training department or by an external training company; (2) determining who in the training organization is accountable for each client need; (3) ensuring the professionalism of all training department employees; and (4) ensuring quality program development and delivery without wasting resources (particularly money and people).
3. *Description of the external environment.* The training department plan might also include an analysis of the external environment and how training enhances the organization's success. For instance, the plan should clarify how training will contribute to the organization if it is faced with increasing competition, an increasingly global marketplace, or the rapid development and implementation of new technologies. In each of these cases, training may be necessary to enhance employees' abilities to produce competitive products, learn how to operate

in foreign cultures, and know how to use new equipment or methods. Characteristics of the labor force that serves as the organization's source of new employees should also be described, especially if the organization will need to hire significant numbers of people during the planning period and beyond. (Exhibit 1 in the first chapter presents some relevant demographic information.)

4. *Description of the internal environment.* The environment internal to the organization should also be described. For instance, an important aspect of the internal environment is the diversity of employees' skills and backgrounds. Age may be an important biographical characteristic, showing the percent of employees in different disciplines and departments who will be eligible for retirement. Many organizations are faced with an older work force as younger employees have been laid of in downsizing the organization. When compared to the aging population and the lower birthrate that influences labor-force availability, retraining strategies for older employees may be critical to the organization's obtaining the skilled personnel it will need in the future.
5. *Data on anticipated training volume.* The plan should include summary data of the numbers of programs to be developed and the number of students participating in these programs during the planning period. Specific data should be available for the upcoming year, and tentative data should be generated for several years beyond. Some plans go out as far as five years or more, although projections beyond one year must be viewed as highly preliminary, having value primarily in highlighting the likely importance of training in certain areas and the need for continuing investment in employee education.
6. *Curriculum strategies.* These strategies should include a description of each curriculum (that is, subject matter) area, the strategic direction it is taking, the numbers of programs to be developed and delivered, the media to be used, and the clients served. Strategic direction for a curriculum would include major goals, such as to increase employees' understanding of a new technology. Names of contacts in client departments and in the training department should be listed for each curriculum.

Operations Plans

Operations plans are elaborations of the curriculum strategies and should include more details, such as descriptions of new programs that are needed. Operations plans may be written for curriculum areas, functions (for instance, the administration of a specific classroom facility or the development of new course evaluation procedures or of training performance tests), client groups served (which may combine curriculum areas), and/or groups in the training department (for instance, the administrative systems group or the counseling, scheduling, and registration group). Also, operations plans can be formulated by each individual employee as the basis on which the employee will implement his or her commitments. Or the operations plans can be written for any combination of employees forming natural work groups or combinations of groups.

Zero-Based Project Planning

The planning process should begin each planning cycle with a clean slate. Existing projects should be prioritized and evaluated in relation to the mission of the organization and the specific goals of client departments. If this is not done, every project will appear to be a top priority, and projects will never be dropped even when they have outlived their usefulness.

A prioritization process should be established involving department training coordinators and training managers who have responsibility for a set of programs in the rating of those programs against criteria relevant to the departments involved. Line managers may serve this function in line departments that do not have training coordinators. Criteria may include revenue generation, cost reduction, customer satisfaction, operating effectiveness, and enhancement of employees' value to the organization. The results can be summarized as input to planning discussions.

This process is useful not only to initial planning but also to later project review, especially if resources become tight and cutbacks are necessary. At such times, priorities should be reviewed to ensure that they still apply in light of new projects that may have emerged since the initial plans were established.

Training Gap Analysis

Training professionals are involved in planning on at least two other levels. They assist client departments in developing training plans for their employees (which plans drive the training department's plans), and they help individuals (or help supervisors to help their subordinates) develop training plans for themselves.

The training gap refers to the difference between the amount of training being provided by the training department or by local training and the amount of training needed. Training deficiencies arise from three causes:

1. *Current skill gap.* This is an estimate of training required to bring the existing work force to the level of technical competence required to do the work that must be done now or during the coming year. This is the amount of training that would be required if all employees were fully trained for their current jobs.
2. *Turnover/growth gap.* This is an estimate of the training required by people entering work groups as new employees, either as new hires, promotions from other positions, or lateral transfers from other jobs.
3. *Evolution gap.* This is an estimate of the training that will be required as a result of the introduction of new products, work processes, operating systems, and technology. (The evolution gap is over and above the current skill gap, which, if eliminated, would mean that all employees are fully trained for their current jobs before any work changes.)

Sources of Information. The personnel data base will be a principal source of information for developing training plans if the data base contains records of training completed for each individual. The records can be used for developing training plans for individuals by comparing the employee's record to the training curriculum required for a specific job. Similar data can be aggregated across employees to examine the training needed by all those in a particular work group. (Chapter Six demonstrates the use of such information.) Data can also be aggregated across work groups to examine training needs for entire departments.

One problem with training records is that they may be outdated or the individual may not have had a chance to use the skills and knowledge learned in the training, especially if a long period of time has elapsed since the training. Another source of data would be to assess employees' skills through a skills analysis inventory. The inventory, in the form of a questionnaire, may ask supervisors to rate each subordinate's skills and knowledge. Employees may be asked to complete the questionnaire about themselves, and this data may be compared to supervisor ratings to determine reliability of the information and to investigate areas of disagreement. (See Lorenzo, 1988, for a description of the use of skills inventories at Ford Motor Company.)

Another measurement method is to ask supervisors to identify training needed by their subordinates. For example, estimating the training gap due to work-force turnover and/or growth may require supervisors to provide judgments of the amount of turnover and growth they expect during the planning period. Estimates of work evolution should come from subject matter experts who are responsible for designing and implementing work-method changes. Line supervisors should also be consulted about when and how quickly such work evolution will affect their units.

In large organizations with many similar departments that are geographically dispersed, a random sample of departments can be included in the gap analysis. The data can be used to estimate the full training gap by increasing the student training days in relation to the proportion of the organization represented in the sample. If a 10 percent sample is taken, then the gap can be multiplied by ten to estimate the complete gap. While the results will not be precise, the general direction and magnitude of the gap can be determined, and this will be an adequate basis for determining the resources needed by the training department to meet customer needs.

Sources of Error. The potential sources of errors in a training gap analysis include:

- Sampling errors due to choosing only a fraction of work groups (For example, employees in some work groups may be better trained than in others.)
- Errors due to incomplete, inaccurate, or missing training records
- Misestimation of the turnover or growth rate
- Difficulty in translating information about work evolution into training days because the training has not yet been designed
- Variability in the evolution gap because all technical advances are not known at the time the study is conducted
- Bias owing to the assumption that all employees must take the entire curriculum for their function to be considered fully trained (Supervisor judgments about the amount of curriculum needed should be factored into the current gap estimate.)
- Bias owing to the assumption that employees need training only in the curriculum required for their function (Cross-training may be desirable, and supervisor judgments on this should be sought.)

Using Gap Estimates

The methods for arriving at solutions to the gap and the solutions themselves are applicable to training departments of any size and scope, although the number of clients involved and the resources devoted to the process will vary depending on need, available time, and the numbers of different vested interests. Some training departments may involve only a few people in a gap analysis and may arrive at solutions relatively quickly, as when an analysis is done for a small client group. When the analysis is conducted for a large organization with multiple departments and functions, as was the case in the following example, more resources are necessary, and input is required from more people. Also, since more people will have to agree to ways for resolving the training gap, the analysis process will take more time.

As the manager of the administrative section for a large training department, I assumed responsibility for completing a gap analysis that had been started just before I took the position. (See Resource A for further description.) The gap data analysis was the responsibility of the planning manager, who reported to me. The study identified a sizable gap. The current need for training to bring employees up to par was estimated at twice the amount of training the department provided in a year. The training need due to turnover and growth for the next three years was equal to the current need for training. The training need due to evolution for the next three years was almost twice the current need for training. After subtracting the amount of training planned by the training department for the next three years, the remaining gap was about three times the amount of training provided in a year. (It should be kept in mind that the gap was over and above the amount of training that would be provided during the three-year planning period.)

We initiated a study to examine the amount of local training provided and found that local training should account for about two-thirds of the training gap. This implied that the local line units were recognizing the need and starting to fill the training gap themselves. However, some of this local training was not aimed at filling the gap, being directed instead at providing new employees with prerequisite experiences and skills in preparation for the training department's curriculum. Thus, even including the local training, there was still a substantial training gap. (Examples of local training needs and solutions were discussed in Chapter Three.)

Training Gap Solutions. The report on the training gap was shared with the training department's board of directors, which was composed of high-level managers in the client departments (and thus peers of the training director.) The board brainstormed potential solutions to the gap, focusing on the following areas:

- *Increasing use of advanced technology and self-paced training* (greater use of videotapes, PC teletraining, computer simulations and CBT, on-the-job training packages)
- *Considering alternatives to training* (more job aids, availability of "hot lines" for employees to call for information on service or product problems, sending new products to work locations so employees could experiment with them)
- *Training and using employees to deliver training on the job*

(encouraging peer training, using subject matter experts as trainers, borrowing field people for short-term assignments as instructors)

- *Enhancing the line supervisor's role in training* (improving supervisors' skills in career development for their staff, rewarding supervisors for planning training for their subordinates)
- *Improving work-force management* (more careful selection of new employees to ensure they have prerequisite skills, controlling work-force movement by not releasing experienced employees for transfers unless they can be replaced with qualified people)
- *Understanding training needs better* (developing a training profile inventory for each work group, identifying skill requirements for all jobs)
- *Motivating employees to increase their skills and knowledge* (providing incentives for out-of-hours training, ensuring that employees understand the benefits of training for improving their employment security).

The Gap Reduction Implementation Team. After generating these ideas for reducing the training gap, the training board of directors assigned a representative from each of the departments to work with a group of representatives from the training department to implement these and other solutions. My supervisor, the director of the training department, asked me to lead the team. There were nine field representatives and nine training department representatives on the team.

We began by making a conference call to get acquainted with one another and review the task. I requested that each team member representing a field organization collect examples of local training that occurred because local management felt a training gap existed. These examples were brought to our first two-day meeting several weeks after the conference call. The meeting followed the processes of a quality improvement team, which called for the group to understand the issues and determine improvement areas for themselves. (See Chapter Eight for a review of how to apply quality improvement processes to training department operations.) We were assisted by a "quality consultant"—an internal company manager whose job was to advise quality teams.

Perhaps because of the quality process or perhaps because all teams wanted to determine the problem themselves, we spent considerable time during the two-day meeting identifying training problems. Rather than take the training gap data at face value, the team members wanted to understand the reasons behind the numbers. The problems discussed ranged from field managers' difficulties in registering new employees for courses to problems involved in developing new training programs, such as not getting methods and procedures from subject matter experts to use as a basis for completing training programs in time for new product rollouts.

We also spent considerable time discussing who the customer was. The issue was whether we should take the perspective of the training director, the training board of directors, the lower-level field managers, the technicians taking the training, or the end customer, the one ultimately affected by the quality of service provided. This was an important question because we believed the answer would determine the focus of our actions and recommendations. When we considered that all these "customers" had common goals, it seemed appropriate to implement the ideas brainstormed by the board of directors. However, when we considered the needs of field supervisors, technicians, or the end users, it seemed that very different solutions would be needed in each location and that a single program or set of actions would not be the best way to solve the gap. The field representatives on the team felt that approaches that could be customized to the needs of specific locations made the most sense. The training department representatives were also anxious to be responsive to the field needs. After our two-day meeting, I talked to our training director about the question "Who is the customer for the team?" He had no hesitation in saying that field managers and technicians were our prime clients because they had direct contact with end-user customers.

During the six weeks before our next two-day meeting, the team members continued collecting examples of local training and also identifying training gap problems in their units and initiating trial solutions. The members were to discuss these trials at the next meeting in the hope that we could all learn from the trials and that eventually we would have a set of suggestions and examples for other field managers to follow. The solutions would evolve from the joint resources of the field and the training department (that is, educational consultants, course material, customized programs, and regular training courses).

These examples and trials were shared at the next group meeting. In addition, my staff had conducted a study of the amount of local training, and the results were reviewed at this meeting. We also devoted time to discussing the needs of three types of fieldwork units. The team broke into three subgroups, with each subgroup focusing on the training needs of the work unit most familiar to them. Each subgroup acted as if it were a local unit, discussing problem areas, identifying possible solutions, and developing action strategies. This was a model we could recommend to the field. The steps in this model are outlined in Exhibit 2 and may be useful to training departments in helping work groups review training needs.

The value of following this type of structured process is that it uses quality improvement principles, such as focusing on one problem, flowcharting current processes, examining root causes to problems and barriers in the normal flow of events, generating possible solutions, and considering the impact of these solutions. This procedure can be done in the group, utilizing the expertise of representatives from the training organization and the work group.

Determining Final Recommendations. Returning to the discussion of the training gap solution team, at the conclusion of the second, and final, two-day meeting, the team agreed on final recommendations to be presented to the board of directors. (Brainstorming and rank-ordering processes were used to arrive at the recommendations.) Therefore, the team felt it had completed its task, having defined the problems leading to the training gap, determined and trialed solutions to meet field needs, and provided suggestions that could be implemented in the field. Moreover, they determined ongoing responsibilities for the team, field managers, and the training department. Several members of the board of directors, after reviewing the team's recommendations, initiated

Exhibit 2. A Team Exercise for Identifying Training Gap Solutions.

1. Select a team leader.
2. Review problems specific to the work group:
   - Results of a training gap analysis study
   - Knowledge of local field issues
   - Knowledge of product/service changes and enhancements likely in the near future that will influence skill needs.
3. For each problem area, flow chart how it works—that is, how the problem would be solved typically.
4. Identify typical barriers and root causes of problems—what gets in the way of solving the problem.
5. Identify actionable root causes—important problems that can be solved.
6. Generate potential solutions to the root causes—distinguish between short-term, informal, and long-term solutions.
7. Project possible effects of the solutions on the training gap for the work group; for example:
   - Student training days reduced
   - Percent of employees in the work group trained
   - Speed of skill acquisition
   - Other benefits.

further activities in their departments to examine training needs closely and to develop training plans.

Some of our recommendations were very general suggestions for enhancing the importance of training and improving efficiency in the training department. Other recommendations were related more directly to reducing the training gap by providing more training. In some cases, the recommendations were similar to those initially generated by the training board of directors, but the team process helped team members feel ownership of these ideas. Also the team was convinced that these recommendations should require the commitment of local managers and be implemented in different ways in the field, depending on local need, with the support of the training department.

The top ten recommendations, and the persons responsible for action, are listed below in order of importance, starting with the most important. These suggestions may be useful to other organizations trying to integrate training department resources with local training.

1. *Train first- and second-level managers in supporting subordinates' development.* This was viewed as the responsibility of educational consultants in the training department and middle and top managers in each department. The team recommended a half-day seminar developed by one client department for managers to review their training goals, resources, and expectations of top management.

2. *Use more modularized training.* This would provide field managers with more flexibility in requesting combinations of training modules to meet their needs. Curriculum review committees and program developers should determine how particular training objectives should be split into modules.

3. *Form local quality improvement teams as one way to address ways to solve training gaps.* Department directors should suggest the need for such teams and support their solutions.

4. *Communicate local training experiences throughout the organization to provide other groups with ideas for reducing their training gaps.* The training department, the gap reduction team members, and departmental training coordinators should assume responsibility for increasing communication of these ideas and examples.

5. *Manage the budget accountability process to ensure that local managers recognize how much training they are using and to ensure that they use the training resource wisely.* The budget/expense system is critical to determining accountability. In our case, the cost of training program development and delivery was absorbed by the training department without usage-sensitive chargebacks to the field. The field paid for travel, lodging, and salaries when people were sent to training. However, one way to enhance local accountability is to charge back for training services. We were not ready to implement tuition, but we wanted local management to track training use and expense, and we suggested that the training board of directors periodically review the chargeback policy.

6. *In large companies, work with other training groups in the firm to avoid redundant program development and take advantage of existing programs.*

7. *Communicate results of training effectiveness to field*

managers. Consistent with the first recommendation for increasing managers' awareness of the importance of training, the field representatives on the team felt that local managers did not have data to show the effects of training programs—whether or not technicians learned the skills and knowledge needed to do their jobs. While in our case there were numerous measures available, the training department needed to do a better job of communicating these to the field rather than just using them internally to guide training development and to report to top management.

8. *Identify and accredit high-quality local training.* The team believed that field managers should have an opportunity to include locally developed and administered training on their technicians' training records. The training department should examine the content and process of the training if the intention is to substitute it for existing courses. Otherwise, there should be no restriction on local managers for including local training experiences on technicians' records. In our case, the administrative systems to do this needed to be developed.

9. *Hold local managers accountable for training plans.* Again, consistent with several of the above recommendations that deal with the importance of local accountability, the team wanted to recognize local managers' responsibility for developing training plans for their groups and for working with subordinates to ensure that each have a training plan. Field directors need to clarify this expectation and reward its accomplishment.

10. *Continue to monitor the training gap by analyzing training plans and skill needs.* This was viewed as the continuing responsibility of the gap reduction team. In our case, my training adminsitrative staff assumed principal responsibility for collecting information and communicating it to the team members and the board of directors. Also, we hoped that local line managers would play a more active role in developing training plans and carrying them out. Then field directors would have a clear understanding of the training needs in their units, and our aggregate data would support that view as well as provide direction for the training department's plans.

While these ten recommendations varied from the board's original suggestions, those suggestions were not forgotten. Many were a part of the local actions taken by the team members. In addition, budgetary pressures led to an urgent search for unit cost-efficiencies. The board suggested that the training department increase the use of advanced technologies, use training alternatives (such as job aids), and borrow field people to deliver courses as ways to improve efficiency in addition to increasing class size and ensuring that classes were filled as close to capacity as possible.

Role of the Educational Consultant

Chapter Three described the position of educational consultant as a training department resource for assisting clients in formulating training plans. Educational consultants design tools and methods and jointly work with managers in client departments in developing training plans.

Training plans help client departments meet their needs for trained personnel and allow the training department to determine needed resources. Training plans are likely to minimize the need for crisis training—that is, training needed immediately by technicians when a new product enhancement is to be installed. Also, training plans are likely to reduce unnecessary training by allowing supervisors to match training to work demands. In one case, a gap analysis based on matching training records to curriculum requirements and work schedules reduced the estimated training requirements by 50 percent. (Chapter Six provides examples of how training records can be used to compare individuals' training histories with the training curriculum required for their jobs. Analysis of individuals' records can be aggregated to examine training needs of work groups. Essentially, this is gap analysis by department.) While there is value in improving every employee's skills, there is little value in providing training that will not soon be used on the job. Employees generally lose skills and knowledge gained in training unless these skills are applied.

The educational consultant role is important in small as well as large organizations—wherever resources are scarce and must be used wisely to maximize benefit to the organization. Educational consulting may be part of a training manager's responsibilities or it may be a full-time position for one or more people. The educational consultant should have good interpersonal and problem-solving skills as well as knowledge of the curriculum and the firm's products and services. The consultant's role includes proactive consultation, which may entail working jointly with individuals and supervisors to establish plans or providing the resources (forms and guidelines) for employees to formulate their own training plans. Objectives of the consultant should be to create the training plans, help schedule training, and provide feedback to the client organization and the training department on the extent to which the plans are implemented.

Overall, the educational consultant function should improve the training department's image in the organization. Instead of waiting for clients to come to the training department, the educational consultant initiates and enhances the relationship between the training department and its clients. The training department should publicize the value of training plans in newsletters or bulletins, describing cases where training plans helped work groups save training costs.

Summary

Strategic planning is the foundation for training operations and should be an interactive process involving clients as well as training personnel. Planning should be based on data about training needs. Strategic plans should be communicated, discussed, and reviewed as they guide operations plans and activities and as new priorities arise. Training gap analysis is a way to involve the training department's clients, increase their understanding of training requirements, and help them agree on solutions.

Policy Opportunities and Recommendations

1. Planning should not be the sole responsibility of one administrative manager, although one such staff member may have responsibility for coordinating training plans. Input from clients, suppliers of subject matter, and training managers is critical for creating a vision of the future that these parties can understand and make a commitment to. What is required is a process for obtaining that input, communicating and discussing plans, and periodically

revising plans in light of accomplishments and priority changes. This chapter outlined such a process; however, the exact procedures and format are probably less important than the fact that planning is a participative process.

2. Strategic planning should be preactive, meaning that it should set a clear direction for the future. But it should also be interactive, meaning that contingency plans should be developed to prepare for changes in direction. Periodic training gap analyses, as described in this chapter, help keep the training organization current on client training needs and able to respond quickly to those needs.

3. Developing training plans and reducing or eliminating training gaps should be the primary responsibility of local managers. After all, they are held accountable for the performance of their work groups, and the skills and knowledge of the people in the group are a determining factor in the performance of the group. Field managers must develop the expertise of their people and, consequently, must have input to the training department's activities. Moreover, the training department should be a resource for supporting local training intitiatives. The training gap reduction team described in this chapter is a way to involve local managers in diagnosing and reducing the training gap in their units while also employing training department resources.

4. The training department should maintain a balance between providing standard training and meeting varying local needs. On the one hand, the department must provide uniformly high-quality training so everyone who needs the same skills and knowledge has the same training. On the other hand, local needs vary depending on employees' backgrounds and on work demands, and local managers may want to design their own training packages for local delivery. Therefore, training programs should be designed in flexible formats—for example, in modules, which can be combined in different ways to meet local needs.

The next chapter examines the budgeting and expense-tracking process. Tracking overall training costs as well as unit costs is key to making sound decisions about alternative training methods as well as to understanding the organization's investment in human resource development.

5

Measuring and Increasing Cost-Effectiveness

Organizations are increasingly concerned about the value of training. As budgets tighten, organizations look for efficiencies—ways to provide the same amount of training or more at less cost. This chapter examines the sources of training costs and ways to reduce training expenses.

The material in this chapter and the next chapter on training measurements can be understood by keeping in mind the variables and relationships outlined in Figure 3. The figure demonstrates the interrelationship among training expenses, outputs, and plans. Unit costs are a function of the integration of expenses relative to the products produced by the training department (for example, student days taught, computer-based programs delivered, new programs developed). Unit costs and evaluations of the effects of training (for example, posttraining test performance and job performance improvement) are the foundation for cost-benefit analyses of training programs. The cost-benefit analyses of training alternatives can be used in conjunction with employees' training histories and performance analyses of fieldwork groups to develop training plans and strategies for individuals, work groups, and the training departments.

Figure 3. Integrated Training Processes.

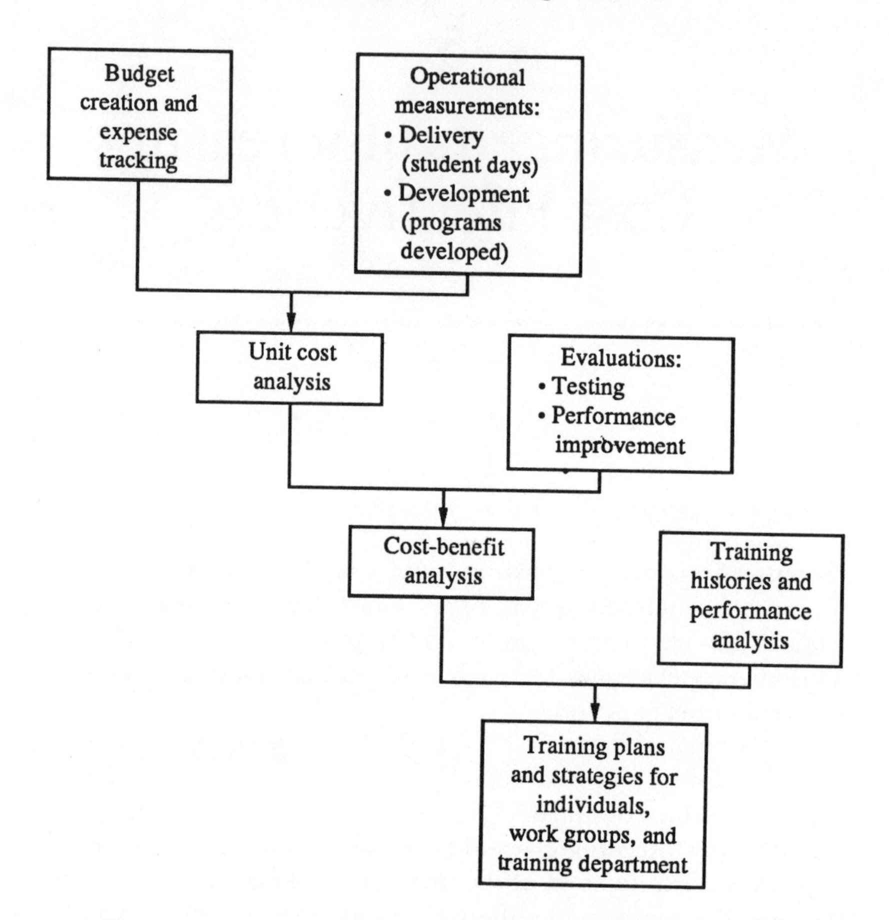

This chapter considers the budgeting process, examining the components of unit costs for training program development and delivery, current ways to reduce unit costs, and how to make training cuts when necessary. Competitive assessment is presented as a way to benchmark or compare the costs of training in the organization to the training costs incurred by competitors and the costs of training if purchased outside the organization. Such comparisons help ensure that the organization is competitive and provides the lowest unit cost for the most value.

Budget Preparation

How should an organization decide how much to spend on training? Often, new training programs are developed as they are needed and old training programs are continued as long as there is a demand, but no attention is given to priorities, long-term organizational goals, or the return on investment. It may seem obvious, but there should be a relationship between business goals and the training resources allocated to accomplishing those goals.

Operations Plans. One way to make budget decisions is to assess the costs associated with projects in the business plan and its associated operations plans. As noted in Chapter Four, operations plans identify programs, describe key projects associated with those programs (such as the curriculum of courses and related training materials), and target the population of training. The objectives and benefits should be stated, including benefits to the customers as well as the relationship of the program to organizational strategies. Actions and critical milestones for accomplishing the program should be listed, and any cross-initiative impacts should be stated (for example, whether the program development depends on other programs such as training in prerequisite knowledge and skills).

The operations plans need to be specific enough so that budget estimates can be derived, and program development and delivery outputs should be detailed. For instance, for program development, the number of course days and associated "people months" (the number of developers multiplied by the number of months required to develop the program) should be determined for new instructional design as well as refinements and enhancements of ongoing programs. For delivery, the operations plans should indicate the number of student days that will be instructor-led (including training delivered at a training site and training suitcased to a work site). The equivalent student days for computer-based training modules and other advanced training media used in the program should also be determined. Then the operations plans should indicate the amount of instructor time required.

The next step is to translate the above resource requirements into dollars. Development costs should be split into capital funds for equipment, namely computer equipment or products employees are learning to use; these costs are depreciated over the life of the equipment. The development budget should also include the expenses associated with program developers, instructional technologists, and others who will work on the project. These expenses include salary, merit pay, pension and benefits, travel, relocation if appropriate, and other money that might be allocated on a per person basis, such as money for office supplies. Capital and expense dollars should also be determined for training delivery. Cost estimates should be made for the life of the program, which may be one to five years in the future.

The operations plans should also include a statement of what would happen if the budget were cut. For instance, what part of the program would be compromised if the budget were cut by 10 or 20 percent? Is the project an all-or-nothing situation? Can minor pieces be eliminated and there still be a useful product? To what extent would quality be sacrificed by cutting corners throughout the project? (Ways to compare the cost-benefit of alternative ways of developing and delivering a training program are considered later in this chapter. This comparison should be made before the operations plans are formulated.)

Unit Cost Analysis. A good way to develop cost estimates and a good basis for comparing the costs of different training methods is to translate dollars into unit costs. However, there is no universally accepted metric for comparing training costs. The training organization must decide what unit to use and then determine what the components of the unit are. Then all cost comparisons must use the same unit and calculate it in the same way; otherwise, comparing unit costs will be like comparing apples with oranges.

One meaningful unit is a student day. The question becomes, how much does it cost to develop or deliver a student day of training? Since instructor-led classroom instruction is still a common mode of training, and probably the most common in most training organizations, this unit is a meaningful metric. However, unit costs for other methods of training must be translated into student-day costs. This is a matter of judgment and, of course, depends on the particular training methods used. The following is a fairly conservative translation:

- *Computer-based training*—2:1 (two instructor-led student days for every one day of CBT; or two hours of classroom instruction for every one hour of self-paced PC training)
- *Videotape and video disk training*—2:1 (the same as CBT)
- *PC teletraining*—1.5:1 (one and a half instructor-led student days for every one day of PC teletraining).

These ratios will vary from one application to another, and it is important to consider such comparisons when examining the cost-effectiveness trade-off of alternative modes of training delivery. Also, in making such comparisons it should be recognized that while the amount of information conveyed may increase considerably with advanced technology training methods, the amount of learning may not. For instance, with CBT the increase in amount learned may be one-third more than for instructor-led training on some content, not two times as much.

As discussed in Chapter Two, each type of training technology is better for some types of training than for others, so the technologies are not completely interchangeable. For example, CBT is an excellent medium for simulating work, especially if the job requires using a terminal and associated software. Video works well for demonstrating new procedures and communications skills, but it may need to be supplemented with instructor coaching.

Unit costs are determined by dividing the total cost of the program by the number of units. In the case of program development, the units are the number of videos produced, the number of days of instructor-led training developed, or the number of computer disks written. In the case of program delivery, the units are the number of students trained, the number receiving the self-paced computer program, the number of job aids distributed, and so on. The resulting unit costs can be translated into equivalent student-day costs using the above ratios.

Determining the costs of delivering a self-paced course or video leads to some questions, such as, how do we know whether the course is actually used or how many people used it? There are some ways to determine use, such as only crediting people who successfully pass a test based on the self-paced course. Another issue that unit cost comparisons address is whether the costs for developing a particular program are appropriate. Perhaps it is less expensive to send students to training offered externally, for example, at a university, than it is for the organization to develop and deliver the program in house.

Another difficulty is determining standard, or average, unit costs for easy comparison. For instance, is developing a one-hour videotape more or less expensive than developing three hours of instructor-led training? A tape may provide more information or a better demonstration while reducing the number of hours students spend in the classroom. But how much more expensive is a tape to produce? Unit costs for the same training medium vary considerably, depending on the purpose and content of the program and the desired quality. A one-hour video can be produced using home video techniques for perhaps $3,000, including several days of the producer's time, the cost of travel to interview experts or to film demonstrations at work locations, and the cost of materials. The same tape could be produced professionally with actors, music, graphics, and other "bells and whistles" for $25,000 to $30,000. Deciding which to use depends on educational value, the impression the organization wants to convey to the student, and the funds available. The professional tape may be better in capturing students' attention and clearer in demonstrating techniques. Also, the extra cost may be small per unit delivered if there is a large audience for the tape.

To examine the variation in components of unit costs for training development, instructional technologists at McDonnell Douglas Corporation calculated the range of time it takes to develop printed materials that yield about one hour of student "contact time" (Lee and Zemke, 1987, p. 78):

- Subject matter expert: 4.8 to 46 hours
- Instructional technologist: 4.8 to 18 hours
- Technical writer: 3.2 to 14 hours
- Graphic artist: 8.8 to 92 hours
- Word processor: 4.8 to 28 hours
- Reviewer: 1.6 to 6 hours

These hours can be translated into cost ranges by multiplying average time by employee-rated expenses. Other time analyses allow comparison of different training technologies. For instance, a video may take 160 to 345 hours to develop for each hour of instruction. Instructor-led training may take from 80 to 315 hours to develop for each hour of instruction (Lee and Zemke, 1987).

Development costs also vary depending on how much "up-front" work is done before developing the program, including whether a job analysis is conducted and, of course, the depth of that job analysis. Another source of costs is field testing before putting the program on line. To some extent, these costs are independent of the training medium in that they are incurred regardless of what medium is chosen. Nevertheless, they must be included in the unit cost calculation. Another cost factor in developing training programs is the expertise and experience of the developers. Computer-based training requires specialized skills that develop over time. The first CBT course developed by a training organization may take much more time—and thus cost more—to develop and may be much less valuable than the tenth CBT course developed.

An analysis of the organization's current unit costs can be of value in understanding and controlling resource expenditures and in setting goals for the future. One training organization examined its training costs in relation to the student-day units produced and delivered. The following unit costs were derived:

Current Unit Costs	*Development*	*Delivery*
Instructor-led	$ 91	$182
CBT and video	228	19
PC teletraining	153	98

The training organization then reevaluated the mix of training media used in its programs and planned ways to reduce unit costs (described below). One way unit costs were reduced was by increasing the numbers of students in a class and by discouraging cancellations (by sending out reminders or charging departments for a seat if the registered employee failed to show up). Since there was a high demand for the training in the organization, this approach made sense. By increasing the number of students in the class, the average unit cost for instructor-led development could be reduced to $69 per student, and the unit cost of instructor-led delivery could be reduced to $138. Many of the courses covered highly technical material taught to classes of six to eight students. The training managers judged that efficiencies in unit costs could be produced by increasing the size of these classes by two or three students without a loss in learning. Programs in management development and technical fundamentals were generally offered to larger classes (twenty to twenty-five students), and these class sizes could be increased further (by five to ten students) to achieve significant economies of scale. In general, when increasing class size, production goals must be considered alongside learning goals. The nature of the material and desirable interaction between students and instructor must be considered to ensure that learning is not compromised.

Another way the organization could have saved money was to increase use of advanced technologies, especially CBT and video, which lend themselves to many subject matter areas. In general, the average cost of instruction using advanced delivery technologies is lower than instructor-led, face-to-face training (Chute, Balthazar, and Poston, 1988), but the cost of development for advanced delivery methods is almost always more. This drawback is offset by the fact that self-paced, advanced technology methods can reach far more people more quickly than face-to-face classroom training, thus defraying some of the higher development costs.

Calculating Cost Avoidance

Since advanced technology training methods generally cost more to develop, a training department usually has to provide concrete justification for their use. This can be done by calculating the costs avoided by using more self-paced training, which reaches more people faster and also increases the rate of learning.

For instance, IBM calculated that in 1988 the increased use of self-paced training and other advanced technology methods decreased the user's costs (that is, student salaries, travel, and lodging incurred by the firm's business units) by $430 million. The company planned to save an additional $300 million in users' costs in 1989 by increasing use of advanced technology methods. However, the increased development costs as well as increased demand for training (resulting from reorganization and work-force redeployment) required increasing the training units' budgets in 1989 over 1988. Nonetheless, the costs avoided were still far higher than the increase in the training budget, and this provided a strong case for spending more on direct training costs.

The value of calculating cost avoidance is that savings can be viewed as money that can be isolated and diverted for other uses, not just as money that does not have to be spent. The corporation must be able to reduce the budgets of the business units and plow the money into other investments or return the savings to the shareholders in the form of dividends. In come cases, the organization may wish to use part of the savings for further enhancing employee education by providing more training than would otherwise be available.

Improving Training Efficiency

As the manager for the administrative staff of a large technical training organization, I was responsible for budget management. I was asked to serve on a steering committee to reduce the unit cost of training development and delivery. The need for improved efficiency arose because the company was trying to reduce overhead wherever possible. Any function that did not involve direct customer contact was considered overhead; thus, training fell into the category of overhead. However, the firm recognized that there was a substantial training gap in the technical training needed by employees and the training that was planned. Therefore, reducing overhead by cutting the training budget and providing less training would increase the training gap, not narrow it. The goal of the steering committee, then, was to provide more training but to maintain a flat budget by improving unit costs.

The four-member steering committee included representatives from the development and delivery arms of the department as well as my administrative staff. We began our work by asking managers responsible for the various curricula to indicate the sources of costs and to identify ways already under way to improve efficiency. We then convened a meeting of representatives from every major development and delivery unit within the department—about twenty people in all. At the meeting, we reviewed the cost data and brainstormed ways to further improve training efficiency. The ideas we generated suggested better ways to improve training program development and delivery, improve unit costs, and, in some cases, reduce absolute costs. These methods are summarized in Exhibits 3 and 4.

In general, development methods can be improved by ensuring that the training content and medium of delivery are appropriate, by reviewing the costs and benefits of alternative training methods, by enhancing course developers' skills, and by mechanizing the workplace for less expensive development and production of materials. Training program delivery can be improved by better planning of the course schedule and use of training classrooms, by determining the best travel arrangements, by improving communications among local work groups and delivery managers and instructors, and by better counseling to ensure that employees have the right prerequisites and job needs to participate in a training program.

Competitive Assessment

Competitive assessment provides an indication of the efficiency of the training organization. Such assessment is the process of comparing measures of training development and delivery in the organization with similar measures from other organizations' training departments. These measures are termed *benchmarks*. Competitive assessment is also the process of comparing the types of training provided to similar types of employees—for example, comparing how companies develop and advance their high-potential managers, comparing the content of a management curriculum, or comparing how much training service technicians in a particular field receive on the products they service.

A caveat in collecting comparative financial data is that the components of the measures must be the same in the organizations used for comparison. Organizations maintain different financial records and use different categories of expenses. Companies often

Exhibit 3. Ways to Improve Development Efficiency.

Ensure all existing and new courses and curriculum

- Match target audience needs
- Use documentation, methods and procedures (M&Ps), and job aids when possible in place of, or in conjunction with, training
- Use alternative, high-tech training media when appropriate
- Teach to objectives (eliminate "nice to know" information)
- Modularize materials for maximum flexibility and use
- Use appropriate media to match the training content and the experience of the student
- Teach systems (generic concepts).

Ensure that cost-benefit reviews

- Examine existing courses
- Perform front-end reviews and performance analyses to identify non-training solutions
- Track development costs and look for improvement areas
- Compare costs of alternative training options.

Enhance course developers' skills in

- Providing better courses
- Allocating training professionals to projects
- Providing comprehensive career planning for training professionals.

Involve training professionals in

- Identifying and implementing efficiencies
- Using quality improvement teams.

Mechanize the workplace by

- Using desktop publishing and computer word processing
- Using computer-based, on-line catalogs
- Making it a showcase for training technology.

---

do not make such information freely available. When financial data are available, it is important to determine how the information was obtained and how figures were calculated. For instance, the cost of delivering one student day of instructor-led training might include the cost of student salaries, travel, and lodging—or it might not. While these problems make competitive assessments difficult, they

Exhibit 4. Ways to Improve Delivery Efficiency.

Plan delivery:

- Improve scheduling and allocation of instructors to classes and training sites
- Review training sites (share and/or consolidate sites with other training departments in the organization)
- Prioritize delivery based on impact to the organization
- Make careful forecasts of clients' training needs (forecasting programs needed and timing).

Decrease travel expenses:

- Negotiate the best travel arrangements (hotel, rental car, and airfare discounts)
- Use training technology for meetings of training professionals and train-the-trainer sessions (for instance, video conferences)

Improve communications among training staff members, field personnel, and students:

- Ensure standard training procedures
- Coordinate local and regional training for continuity and avoidance of redundancy
- Provide accurate, up-front information to students and instructors (such as dates, locations, and times)
- Inform students and field supervisors of program availability.

Provide convenient registration:

- Ensure that educational consultants, training counselors, and registrars are accessible.

are not insurmountable barriers. Competitive information should be sought, scrutinized closely, and compared to current operations to identify areas and ideas for improvement.

The organizations included in a competitive benchmark analysis must be meaningful as comparisons in terms of the type of training provided. In general, organizations should compare their costs to their major competitors—firms that are in the same or in a similar business. Such comparisons can identify not only the efficiency of the training department but also the competitiveness of the organization as a whole, using as a basis the amount and the ways money is invested in developing employees and customers.

Sources of Competitive Benchmark Data. There are many sources of useful competitive information. Periodicals such as *Training* and the *Training and Development Journal* often publish articles comparing companies' training, as do journals that focus on a specific segment of the training industry or on a technology that is applied to training—for instance, the *CBT Report, Telespan,* and *Videodisc Monitor.* Other good sources include the Training Director's Forum *Newsletter* and the newsletters of associations of training professionals, such as the National Society for Performance Instruction and the American Society for Training and Development. Valuable competitive information can be obtained by attending conferences sponsored by training associations. Business periodicals, such as *Fortune, Forbes, Business Week,* and the *Wall Street Journal,* occasionally have articles that refer to a firm's training programs.

It is possible to commission business research organizations and management consulting firms to conduct a special competitive benchmark study for a specific organization. The research firm mails or does telephone surveys of the organizations to be used as a basis for comparison; the surveys can be done without mentioning the name of the initiating firm. The cost for such work will vary considerably depending on the firm hired and the amount of work done. Hiring a well-known consulting firm to understand the specific goals and strategies desired and to design the study, report the results, and make recommendations will be far more expensive than designing the study internally and hiring an outside firm to obtain answers.

Some organizations work together as a consortium to sponsor a benchmark study among themselves and then share the results. Companies such as Kodak, IBM, and AT&T have organized such groups. Training departments interested in participating in such a study could contact the American Society for Training and Development, headquartered in Alexandria, Virginia, or could contact training directors in major companies for information.

Types of Competitive Information. Competitive benchmark data are available on the cost of training, how much and what type of training is provided to employees, the effectiveness of the training, what training media are used, how training is structured in the organization, and how training fits into the organization's strategies. Sometimes this information is specific to single organizations, as in, for example, journal articles on how new managers are developed at General Electric (Komanecky, 1988) or on how Motorola uses training to prepare employees for technological change (Doyle, 1986). Other times this information is specific to an industry overall, being derived from a survey that included a number of different firms. (See, for instance, Stephan, Mills, Pace, and Ralphs, 1988, who report the results of a survey of human resource managers in 179 *Fortune* 500 companies responding to a questionnaire about management development and human resource practices.)

Competitive benchmark information is fluid—that is, it applies only to the time the data were collected. After all, organizations frequently change how they operate, often in response to competitive benchmark information. Consequently, collecting comparative information should be done periodically. Another issue to consider is the reliability and comprehensiveness of the data. Firms will guard proprietary information and may be reluctant to provide complete information on their training strategies and programs. However, organizations also recognize that they benefit from sharing information. One way to collect such information is to promise to share the results with the participating organizations and to ensure that the firms are not mentioned by name.

Several examples of competitive benchmark data are presented in the following subsections. This information was derived from public sources that name companies or provide generic information. Since specific figures are likely to change over time, general information and, in come cases, examples of specific firms are provided for illustrative purposes.

Training Costs. Comparative figures are often available on the amount of money organizations spend on training employees. For example, figures from four major organizations in the telecommunications industry indicate that money spent per employee per year in 1986 ranged from $350 to $822 and that the average spent in the United States on training was $283 per employee (American

Society for Training and Development, 1986). If this information is not available in this form, it can be calculated by dividing the total training expenses by the total number of employees in the firm, if this figure is available elsewhere.

Another index of expense is training costs as a proportion of salary. Data from eight high-tech companies indicate that training costs made up 1.5 to 7 percent of salary costs. Other indicators of expense are training budget as a percent of the total corporate budget (which was about 1 percent in two telecommunications companies), training budget as a percent of payroll (1 to 2.5 percent in serveral high-tech firms), and training costs as a percent of after-tax revenue (2.5 to 3 percent in a major reprographics company).

Such information is based on responses to surveys, and the extent to which such information is accurate and can be extrapolated to the whole country may be questionable. An important need continues to be a more accurate assessment of training costs across the country. Some large companies, such as IBM, have made the effort to understand their total training costs and the components of these costs (Galagan, 1989) and provide a model of what other firms could do in this area. (See the description of IBM's cost structure in Resource B.)

Amount of Training. In 1986 the national average of the number of days an employee spends in training per year was 4.4 days (Bureau of National Affairs, 1986). The data for this category shows a considerable range, with some firms reporting that employees spend as little as three days per year in training and other firms reporting as much as ten to fourteen days. It is also important to determine whether the training employees receive outside the organization is included, but doing so is difficult, since firms may not collect this data. Variance can also occur if the organization includes on-the-job, in-class, or self-paced training; the inclusion of any of these can raise the training figure significantly.

The amount of training employees receive depends on their position in the organization and varies by industry (Ballman, 1987). Middle managers, executives, and professionals tend to have more training (twenty-seven to fifty-one hours per year) than do sales representatives, production workers, office/secretarial personnel, and customer service representatives (eleven to forty-four hours per year). There are some exceptions: in the educational services industry, sales representatives spend an average of 81.5 hours a year in training, and customer representatives spend an average of 70.6 hours per year in training (Ballman, 1987).

For comparison, it is useful to know how much competitors spend on training and how much training is provided. Such information must be interpreted in light of the firms in the study and the changes in the industry. More money spent on training may suggest that the competitor is doing a better job in keeping pace with new technology, or it may imply that the competitor is a new entrant to the market and needs to catch up by improving employees' skills. A company that spends less on training may be falling behind in the marketplace, or it may be acquiring skilled employees in other ways, such as raiding your firm!

Types of Training. Training is important for helping employees perform well in their current jobs, for keeping employees informed of technical and procedural changes, and for helping employees qualify for future jobs in the organization. Knowing what types of training competitors provide to employees indicates the types of skills and knowledge competitors consider important to success in the marketplace.

Most large firms offer a variety of technical and managerial training. Some firms have recently revised their curricula to include training on principles of quality improvement, project management, software engineering, and automated manufacturing—areas that are becoming key in manufacturing and high-tech organizations. In some firms, the emphasis has shifted from generalized education to training directed almost exclusively at job-relevant skills and knowledge.

As an example, Corning Glass focuses on quality in all its training programs. Managers can take courses on planning, delegating, time management, quality control, interpersonal and communications skills, statistical problem solving, and experimental design and analysis. Engineers and scientists have the same course opportunities and, in addition, have the chance to take courses in project management and quality support as well as in engineering and technical disciplines. All employees are encouraged to develop "team competencies," such as effective group participation, problem solving, and statistical data gathering.

IBM is focusing on technology and quality. Its major areas of education include technical training, marketing and product information, financial planning and analysis, office systems education, and management development training. Other themes emerging in corporate training curricula are managing change, career planning, supporting subordinate development, strategic planning, designing organizations, improving customer interface skills, as well as quality control, marketing education, and participative management.

Needs Assessments. It is instructive to know how organizations decide what training to offer. The American Society for Training and Development (1986) found that needs analyses are done 50 percent of the time or less. Firms most likely to conduct needs analyses prior to developing training are those that have met their financial goals, those that training executives describe as innovative, and those in which the most senior training managers' roles involve being key members of a corporate team. Less successful and less innovative firms are quick to adopt a training program without considering whether other options might be better. The most frequently used methods of needs assessment are interviews with employees and direct observation of work (used by 80 percent or more of firms doing needs analysis). Other methods include examining performance or productivity measures, questionnaires about skill needs, and task analysis (used 60 to 75 percent of the time).

Training Evaluation. Knowing the effects of training in other organizations suggests directions for training and provides a basis for analyzing whether and how training can be made more effective. However, evaluation of return on training investments does not occur with much regularity, at least as shown in the *Fortune* 500 survey of HRD practices (Stephan, Mills, Pace, and Ralphs, 1988). Self-evaluation or supervisor judgments are usually considered measures of training success. Consequently, organizations that do assess the effects of training on job performance and organizational effectiveness are probably at a competitive advantage, being able to guide wisely the use of training dollars. (Evaluation methods are described in Chapter Six.)

Training Media. As noted earlier in this chapter, alternatives to instructor-led training are becoming the norm rather than the exception. For instance, IBM's goal for electronic training is to provide 50 percent of all training using computer-based methods. Further, IBM intends to have 10 percent of its training delivered by satellite by 1990. This technique works well for delivering training on product updates to branch sales offices and to remotely located service technicians. By 1990 only 40 percent of IBM's training will involve the traditional instructor-led class. A similar trend is occurring in companies such as DEC, Hewlett Packard, Apple, and GTE. In 1988 the majority of training in these companies was still instructor-led (about 65 percent). However, about 15 percent involved computer-based training or PC conferencing, 15 percent was hands-on lab training, and 4 percent utilized some other media, such as satellite or video.

Innovative approaches to training are evident in how training is described to employees. For example, Aetna's charter for its Institute for Corporate Education mandates experimenting with new learning technologies; the company's course catalog was replaced by a directory of "learning events." Rolm includes job sharing, job rotation, coaching, and mentoring in its schedule of courses. GE encourages "action learning," and includes "outward-bound" events (challenging group physical activities) in its management development programs. Honeywell uses "action learning workshops" to solve actual business problems while teaching new problem-solving techniques (Churma, Henton, and Melville, 1987).

When human resource managers in a study of 179 *Fortune* 500 companies were asked about the use of alternative training technology, the results showed that while many firms use advanced technology, such use is limited (Stephan, Mills, Pace, and Ralphs, 1988). While the respondents may not have been completely knowledgeable about all their company's training programs, the results of the study are interesting and point to the need for more research. Specifically, the study asked, "How often are the following technologically advanced techniques used for training in your company?" The response scale ranged from 1 (almost never) to 5 (almost always), and the following results were tabulated (p. 30):

	Percentage Using Scale Points		
	5 only	*4 and 5*	*Mean*
Computer-assisted instruction	3	17	2.42
Interactive video	4	17	2.24
Teleconferencing	1	5	1.59
Satellite TV networks	1	6	1.44
Artificial intelligence	1	3	1.41
Electronic workbooks	1	2	1.37

These mean scores are very low. However, as many as 17 percent of the firms rely on computers and interactive video enough to provide a rating of 4 or 5. The implication is that training departments that are still using predominantly instructor-led training and are not moving to other media are probably much less flexible in the training provided and are probably incurring more delivery costs than necessary. However, as noted earlier in the chapter, technology-based training is often expensive to develop, and the cost-effectiveness of such methods depends on the specific media, the sophistication of the user, and the ease of adapting the subject matter to the training technology.

Organizational Structures and Strategies. Finding out how other organizations structure and deliver employee training can be useful in gauging the efficiency of a training organization and can, at least, suggest other ideas for improved operations. Many organizations have central training divisions; others centralize program development and deliver the programs in each department. American Express centralizes training delivery separately within each subsidiary. Another approach—taken by such firms as Westinghouse, Shell Oil, GM, Xerox, and AT&T—is to have a mix of centralized and decentralized training.

Degree of training centralization, as discussed in Chapter Three, is as much a matter of management philosophy as of economics. The philosophical rationale for increased decentralization is to develop an educational program that is directly tied to the needs of each department. The rationale for centralization is to convey an organizationwide message that emphasizes overall goals and encourages all employees, regardless of department or function, to work toward a common goal and feel a common identification with the firm. IBM takes such an approach in its central training department, expecting employees to complete a specific set of courses as they move up the organizational hierarchy.

Most organizations now view employee training as an integral part of overall corporate strategy. This belief has an effect on how training is organized. At Corning Glass, training managers within a division report to a senior vice-president for the division and also report to a corporate director of training. This matrix of reporting relationships encourages cross-functional identification of training needs and allows training managers access to human resource managers and other training managers as well as to top management in their departments.

General Electric has an engineering advisory council that directs their engineering continuing education program. Senior managers from all major technical areas as well as marketing and business planning advise the training department on technological change, suggest needed courses, and provide guidance on course content and choice of instructors. At GE, employees are evaluated on how well they keep current; failure to attend to personal development weakens the likelihood of further advancement.

Budgeting. Information about how other companies allocate training resources indicates the attention given to training. At Pacific Telesis, the human resource central staff examines business strategies and then targets the amount to be spent. Line managers are responsible for the allocation of the funds within the targeted amount. At Corning Glass, the budget is decided and targeted at each unit by identifying training needs and calculating the cost of these needs.

Making Conclusions and Recommendations from Competitive Assessments

Competitive assessments should lead to conclusions and recommendations for improvement. Consider the following possible results from such an assessment for a fictitious firm, BBB, Inc.:

- BBB spends much less per employee on training than other firms in the industry.
- BBB provides less training per employee than its competitors.
- BBB devotes roughly twice the training resources for management and administration of training than its competitors.
- Major firms in the industry report sizable savings through self-paced training using computers, videos, and workbooks. BBB uses a much smaller percent of self-paced training than its competition.
- Competitors plan to allocate more resources to self-paced training in the next few years; BBB has no such plans.

Such conclusions suggest that training is not as important in BBB as in other similar firms. This may be because BBB is a new firm and has younger, more recently training employees. If such is the case, BBB should evaluate its long-term strategy for employee development. Training may not now be necessary but may be critical as technology develops and as trained people become less plentiful. On the other hand, the conclusions may be the result of lack of managerial foresight. The results may be a precursor to increasing unresponsiveness to customer needs and an eventual downturn in BBB's profits.

In general, training managers must be willing to collect competitive assessment data and then analyze it critically to ensure it is accurate and a meaningful basis for comparison. Then training managers must be prepared to act on the results by implementing programs. In the case of BBB, a wise move may be to form training councils to oversee the analysis of training needs and then to allocate financial and human resources to training methods and training content that meet short- and long-term organizational needs. Resource B provides an in-depth view of how two companies—Motorola and IBM— operate their training departments.

Determining When Training Is Needed

Since this book is not on training design or instructional technology, needs analysis methods are considered only briefly. However, several methods that help in determining whether training makes good financial sense are presented in the following subsections.

Performance Analysis. Performance analysis is the process of examining performance problems, estimating their cost, and identifying potential solutions. The costs of these solutions are estimated along with their likely effectiveness. Performance analyses ensure that when training is implemented, it is related to a definite need and that other solutions were considered and determined to be less beneficial than training.

A sample worksheet for conducting performance analysis is shown in Exhibit 5. Performance analysis begins by recording behaviors and examining work outputs. Reasons for deficient outputs must be examined. When they can be attributed to employee behaviors—for instance, lack of necessary individual action or poor communication—then the context is examined to determine possible causes. Skill and knowledge deficiencies might suggest the need for training. However, other factors—such as a weak communications system or a slow financial reports system—may be the cause of the ineffective behavior. If skill or knowledge deficiencies are identified, then possible solutions should be developed. Training may be one solution, but there could be others, such as improved selection systems that ensure that people hired have the needed skills. Job simplification may be another nontraining solution.

The cost of performance deficiencies should be estimated by adding the costs of lost person hours, additional materials needed in redoing the work, use of equipment, and lost revenues. Next, the costs of alternative solutions should be estimated. For training, this includes the cost of up-front job analysis, program development, materials, training facilities, instructor salary, vendor charges (if a vendor is involved in providing all or part of the training), travel and lodging for students and instructor, and student wages. Costs of different training alternatives must be determined—for example, the cost of a video versus the cost of a written job aid versus the cost of classroom instruction.

Finally, the cost of the problem must be compared to the cost of the solution. Training will be worthwhile if it saves more than the cost of the problem. In addition to cost avoidance, the benefits of

Exhibit 5. Performance Analysis Worksheet.

1. What specific skill has been observed to be lacking?

2. How often has this been a problem?

3. How many employees are involved?

4. In what job is this a problem?

5. What solutions are possible?

6. Is training a legal requirement [as it is in some regulated industries]? Or is training required by a union contract? [If training is required, the cost-benefit analysis should focus on a comparison of alternative training methods, not on whether training is needed.]

7. Lost opportunity analysis:

a.

Costs	*Number of Employees*		*Hours*		*Wages per Hour*		*Total Cost*
Person hours lost	______	×	______	×	______	=	______
Redoing work	______	×	______	×	______	=	______
Equipment							______
Materials							______
Total estimated skill deficiency costs						$	______

b. How much was work load reduced per employee because of the skill or knowledge deficiency?

c. Total lost opportunity cost = 7a + 7b

Exhibit 5. Performance Analysis Worksheet, Cont'd.

8. Training cost analysis:

a. Course development costs:

Costs	*Work Hours Required*		*Cost per Hour*		*Total Cost*
Up-front performance analysis	______	×	______	=	______
Program development	______	×	______	=	______
Materials					______
Total development costs					$ ______

b. Outside vendor costs (if applicable).

c. Instructor costs:

Food + travel + lodging = $ ______
Hourly rate × number of class hours = $ ______
Total instructor costs $ ______

d. Student costs:

Food + travel + lodging × number of students = $ ______
Hourly rate × number of class hours × number of students = $ ______
Total student costs $ ______

e. Total training costs = 8a + 8b + 8c + 8d

9. Cost-benefit analysis:

Cost-benefit = 7c – 8e [A positive number suggests that lost opportunities are higher than the cost of the training required; thus, training is likely to be cost-effective.]

Source: Adapted from a form used by an electric utility company to analyze performance and determine the effectiveness of training.

other solutions should be determined. For instance, the training may result in higher productivity, which in turn increases revenues. This is discussed in following subsections.

Cost-Effectiveness Analysis

Cost-effectiveness analysis is a way to determine the monetary benefits of a training program over and above the costs of the program and in comparison to other training programs (or to no other programs). There are several steps to follow (adapted from Cascio, 1982; and Cullen, Sawzin, Sisson, and Swanson, 1978):

1. *Determine the cost of training development.* This includes the costs for performance and job analysis (including salary, benefits, and overhead), design, material, instructional software, videos, and so on. These costs may be divided among the salary and benefits of program developers, subject matter experts, and contractors, or allocated in costs of supplies; clerical and graphic services; computer time, hardware, and other equipment; and travel and lodging. The training department's administrative costs can also be allocated against training development, depending on the proportion of development work in the department relative to other functions (for example, training delivery).
2. *Calculate the training cost. Fixed costs* include the cost of training facilities, videos, slides, and other material that is reusable. These costs can be amortized over the course of the training, and the cost per student decreases as more students participate in the training. Registration costs and other administrative costs (data systems, the training department's administrative staff) can also be allocated against training delivery. *Variable costs* include the costs of materials and time associated with each student's participation in the program. The total variable costs will depend on the number of students, but the costs of items in this category probably are fixed per student (except when materials are cheaper owing to large orders.) Also, each student incurs costs for salary and benefits and travel and lodging. Costs associated with instructors

(salaries, travel, and so on) may be variable if instructors are paid by class (as they would be if contractors were hired by class). Instructors who are full-time employees also present variable costs if they do other productive work when they are not teaching; and thus, their salaries and associated costs can be allocated to these other non-instruction-related functions.

3. *Assess losses resulting from training.* These costs are the result of lower rates of production, errors, and inadequate skills or knowledge.
4. *Estimate the financial value of each possible return from the training.* This is the monetary value derived from each output learned in the training program and could include the value of increased production rate, higher-quality products, less wasted material, increased sales, and so forth. Converting performance information to dollars may be done objectively when performance can be quantified (for instance, units processed), and the cost of each unit can be determined. However, performance, particularly on managerial tasks, is often a subjective assessment. Supervisors are usually asked to judge the monetary value of each important performance element. (See Cheek, 1973, and Cascio, 1982, for such assessment methods.)
5. *Compare the cost of training to the benefits.* The financial gain from the training is subtracted from the cost of training to determine cost-effectiveness. For example, Motorola determined the value of a program to teach employees principles and methods of statistical quality control. They estimated that three Florida manufacturing facilities saved $5.2 million in two years through the application of the skills and knowledge learned in the program (Galazen, 1986). In another analysis, Motorola showed a 30-to-1 return on a sales training program.

Utility Analysis. Utility is the increased value of the training to the organization over the cost of the training. It is a function of the effect of the training on job performance and the monetary value of an improvement in performance (Godkewitsch, 1987) and can be represented as:

$$F = N[(E \times M) - C]$$

where F = financial utility
N = number of employees
E = effect size (in standard deviations)
M = monetary value of one standard deviation of job performance
C = average cost of training per employee

In addition:

$$\text{Payback period} = C/(E \times M)$$

$$\text{Return on investment (ROI)} = [(E \times M) - C]/C$$

These formulas can be demonstrated practically if we make certain assumptions; for instance, consider effect size. Training generally has a fairly strong effect on productivity compared with other organizational interventions; however, the strength of the effect depends on the performance criterion used as well as the particular training program (Guzzo, Jette, and Katzell, 1985). The exact amount of effect a training program has can be determined by relating the amount of participation in the training to later performance. Such evaluation methods are discussed in the Chapter Six. For now, we will assume that the effect is 0.49.

Next, we will assume that the monetary value of one standard deviation of performance is worth 40 percent of a student's average annual salary. Assume the average salary for employees who are the target for the particular training program is $35,000. There are other ways to estimate the value of one standard deviation of performance. For instance, one method asks supervisors to evaluate the worth of employees who perform at the fiftieth percentile—the level of performance at which 50 percent of the employees are lower and 50 percent are higher. Supervisors are then asked to judge the value of performance at the eighty-fifth percentile (the point at which 85 percent of the sales managers are lower and 15 percent are higher). The difference between the fiftieth and the eighty-fifth percentiles is taken as the average (or standard) deviation of employees' performance. (See Cascio and Silbey, 1979; and Cascio,

1982, for descriptions of this approach as well as other more detailed approaches.)

Now, we will assume that the cost of the training is $1,620 per employee. This figure is based on a program that costs $965 per employee, plus travel, lodging, and student salaries and benefits as well as the costs of instruction and the costs of program development distributed over the number of students in the program. Let us further assume this is a program that is applicable to all employees in a major division of the firm and that there are 62,000 employees in the division. Therefore:

F = 62,000 [(0.49 × $14,000) - $1,610] = $325,500,00

Payback = 1,610/6,860 = 0.23 years (or 3 months)

ROI = (6,860 - 1,610)/1,610 = 3.26, or 326 percent

Utility analysis can be much more sophisticated. More detailed formulas take into account financial discounting, depreciation, contribution of the program to pre- and posttax profit, fixed and variable costs, and other elements of accounting and capital budgeting (see for instance, Boudreau, 1983; and Cronshaw and Alexander, 1983). The computational model that is used should fit the case and the available data (Hunter, Schmidt, and Coggin, 1988). For instance, computing return on investment (ROI) makes sense if the training program development and delivery require an investment. However, such development and delivery may not involve an investment of funds. For example, a change in a training program's design may be made with little or no cost, as is the case when more group exercises are designed in order to replace a lecture. Or the result may be a major benefit to the success of the program. In such a case, ROI should not be computed when comparing the new design to the old.

Chargeback Policy

The policy of whether to charge back client departments for training costs has implications for how training is viewed in the organization—that is, whether it is seen as a free commodity or whether it is treated as a resource that must be managed as other scarce resources. If tuition is not charged back and the organization pays for the training by funding the training department directly, supervisors may not be as careful in determining who attends training.

Charging back tuition holds clients accountable for how they spend their training resources, in that clients must ensure that the people who need the training get it. However, clients may cut costs by reducing needed training, thereby making it difficult for training managers to predict volume of students. But, after all, most businesses are at the mercy of customer demand. Having to satisfy clients should lead to more cost-effective training.

A disadvantage of charging back tuition is that the firm incurs bookkeeping and processing costs that could be avoided by agreeing with a client department on the approximate amount of training to be provided to the department during the year and then billing the department for that amount at the start of each year. The cost of program delivery could be calculated and charged back separately from the cost of program development. The department would pay one-twelfth of the cost each month, with a tallying-up at the end of the year to reflect actual usage.

The advantage of this method is that the training department has a fairly accurate prediction of the volume of work that needs to be done during the year and therefore can plan accordingly. The client department still has the option of changing the contract but can perhaps provide several months' warning to the training department. The training department still must track usage and report this to the client department each month. IBM uses this approach, as described in Chapter One. The key to IBM's effectiveness in this area is that each employee has a training plan at the start of the year and that the training plans can be aggregated across supervisory groups to determine the department's annual training plan. The accountability for training still rests with each individual employee and supervisor.

This method of charging back can be abused if employees frequently register for classes and then fail to show up or cancel too late for the training department to find a replacement. One solution is to charge the supervisory group the tuition for no-shows or late cancellations. The employee's immediate supervisor thus has a vested interest in ensuring that subordinates participate in the training when they register. Otherwise, supervisors may feel free to pull employees out of training without realizing the cost to the organization as a whole.

Training External Customers

Training a firm's customers can be a source of revenue for a training department and a strategic initiative for the company. Strategically, customers who understand the value of the firm's products and services will be likely to purchase them. Also, a customer will be more likely to stay with a firm's products when the customer's technicians know how to maintain the products. Training customers also reduces the time account representatives spend educating the customer.

IBM directs 52 percent of its training resources toward its customers. The company has over fifty education centers in the United States, which offer approximately 3,500 scheduled courses every year to external customers. Most of this education is fee based and generates over $88 million in revenue (only about 0.2 percent of IBM's total revenue). Some of the courses are by invitation only and are tuition free, and the IBM marketing representative helps to determine courses of value and make reservations. The courses are aimed at helping management information systems managers stay in touch with advancements in the field and preparing them for higher-level management positions.

Other companies also offer substantial customer training. Digital Equipment Corporation focuses 65 percent of its training resources externally. While such firms offer excellent service as a competitive advantage, they recognize that there is more profit in selling products than in servicing them and that customer training can increase sales revenue. The revenue generated from customer training is trivial to these firms in light of the strategic advantage it provides.

Cost Cutting

Improving efficiencies, as noted earlier, is always desirable, and reducing unit costs is a way to get the most for the organization's training investment. However, when budgets must be cut, unit-cost improvements may be lost. For instance, a budget cut may mean less money for developing videos to replace instructor-led training, since videos are more expensive to develop than classroom training. (But another factor to consider is that videos are much less expensive to deliver and can impart more training per student hour than instructor-led training.)

In addition to endangering efficiencies, budget reductions generally mean doing less. Determining what to give up can be accomplished by a systematic priority-setting process, such as zero-based priority setting, discussed in Chapter Nine. Whatever the process, the users (clients) of the training department must be consulted.

Impact analysis. Budget cuts should include an impact analysis that covers the following areas for cost reduction and their potential impact:

1. *Enforce strict control of discretionary employee-related items.* For instance, travel only when necessary, limit daily meal allowances, use hotels having discount contracts with the organization for employees attending training, limit the amount of employee overtime, and restrict the use of consultants and temporary personnel to essential functions. The intention is to work smarter, not to do less.
2. *Reduce management education.* Such reductions may seem obvious, since courses on supervisory skills often seem softer and less directly applicable than technical courses. (As a balancing consideration, however, better management may save the organization money in the long run.)
3. *Cut delivery personnel.* That is, provide less training to the organization. Cutting delivery personnel is an easy way to save a lot of money when training programs are instructor-led as opposed to self-paced. Areas for cutting back can be identified by setting priorities with clients. Or there can be an across-the-board cut in the amount of all training, so that all employees reduce their annual training days. Special training-seat allocations may be needed to ensure a fair distribution of training.

Reduction of delivery personnel may be alleviated partially by "borrowing" instructors from field forces.

4. *Close one or more training centers.* This may save rent and building expenses and some administrative expenses. However, while it may help the training department's budget, it may increase clients' costs, since students will incur increased travel expenses in attending remote training sites. Also, eliminating a training facility may decrease the total amount of training available.
5. *Reduce or eliminate measures of training effectiveness.* Such measures include course evaluation questionnaires and post-course performance testing. The problem is that such cuts reduce the training department's ability to ensure that it is meeting client needs and expectations and also limit the ability of the department to quantify the effects of training on employee development.
6. *Cut training support services.* Such support services include registration, counseling, and administration (as described in Chapter Four). Some administrative functions may be luxuries, such as a training department newsletter. However, reducing the number of people in other support functions, such as registration, limits responsiveness to clients. Reducing the counseling function curtails the training department's ability to understand and effectively meet client needs and may also contribute to employees registering for training they do not need.
7. *Reduce course development.* This may mean that new courses are not available to those who need them because the courses are never developed. For this reason, cutting training delivery may be better than cutting course development.

Each of the above points includes reasons why the cuts should not be made, or at least dangers that should be considered before making the cuts. Being "penny wise and pound foolish" should be avoided; cutting training costs might result in increasing organizational expenses and loss of revenue. However, the training department may need to face up to a budget cut and thus provide fewer services or less training. Doing so requires knowing what the organization needs. As stated above, the best way to know this is to involve clients in setting priorities and to let clients know the impact of training expense reductions on their operations.

Summary

This chapter covered financial aspects of training administration, including the sources of training costs, the budgeting process, how to identify unit costs, and suggested ways to reduce unit costs. The second portion of the chapter described competitive assessment, including the sources and types of competitive data available. Performance analysis methods were reviewed and applied to evaluating the cost-effectiveness of training. Finally, the chapter reviewed ways to cut training costs when budgets must be reduced.

Policy Opportunities and Recommendations

1. The cost-effectiveness of current training programs should be reviewed, and ways to revise them to improve the costs per student should be determined. For example, high-volume courses, perhaps courses in fundamentals of management that are applicable to most managers in an organization, could be updated to use more self-paced training in place of instructor-led, classroom training. In such a case, the additional costs of development must be weighed against the savings.

2. The costs of alternative approaches to training (for example, different training media) should be considered before deciding on the format for a course. Too often, program developers have a favorite training method or they assume that the content requires a certain type of media when other types may be possible.

3. Operations plans should be formulated to integrate training development and delivery. Plans should focus on client groups rather than on courses for development or on delivery requirements in a geographic location. Joint planning by program developers, instructors, and training counselors will enhance communication as the program is developed and facilitate identifying and implementing improvements once the program is operational.

4. Training managers should be involved in identifying

cost-saving ideas. Also, training managers should be held accountable for implementing these ideas and tracking their success.

5. Training departments should learn from competitive assessments. Training managers should be sensitized to look for competitive information in the business press and journals aimed at training professionals. These managers should also be encouraged to collect competitive assessment data, especially before major new initiatives are undertaken. Training managers should also be sensitive to what ideas are and are not transferable from other organizations. What is right for one organization may not be right for another.

6. Performance analyses should be conducted to identify client problems and to establish whether or not training solutions are justified. The cost-effectiveness of alternative solutions should be considered (for example, the cost of training versus the cost of a more restrictive recruitment and selection effort versus a combination of more rigorous selection and training).

7. When cutting the training budget, clients should be involved in determining training priorities and establishing the impact of training cuts. The training organization does not want clients to be surprised when training is not readily available.

8. Avoid being penny wise and pound foolish when reducing the training budget. A savings to the training organization may cost the organization more if other departments must incur higher costs to meet the need for skilled employees (for example, cutting a training facility and thereby requiring employees to commute long distances to other facilities; cutting a training program and thereby requiring clients to purchase the training outside the organization at higher cost; or obtaining skilled employees in ways other than training, such as paying higher wages to attract already skilled employees away from the competition).

6

Tracking the Return on the Training Investment

Training measures are the way an organization tracks the return it receives for its training investment and indicate whether the training department is meeting its clients' demands. This chapter examines indicators of training success—in terms of the quality of the programs developed, the efficiency of the development and delivery processes, and the effects of training on employees and their departments. Also described are a number of measures, measurement procedures, data-base management issues, report designs, and evaluation procedures. The goal is to suggest practical methods that can be utilized by training departments and their clients for tracking and improving the quality of employee development. We begin by considering who uses training measures and sources of information.

Training managers, especially the most senior managers, are often reluctant to pay for and use evaluation data, perhaps because they do not understand how to use the information. Or the evaluation may lack credibility, and the results may seem inconclusive. The data may not seem accurate or the results may not seem to be applicable to other settings in the organization. This chapter will highlight the uses of evaluation data and describe methods to enhance reliability and validity.

Clients for Training Data

The training measures that are collected and the frequency with which they are collected and reported depend on the users' requirements. The various uses and clients for training data are discussed below.

Training Managers. Managers responsible for training program development need to know how many and what types of programs are being developed and the progress being made. Managers need to know what process is followed to identify customers' needs, analyze job and skill requirements, and design a program that will impart the knowledge required. Basically, managers who are responsible for program development want to track the quality and quantity of the programs for which they are responsible. Delivery managers need data to track the efficiency of utilizing the training department's resources. Is instructors' time being utilized effectively? Or is it being wasted? Are seats in company classrooms unfilled? Are courses offered when clients need them? Are instructors effective in engendering learning?

Training directors need the same information as development and delivery managers except perhaps in less detail and less frequently. Their concern is keeping up to date on the department's progress in meeting the needs of client departments. Training data summaries may be needed for review meetings with department heads and for evaluation by training managers.

Client Department Supervisors. Managers who send their employees to training want to know that the employees successfully completed the program and can apply new skills and knowledge on the job. Moreover, supervisors want to know whether applying the new skills makes a difference in job performance.

As an example, Digital Equipment Corporation provides line managers with training data that are truly important to the work group's ability to meet customer needs for product installation and repair. One type of report provides information on a course's "hit rate"—data on the products an engineer has worked on during a given period of time compared with the products on which he or she has been trained. (This requires integrating the firm's training records data base with the data base on engineers' work assignments.) The data determine whether the engineers have been trained properly to meet work demands. Other data compare the mean time for completing installation and maintenance functions for engineers who have received the training versus those who have not. This demonstrates to line managers the value of the training for their work groups. Still other data show engineers' success in passing end-of-course tests to show line managers whether their people are getting the most out of training. Engineers must pass the test to obtain certification for working on a product.

Students, Instructors, and Program Developers. Employees who participate in training programs need feedback about how well they are doing while they are involved in the training. They can also benefit from feedback about how well they are applying their learning on the job. Training professionals also require feedback about their performance. Measures of their performance from multiple sources can be valuable inputs for appraisal as well as a guide for development.

Sources of Information

Training data come from students, instructors, employee records, and registration data bases.

Students, Instructional Technologists, and Supervisors. Students can provide objective and subjective data about training effectiveness.

- Information about students' skills and background can be used as a guide for selecting needed training.
- Evaluating test scores on job-related performance measures is another means of ensuring that students are directed into the training programs they need. Test scores also can demonstrate that the student has the prerequisite knowledge before taking a particular program.
- Student opinions about the program are another source of information. Such measures provide an indication of client satisfaction with the content and the quality of instruction.
- Posttraining test performance indicates the student's success in acquiring the knowledge the program was intended to convey.

- Measures of the student's job performance before and after the training indicate performance deficiencies and whether the training was successful in correcting the deficiencies.

Instructional technologists are trained to observe instructors and provide feedback. This feedback can be valuable developmental information for instructors. Supervisors can be asked to evaluate students' performance and offer opinions of the students' ability to apply the new knowledge to the job.

The Registration System. The registration system is a centralized data base that contains scheduling, registration, course, instructor, training center, and student information. The numbers of employees enrolled in different courses, the numbers on wait lists, and the numbers completing programs indicate the demand for training and the rate at which the demand is met. The registration system also provides information on instructor utilization, such as the extent to which classes are filled.

Data Reliability and Validity

Reliability refers to the accuracy of the data. There are a number of threats to reliability. For instance, a measure of employee satisfaction with a course may be biased by how the questions are phrased or by an instructor's hints that the employee's evaluation will affect the instructor's performance appraisal. Some data may be inaccurate or incomplete, for example, a record of an employee's training experience may not be updated or may be confused with another employee's record. Because of these threats to reliability, it is often worthwhile to have multiple sources of information. Employees' attitudes about the course and instruction may be supplemented with ratings by an instructional technologist who periodically observes classes. Measures of posttraining test performance are supplemented by indexes of on-the-job performance.

Validity refers to the meaning of the measure—for example, the extent to which it reflects the amount of new learning, the applicability of the learning to the job, or the effects of the learning on improved job performance. These are indicators of training effectiveness. Another effectiveness measure might be simply whether clients (department managers and their employees) are satisfied with the training.

Other measures indicate training efficiency—for example, instructor platform time (the number of available days an instructor spends teaching), the time required to develop a program, the number of training days or hours developed, and the number of videotapes produced in a given length of time. However, training managers must determine what is important to the department's operation and whether the measures drive the right behavior. For example, the number of instructor-led training days developed in a six-month period can be an indication of course writers' efficiency. But it might be better to spend more time developing fewer training days if the days that are developed convey more information or use more powerful learning techniques. This would save the organization money in the long run by reducing training time, thereby delivering the training to the field faster.

The measures chosen can affect learning behavior. People attend to what is being measured. Therefore, the measures selected must be tempered by what the organization is trying to accomplish, and training professionals should understand clearly what is being measured and what measures are being used to evaluate their performance.

Training Records

One source of information about training needs and employees' training progress is a personnel data base where training programs completed are recorded. With the appropriate software and programs, these records can be compared to curriculum paths to indicate what training is needed and what progress the individual is making on the curriculum. Exhibit 6 provides an example of an excerpt from a training record comparing the employee's training to the curriculum for the employee's current position.

Some of the programs in this example may be instructor-led courses. Others, perhaps Product Testing, may be self-paced, computer-based instruction with an accompanying workbook and a written job aid. The supervisor and the employee need to judge what training is necessary before the individual can be productive

Exhibit 6. Excerpt from Employee Training Record.

Name: John Crane | *Department*: Operations
Years service: 12 | *Assignment*: Technician II
Time in current assignment: 4 months
Curriculum: Technician II

	Programs Completed
Product Overview	x
Installation Procedures	x
Customer Interface Skills	x
Product Testing	
Technological Foundations	
Advanced Product Testing	
Systems Analysis I	

on the job. Also, they can work together to determine when the additional courses should be taken. The supervisor's assessment will depend on the level of training of other workers in the group. If there are a number of experienced technicians, it may be less critical for John Crane to take all the training courses, since more experienced co-workers may be able to train John on the job. However, if most of the workers are new to the unit, then the supervisor may want to accelerate John's training program.

The training record is a valuable tool managers can use in tracking subordinates' competence and development. It is also a useful tool for facilitating transfers in that it helps identify qualified internal job candidates. The training record can also be used to counsel employees about what courses they should take for their present jobs and what they should do to prepare themselves for other jobs.

On a departmental level, the training records data base is a way to track skills residing in a department and to determine whether and to what extent there is a training gap (as described in Chapter Four). The data base can be used to help supervisors and training coordinators plan training for individuals in the work group. Exhibit 7 shows a summary of the training records of all employees in a work unit compared to curriculum requirements.

The training records data base can be used to summarize training experience across a number of units or across the entire

Exhibit 7. Summary of Employee Training Records Compared to Curriculum Requirements.

Department: Operations *Unit*: I *Supervisor*: Ed Green
Job Category: Technician II *Number of Employees*: 8

Curriculum: Technician II	*Employees Completing Program*	
	Number	*Percent*
Product Overview	8	100.0
Installation Procedures	8	100.0
Customer Interface Skills	6	75.0
Product Testing	7	87.5
Technological Foundations	3	37.5
Advanced Product Testing	1	12.5
Systems Analysis I	0	0

organization. When combined with skill and function codes, the data base can be a valuable tool for human resource forecasting and planning and can be used by the training department to predict demand for education.

Digital Equipment Corporation uses a training records data base to recommend the number of engineers to be trained on a given product or service. The program accounts for the company's recommended "training intensity"—the number of engineers to be trained for every system in the field. The program accounts for the estimated number of product installations, maintenance, and removals in the forthcoming quarter and can tell a manager the number of additional engineers in his or her group that should be trained in the coming quarter. The program includes data for the past quarter on how long it takes to perform various functions on a given product and how much less time it takes if the engineer is properly trained. Thus, the program and data base are planning tools used continuously by line managers to ensure that their work groups are prepared to meet customer requirements each quarter.

Obviously, training records must be accurate and complete to be useful. Many organizations transfer people regularly for career development purposes and for purposes of restructuring departments to improve effectiveness. In addition, people may leave temporarily (for instance, maternity leave), or computerized records may be inadvertently deleted or mixed when computer systems are updated and software is enhanced. As a periodic check, employees should be sent copies of their training records and asked to review them with their supervisor for accuracy.

To make this process less burdensome, employees can be asked to verify their training records when they register for a course. If the record has been checked within the last year (because a student registered for another course), the computer can avoid asking for a check. Every two years, employees who did not take a course within that time period can be asked to verify their records, but this check should entail more than verifying a record. It should also include considering what training may be lacking. For instance, performance appraisals might be reviewed (in addition to the regular annual—or more frequent—supervisory reviews of performance and development). If performance on the present job is lacking in some way, then training may be needed. Or if the performance appraisal indicates that the employee has potential for promotion, the appropriate education should be provided.

Student Satisfaction Data

Student satisfaction questionnaires are used to collect the attitudes of students about a training program after they have completed the program. Usually, questionnaires are distributed by the instructor at the conclusion of the course. Self-paced computer-based courses might have a questionnaire included at the end as part of the programmed instruction. An example of a typical posttraining survey used in classroom instruction is provided in Exhibit 8.

The completed course evaluation questionnaires should be available to the instructors after the course and also should be made available periodically to course developers so they can track student response to the material. Instructors and developers should work together after the course is on line to develop refinements based on student reactions.

In addition, the data should be entered into a computer data base, and summary reports should be produced for training managers as well as instructors and developers. This information

Exhibit 8. A Sample Student Opinion Survey.

Course number: ________ Course title: ________________
Course location: ____________________ Date of course: ________
Instructor(s) 1. ____________________
2. ____________________
3. ____________________
4. ____________________

Please read each of the following items carefully and circle your response, using the following scale:

5 = strongly agree
4 = agree
3 = neutral
2 = disagree
1 = strongly disagree
NA = no answer, question does not apply

Course Administration

1. The course description accurately described the course. 1 2 3 4 5 NA

Comments: ____________________
____
____

2. My enrollment in this course was handled to my satisfaction. 1 2 3 4 5 NA

Comments: ____________________
____
____

Learning Environment

3. The classroom facilities were conducive to training. 1 2 3 4 5 NA

Comments: ____________________
____
____

4. The equipment (audiovisuals) was conducive to learning. 1 2 3 4 5 NA

Comments: ____________________
____
____

Exhibit 8. A Sample Student Opinion Survey, Cont'd.

		1	2	3	4	5	NA
5.	The course materials were useful.	1	2	3	4	5	NA

Comments: ______________________________

____

____

Course Design

6.	The goals and objectives of the course were clear.	1	2	3	4	5	NA
7.	The pace of the course was appropriate for me.	1	2	3	4	5	NA
8.	The exercises and job simulations helped me learn.	1	2	3	4	5	NA
9.	The topics were presented in a logical order.	1	2	3	4	5	NA
10.	There was sufficient time for questions.	1	2	3	4	5	NA
11.	There was sufficient time for practice.	1	2	3	4	5	NA

Comments: ______________________________

____

____

____

____

____

Instructors

Instructor 1 (name): ______________________________

12.	The instructor was knowledgeable.	1	2	3	4	5	NA
13.	The instructor presented the material clearly.	1	2	3	4	5	NA
14.	The instructor involved students in the learning.	1	2	3	4	5	NA
15.	The instructor held my attention.	1	2	3	4	5	NA

Exhibit 8. A Sample Student Opinion Survey, Cont'd.

16. The instructor took enough time to answer questions.	1	2	3	4	5	NA
17. Overall, the instructor was effective.	1	2	3	4	5	NA

Comments: ____________________

____

____

____

____

____

[Additional sections would be added for other instructors.]

Job Applicability

18. This training will increase my productivity on the job.	1	2	3	4	5	NA
19. I can use the printed materials on the job.	1	2	3	4	5	NA
20. I would recommend this course to others.	1	2	3	4	5	NA

Comments: ____________________

____

____

____

____

____

Student Background

21. How did you hear about this course? (Circle all that apply.)

1 Course catalog
2 Company bulletin
3 Co-workers who attended the course
4 A supervisor
5 A registration counselor or education consultant
6 Other (please specify) ____________________

____

Exhibit 8. A Sample Student Opinion Survey, Cont'd.

22. Why did you take this course?

    1 Required for my job
    2 To prepare for another job
    3 For my career development
    4 To keep pace with technology
    5 To learn new skills
    6 Other (please specify) ____________________

23. Your current job title: ____________________

24. Time in your current job: ________ years ________ months

25. Time with the company: ________ years ________ months

Note: Some evaluation questionnaires may ask for the student's gender and race for purposes of tracking equal opportunity to attend training. The student generally has the option not to respond to these questions.

could be part of a monthly tracking report on training effectiveness. (Such a report is described later in this chapter.)

Follow-Up Evaluations

The goal of follow-up evaluations is to determine whether the training has been applied on the job and whether the methods, procedures, and technologies used in the training match those employed in the work setting. A random sample of students can be contacted sixty or ninety days after the training, and data can be collected by telephone survey or by a mail questionnaire. Similar data can be collected from supervisors of students to determine whether they saw a difference in their subordinates' performance after training. Sample questions used on a follow-up evaluation telephone survey are included in Exhibit 9.

Questionnaires and surveys such as the ones in Exhibit 9 can be useful for ensuring that the students were part of the target population for the course. Supervisors can be questioned on how

Exhibit 9. A Sample Follow-up Evaluation: Telephone Survey Questions and Response Alternatives (for Students and Supervisors Ninety Days after Training).

1. Would you say that the class related to your current job? (yes, no, do not know)
2. If not, why not? (changed jobs, the job has changed, no occasion to use the knowledge, the course was for personal development, other)
3. Would you say that the course had a positive effect on your job skills? (yes, no, do not know)
4. What was the effect of the course on your productivity? (ask for percent increase from 0 to 100; do not know)
5. Will you use the information in the future? (very likely, somewhat likely, not too likely, not at all likely, do not know)

Note: Additional questions can ask about the method of instruction (for example, classroom, self-paced, video, PC teletraining), the number of instructors, the effectiveness of the instructors and material, and the usefulness of the handouts and job aids. These and other questions might be the same as those used in the course evaluation questionnaire filled out by the students immediately after the training.

they assign subordinates to training to determine whether the people who need the training the most are attending the course. Often, open-ended questions or comments related to structured response questions can be particularly valuable. These can be typed and made available as part of the report on the follow-up evaluation.

Client Satisfaction Surveys

Another type of information is a telephone or mailed questionnaire survey of managers at all levels in client departments to assess the effectiveness of the training department. In small organizations in which the population to be surveyed is in one location, information should be gathered face to face. This data can be used by the training director and training managers to determine overall client satisfaction with the training department's services and products. The information gained should help focus attention on possible weaknesses in the training operation that need to be corrected as well as provide a better understanding of the department's strong points. A sample of questions for such a survey are provided in Exhibit 10.

Training Test Performance Measures and Feedback

Tests may be used after training to indicate whether the students recall and are able to apply the information provided in the training program. Tests help detect problems trainees have learning course content. Scores can help trainees and their supervisors understand the trainees' level of ability. Also, performance tests are a means of review for students who were not successful on their first attempt at the course.

An advantage of performance test feedback is that students and their supervisors know shortly after completing a training program whether or not the student has the skills and knowledge necessary to perform the job. Scores can distinguish between students who have acquired a minimal competence and those who have attained a level of mastery. In general, tests lend credibility to a training course. Managers are likely to feel that their employees will take the training more seriously when they know they will be tested.

Performance test results tell course developers, instructors, and instructional technologists how a course is measuring up and, if necessary, what areas need improvement. Tests may also be used to determine whether an employee has enough knowledge to waive the course. To do this, alternate forms of the test must be given to students before and after training.

Unions and government agencies concerned about equal employment opportunity may use training performance tests to monitor this area. Both sectors are concerned that tests be administered fairly, and for this reason, performance tests must be developed with the same care given to developing course content. Job analyses should be the foundation of the course as well as a test to ensure that the course embodies skills and behaviors required on the job.

To ensure that tests are not used improperly, some organizations do not use the tests on a pass/fail basis. Instead, the tests are

Exhibit 10. Sample Questions for a Client Satisfaction Survey.

The Training Process

Please rate the following six items in two ways: *importance to you the respondent* (very important, somewhat important, not too important, not at all important, not sure or don't know) and *performance of the training department* (excellent, good, fair, poor, not sure or don't know).

1. Availability of training *when* it is needed

2. Availability of training *where* it is needed

3. Timely response to requests for new training

4. Effective use of client resources (for example, student time)

5. Feedback given to supervisors on students' performance in the training

6. View of the training department as the primary source of training

The Registration Process

7. How satisfied are you with the registration process? (Indicate any problems, such as slow response, not receiving registration confirmation, and so on.)

Recent Experience with the Training Department

8. Did you personally attend training within the last twelve months?

9. Have you sent a subordinate to training within the last twelve months?

10. Do you consult with the training organization about your subordinates' needs for training? How satisfied are you with the response you have received?

11. Do you provide input to training program design? Are you satisfied that your input is used?

---

used to indicate whether the student has accomplished the goals of the course. Students who do not complete the exam satisfactorily can take it again later and as many times as necessary to ensure they have mastered the program's objectives.

Program Development Tracking System

Measures of the progress being made on training programs under development may be tracked using monthly reports completed by program developers. Exhibit 11 provides a format for collecting data that can be used in a standard project tracking report. A report sheet should be prepared for each project; this allows training managers to determine a project's status on request by clients. In addition, reports can be developed on all projects in a particular discipline or on projects under a particular person's purview to indicate the extent to which development work is on target.

Information on a program development tracking system will be valuable to training managers in dealing with their client departments, allowing training managers to determine the current status of any given project that might be of interest to a client. The information also serves as a management tool for determining whether some projects may need more resources and for evaluating the performance of program developers.

Instructor Reaction Reports

Just as students may be asked to complete a course evaluation questionnaire, a similar form can be prepared for instructors for evaluating the course from their perspective. Questions might cover how well prepared the students were for the course, whether students were attentive, whether the materials were ready, areas of the program needing revision, whether media used were adequate, any classroom problems, and so forth.

Commitment Measures Versus Operational Indicators

It was noted earlier that training managers should determine which indexes are important to the department and should be used to drive behavior. These indexes are commitment measures and involve standards, expectations, or excellence criteria. Achieving a certain level on these indexes will ensure that the training department is successful—that is, has achieved a goal or commitment.

Exhibit 11. Training Program Development Tracking Form.

Project name: ______________ Date of last update: ________
Course number: ______________ Project start date: ________
Program developer: ______________
Target completion date: ______________

Development Team

Developer: ______________
Key instructor: ______________
Instructional technologist: ______________
Subject matter experts: ______________
____
____

Critical Dates

	Initial Target Date	*Current Expected Date*	*Date Completed*
Analysis	________	________	________
Development	________	________	________
Subject matter expert review	________	________	________
Pilot	________	________	________
Delivery turnover	________	________	________

Description of Current Status

____
____
____
____
____

Such measures are instituted or modified when commitments and objectives are established or changed and are used as a basis for performance appraisals.

Any of the methods of gathering information discussed in the preceding sections may be used as commitment measures, depending on what the department wants to accomplish. For instance, a target for delivery managers may be a 95 percent student satisfaction rating on the course evaluation questionnaires. Development managers may commit to completing projects within one week of the promised delivery date. The organization may want to move from 20 to 40 percent self-instruction.

The indexes may also serve as operational indicators—that is, data that are used to monitor the health of the training department and the use of training in the organization for planning and decision making. Such information is collected regularly to cover all significant training processes and outputs. However, unlike commitment measures, operational indicators do not specify excellence criteria or specific objective levels of performance and should not be used in the appraisal process unless designated as such. Exhibit 12 lists a number of operational indicators reflecting program development and delivery.

A participative process should be used to determine which indexes are worthwhile collecting and which should be used as performance commitments. Specifically, groups of representative training professionals should identify measures that reflect their activities and their performance. As individuals, they should work with their supervisors to agree on which measures they will use to measure their performance and the level they will set as performance objectives. Also, they should agree on which measures will help them guide the operation but will not be used to measure performance.

For example, delivery managers may agree to a certain level of instructor time in the classroom as a target (say 60 percent of instructors' time on average). However, they may not commit to a certain level of instructor time spent in professional development or in serving as a key instructor in the program development process, since these activities will depend on need in the department and the instructor's need for training. Nevertheless, it may be important for delivery managers to have this information to understand how instructors' time is allocated and how instructors might spend their time more fruitfully.

It is important to delve into the meaning of the indicators, and, in some cases, take immediate corrective action. For instance, the number of course cancellations may suggest a poor job of analyzing needs, of communicating the availability of the class, or of class scheduling. Similarly, there may be several reasons for no-

Exhibit 12. Possible Operational Indicators.

Class Utilization

A. Course name: ______________
B. Designed course size (number of students): ______________
C. Number of times offered in the measured time period (one month, one quarter): ______________
D. Maximum number of students: B × C
E. Actual number of students: ______________
F. Class length (number of days): ______________
G. Maximum student days: D × F
H. Actual student days: E × F
I. Efficiency: H/G

Instructor-Led and Self-Paced

A. Course name: ______________
B. Delivery mode (instructor-led vs. self-paced): ______________

For instructor-led:

C. Number of times offered in the time period: ______________
D. Total number of students attending during the time period: ______________
E. Average class size: D/C
F. Class length (days): ______________
G. Student days: D × F

For self-paced

H. Number of times offered: ______________
I. Number of students participating: ______________
J. Average size: H/I
K. Program length (days for completion): ______________
L. Student days: I × K
M. Proportion total self-paced training: L/(G + L)

Other Relevant Indexes

- *Unsatisfied demand*: Number of students on a wait list divided by the total demand for a program (number of students who participated in the program plus the number of employees on the wait list).
- *Instructor utilization*: Total number of instructors; percent of instructor time spent teaching, preparing for class, helping to develop programs, attending train-the-trainer classes, involved in other developmental activities.
- *Number of course cancellations*: Cancelled by the client and cancelled by the training department because of too few students or inadequate planning.

Exhibit 12. Possible Operational Indicators, Cont'd.

- *Number of no-shows*: Number of students registered who fail to show up for training.
- *Program incompletes*: Proportion of self-paced courses sent out that are not followed by completed performance tests.
- *Unit cost*: Cost to deliver one instructor-led student day to one student, cost to develop one instructor-led day of program material, cost to develop a CBT self-paced program, and so on (see Chapter Five).
- *Effectiveness of instructors, as observed by instructional technologists.*
- *Percent of programs developed with detailed front-end analysis.*
- *Percent of programs developed on time.*
- *Percent of time a front-end analysis results in a recommendation for a nontraining solution.*
- *Percent of courses developed under direction of a curriculum review committee.*
- *Percent of projects under development that are off schedule.*
- *Percent of student satisfaction on course evaluation questionnaire items.*
- *Percent of supervisors indicating performance improvement after employees take the course.*
- *Percent of courses with posttraining performance tests.*
- *Percent of students satisfactorily completing performance tests (for courses with posttraining tests).*

Source: Based on contributions from Michael Goodman, Robert Almquist, and Raymond Pardee.

shows, and action may be needed to reduce the number of no-shows (for example, charging client departments for seats that are not cancelled within a certain period of time before the class).

The meaning of the percentages suggested as operational indicators in Exhibit 12 should be considered carefully. Consider, for instance, the percent of time a front-end analysis results in a recommendation for a nontraining solution. The information may suggest that nontraining solutions are never considered, which may suggest that training is relied on too much to solve performance problems. But there is no necessary right percentage, unless training managers want to set a target simply for the sake of encouraging change. Training managers must determine which operational indicators are meaningful to them, which ones they want to view as signs of health of the organization, and what the proper levels should be.

The cost of measurements should be an important consideration in determining what indexes will be collected. When administrative data systems exist, such as a computerized registration system, it may be easy to collect a good deal of information about instructor utilization, class fill rates, cancellations, no-shows, and wait lists. When such systems do not exist, they may need to be created in order to track desired indexes. Or it may be necessary to collect data manually, which can be time consuming and costly.

System Requirements

Measurement systems require efficient, cost-effective processes. For instance, consider the operation of a training performance and feedback system, which must meet the following requirements:

- The tests must be reliable and valid indicators of the training content or its application on the job. Therefore, the system requires producing the tests based on thorough job analyses and knowledge of training content.
- Instructors must be trained on how and when to administer the tests.
- A timely process must be established for sending the tests to a central center for scoring or for instructor scoring.
- The tests must be scored accurately.
- Confidentiality of test responses and scores must be maintained. That is, only managers with a need to know the scores and who will use the scores in the manner intended should have access to them.
- A procedure may be needed to put test information on the student's employment record (for example, that the student successfully completed the course). This may require a computerized or manual interface between the training administration system and the personnel data base.
- A nonthreatening process must be established for feeding back results to students and supervisors. For students whose test scores indicate that they did not learn the course objectives, suggestions may be made for how they can obtain the knowl-

edge—for example, through further reading, special job experiences, or more training.

In one case, a training test performance system was slowed up by a slow turnaround time for scoring and feedback. This problem was identified by a quality improvement team led by the administrator of the testing system and composed of representatives of the clerks who processed the tests. They interviewed users of the system (supervisors, instructors, and course developers) and developed a flowchart of the various steps and the people and systems involved. They found a variety of delays in the process, such as the following:

- Instructors waited as much as five days after the class to send in the tests for scoring.
- The computer scanners for scoring the test broke down frequently.
- The clerks responsible for inputting test scores into the registration system (for computer transfer to the employee training records) let tests back up.
- The staff checking the accuracy of the scoring and the training record were slow.
- There were frequent delays in mailing tests in for scoring and in sending scores and accompanying explanation to supervisors and students.

The quality improvement team brainstormed ideas for reducing instructor delays in mailing the tests. The team decided to send two letters to instructors. Instructors who were consistently meeting the specified turnaround time would receive a "thank you" recognition letter, with a copy sent to the instructor's supervisor. The instructors who were late sending the tests would receive a letter asking them to do better and to be aware of students' need for feedback as soon after the course as possible.

The team solved the scanner delays by pressuring the vendor to install a new scanner with a backup. The mail delays were found to be due partially to an error in the addresses in the registration system and were corrected easily. The result of these changes improved turnaround time from forty days to twelve days after training. Also, the team continued to identify ways to improve the process. For instance, they evaluated the usefulness of the tests by surveying line supervisors to determine how the tests were used.

This quality improvement process demonstrates the complexity of instituting a training performance system. Similar complexities arise in the administration of other measurement systems as well, including course satisfaction questionnaires. The size of the training department (number of different courses and the number of students) will determine the need for computer systems and support personnel. The more complex the system, the more it adds to training overhead costs. The goal must be to obtain the most efficient systems for economies of scale (for example, low unit costs).

In small organizations that do not need large computer systems to track training operations, the processes for recording training data should be simple and the data well organized. Tracking information is desirable in small organizations, although the number of operational indicators may be fewer than in large organizations having registration systems that produce vast quantities of data. In small organizations, personal computers can be an extremely useful way to store information; however, attention must be paid to the security of the data.

Measures of Training Department Effectiveness

Measures of student days (or student hours) are commonly used to track the performance of a training department and to calculate unit costs, as indicated in Chapter Five. A difficulty with student-day measures is that they may encourage the wrong behavior. A training department's goal may be to increase delivery, as expressed in terms of increased student days. Or the goal may be to increase efficiency, as expressed in terms of lower cost per student day. However, more student days do not necessarily mean more learning if the training method is inefficient. Nor do they necessarily mean better job performance or fewer performance problems. Also, increasing student days will cost more in student time and expenses and take employees away from their jobs for longer periods of time, lessening the department's productivity. If course developers are measured on the number of student days developed, they may design longer, less efficient courses.

A better measure that more accurately reflects the goals of training and education would be the increase in skills and knowledge. Such a metric would require a common unit across different types of training methods and content for comparing and evaluating various programs. This measure would be particularly useful in comparing the learning derived from different training technologies. One way to express the value of increased skills and knowledge is in terms of changes in test-score performance. However, tests are specific to the content area and do not aid in determining whether a particular method is as good for training on one type of subject matter as on another.

Another metric would be to express the value of increased skills and knowledge in terms of the benefits to the department or company. This might be done by asking supervisors to judge the dollar value of various skill-improvement levels and then calculating the utility of the training program. (The formula for this calculation is provided in Chapter Five in the section on calculating financial utility.) The increased value to the organization of a training method may then be averaged across different content areas (for example, the average value of using computer-based training averaged across all computer-based courses offered by the training department). The overall value added by the training department as a whole can be calculated at the end of each year or each quarter during the year if the utility of each course is determined.

Utility measures are often avoided because training managers are not aware of ways to make the calculations and because they depend on the judgments, instead of concrete measures, of the worth of increased productivity and the effect training has on productivity. Student-day measures are the norm because they are easy to track and easy to understand. Training departments should understand the impact of the measures they use and should try to identify measures that will reinforce their ultimate goal: increased learning leading to increased dollar value to the firm. Experimenting with utility measures and communicating their results along with measures of training volume (student days) may enhance recognition within the firm of the effects of training on the firm's bottom line.

Monthly Tracking Reports

One of my responsibilities as head of an administrative group for a large training organization was to produce a monthly tracking report of commitment measures and operational indicators. This report included the following sections:

- Monthly and year-to-date budget and expense data
- Student days by curriculum and by location
- Summary of student satisfaction and performance from post-training course evaluation questionnaires, test scores, and follow-up telephone interviews with students, supervisors, and department managers
- Total number of employees on the training staff
- Transfers and promotions in and out of the training department
- Narrative write-ups of major accomplishments and progress on important projects in the training department.

The tracking report was used by the director of the department as well as his supervisor to track efficiency and effectiveness of the department and to share with client departments during training review sessions. While this tracking report captured information that reflected the total training department's activities, development and delivery managers collected specific information that pertained to their parts of the operation. In addition, some directors of client departments wanted quarterly updates on training activities in their departments, and it was our responsibility to provide this information.

Training Research and Program Evaluation

Research tests the effects of different conditions or variables (such as different types of training methods) on other variables (such as learning and job performance). Research may be conducted to compare a new training method to an existing method or to answer a basic question (for instance, about the type of people most likely to be receptive to a certain type of learning method). Program evaluation is the process of examining the effectiveness of ongoing or newly implemented programs. Both research and evaluation rely on similar methods, and in both cases, it is important to account for and control variables that may lead to erroneous conclusions. Evaluation is generally less rigorous and less precise than research, although evaluation must be designed, and results reviewed, with attention to possible confounds. Both research and evaluation may use the procedures described in the following sections. Training managers should know of these procedures, and should know how to apply them, how to manage others conducting research or program evaluations, and how to critically read research and evaluation reports to understand their applicability.

Organizations are concerned about evaluating training programs because they spend large amounts of money on training and expect a definite return for this investment. In the long run, this return is manifest in the performance of the organization. However, it is difficult to determine the effects of training from other effects—such as competition and demand for the organization's products and services—on bottom-line organizational performance. Consequently, organizations look for more direct measures of training effects.

Organizations that have assessed the effectiveness of their employee training programs have been surprised by the strong impact these programs have (Chmura, Henton, and Melville, 1987). For example, Honeywell found in a survey of its managers that 20 percent of managers' expertise came from formal company-sponsored training. Other companies, such as Motorola and IBM, have found from controlled experiments and formal evaluations that training results in considerable cost savings. (Chapter Five described ways of evaluating the cost-effectiveness of training.)

The following section presents research and program evaluation methods that can be used in making reliable assessments of the effectiveness of a training program. Making such assessments requires going beyond simply measuring and reporting results to understanding the accuracy of the measures and the factors that may confound results and create misleading conclusions.

Measurement Design

As evident from the discussion in the first part of this chapter, training indexes vary along a number of dimensions. Some are subjective (for example, opinion data), and others are objective (for example, numbers of employees taking different courses). Some reflect the skills and knowledge conveyed in the training (for example, test performance measures), and others reflect the application of those skills and knowledge to the job (for example, supervisor judgments of productivity improvements following training). Still other measures reflect the results of the training (for example, its return on the organization's investment [Kirkpatrick, 1983]).

Also noted was the importance of reliable measures unaffected by bias or errors. Training managers should recognize the possible weaknesses in such measures. For example, they should understand that students' ratings on a questionnaire may be biased by a tendency to rate all elements of the training similarly (halo error). Supervisor ratings of changes in subordinates' behavior before and after training may be biased by their forgetting information or a lack of time to observe subordinates on the job.

This chapter has already considered the multiple indexes of training outcomes and processes and now will cover when and how measures should be used to evaluate a training program.

Research Design

This section examines three approaches to research and evaluation. One uses experimental methods to assess the effects of a program before it is introduced to the field. This test may compare one training program or method with another. A second approach is to track the effects of a program once it is operational. This is an action research approach because the data collected are used to identify ways to improve the program. A third approach examines training data after a large number of sessions of a program have been held. This approach concerns relationships among variables relevant to the training, such as individual student characteristics, instructor characteristics, and a variety of training outcomes. Each of these methods is described below.

The purpose of an experimental research design is to evaluate the effects of a change or intervention (such as training) while eliminating rival explanations. There are two general types of threats to a research design. One threat is to the accuracy of the measures and the certainty that the study is testing what the researchers believe it is testing—that is, the study's internal validity. Threats to internal validity include inaccurate measurement, researcher bias, participant sensitivity to what is measured, history (changes that would have occurred over time regardless of the intervention), and other intervening variables, such as the context in which the study is conducted. (See Cook and Campbell, 1976, for a variety of research designs to overcome these threats.)

The most rigorous research designs eliminate as many threats to internal validity as possible. They do this by having multiple comparison groups with different treatments of the intervention and control groups that receive no intervention. People are randomly assigned to groups with the hope that individual characteristics influencing the effects of the intervention are randomly distributed within each group; hence the groups will not differ in having more or less of these individual characteristics. In addition, half the subjects are measured before and after the intervention, and the other half are measured only afterward, thereby allowing a test of the effects of early measurement on later measurement and controlling for the effects of early measurement on reactions to the intervention. Some research designs make these measurements multiple times before and after the intervention to track the effects of history.

Another important aspect of a research design is whether the results transfer beyond the experimental situation. Will the same training program be equally effective in all departments at other times? This is the issue of generalizability, or external validity. The subjects and setting of the study must be similar to the situation to which the researcher wants to generalize. For instance, a training program may work well in one department because the people need the training, but its value may not generalize to the entire organization.

The rigor of a research design may affect the likelihood of finding positive results. (Resource C reviews different degrees of research rigor, with examples, and the advantages and disadvantages of alternative research designs.) A review of ninety-eight studies on the effects of a variety of organizational change efforts, including training, on measures of productivity found that the smallest effect sizes occurred for the more rigorous designs (Guzzo, Jette, and Katzell, 1985). That is, results were less likely to be significant when the research design used random selection of people to groups and included control groups that did not receive the intervention as opposed to designs that used comparison groups with people who were specially selected for, or withheld from, the study. The largest effect sizes occurred when there were no comparison groups but when before-and-after measures were available for the group experiencing the intervention. The longer the interval between the intervention and the measurement, the less the effect.

Hence, training programs that are evaluated using before-and-after self-report measures of knowledge are likely to show positive effects. Results are less likely to be positive for studies that randomly select employees to a training group, include a control group that is not given training, and use objective measures of job performance six months before training and six months after training.

The review by Guzzo and colleagues (1985) showed that overall, productivity programs such as training do make a difference, but many factors contribute to success besides the programs themselves. These factors include the organizational context, the research design, and the particular measure of productivity, as well as what the program was intended to do. The finding that less rigorous research produces more significant effects suggests the need to understand the multiple factors that may unintentionally affect the training program. For instance, when random assignment to groups is not possible, the group chosen for the training may be the one needing it the most. Perhaps because of this, the group chosen may be the most likely to succeed. Comparison or control groups may not have been selected for the training because they were likely to fail.

The difficulty involved in measurement and research design does not mean that training programs should not be evaluated.

Program evaluations are needed to help management decide whether to adopt, continue, or revise programs to make them more effective. Recognizing the multiple factors that may influence evaluation results will lead to more reasoned judgments and avoid the possibility of disappointment if a program or modification to a program fails.

An Action-Research Process Approach to Evaluation

A process approach to evaluation requires taking a realistic, practical, and long-term view of evaluating the effects of a program. The evaluation focuses on developing goals, identifying and trying different processes or applications of the program, and observing the incremental change, rather than evaluating whether predetermined objectives were achieved (Blacker and Brown, 1985). This action research model suggests the need for evaluation while a training program is being implemented.

Rather than focusing on a predetermined hypothesis or target, the process approach focuses on the process of learning and the process of change. The users of the program (for example, department managers and subject matter experts) are involved in the program's design as a way to increase its applicability and likelihood of acceptance. Program developers must be willing to adapt the program to the users' needs.

It helps if program developers are not also responsible for evaluating the program. Keeping these functions separate will increase objectivity in identifying the multiple factors that can influence the effects of a training program. However, the evaluator and developer should work together to outline the scope of the study, agree on roles, determine the criteria of success, and decide on program modifications as the trial continues (London, 1988).

In the following examples of the process approach to program evaluation, three descriptions are provided of how to combine program evaluation with the operation of a training program.

1. *Evaluating training for new technology implementation.* This evaluation examined the effectiveness of training managers in the use of a new telecommunications system. Another part of the

study was designed to evaluate sources of stress experienced by the people responsible for both installing the new system and training employees to use the system. Questionnaires were distributed to the managers who were trained as well as to the installation people. The results were fed back to the installation group to generate ways to lessen stress. Also, the results were used to determine how the implementation process could be improved at new locations.

The study of the training indicated that the information on the new system should be disseminated more widely and with more detail than was done the first time the system was implemented. Research on the pressure experienced by the installation group revealed that their work was highly stressful. The questionnaire was a way for the installation employees to communicate concerns to their bosses, namely, that the bosses often did not listen to employees' concerns; that employees did not have proper training before being asked to perform a task; that the installation team did not work together well; that there were no written procedures about how to do the job correctly; and that employees were expected to accomplish the installations and training in an unrealistic time frame. These results were the basis for discussions with group members about how they could reduce stress even though they had to continue working at an accelerated pace. The members came up with ideas for more flexible work hours, more extensive training, and a better team spirit.

This example shows that training should be evaluated in the context in which it is used. Rather than evaluate the program to train managers in how to use the new system, the evaluation focused more broadly on the installation process and the people responsible for installation and training.

2. *Evaluating employee education.* During the last several years, I have been involved in several efforts to evaluate the effects of costly employee education programs. One project evaluated a study-at-home program that allowed employees to obtain course material and study on their own. The courses focused on management and technical skills needed to prepare occupational workers for growing areas of the business, such as data systems. The research focused on assessing employees' awareness of the program, participant reactions to the courses, and why some participants did not complete

the courses. In addition, the research evaluated the impact of course completion on employees' careers. Questionnaires and interviews with participants and nonparticipants were employed as methods of data gathering.

3. *Evaluating a job rotation program.* A research and development (R&D) unit of a large industrial corporation established a rotation program for early-career scientists and engineers (those with two to five years' experience) in the R&D community to give them job experiences in the firm's business units. These would be six-month to one-year assignments. The objective was to have R&D personnel become more aware of how research and development is applied and marketed by the firm. Also, the hope was that R&D would be more appreciated by business unit managers and executives.

The positions the participants moved to were "real" jobs—not jobs created especially for the R&D staff but assignments on important line or staff projects in the business unit. The positions were chosen to match learning objectives established for the employee. The R&D home department continued to pay participants' salary, and the business unit paid travel and lodging expenses. A central office in the R&D unit's training department coordinated the moves, identifying positions and matching qualified personnel. The learning experiences were monitored by the program coordinator, the employee's supervisor in the business unit, and the supervisor in the employee's home department.

In addition to moving R&D staff to business units, the program included rotations from the business units to the R&D department. However, it was more difficult to find qualified business unit managers who had the educational background necessary for a "real" R&D job. Also, it was more difficult to find business unit managers who would give up people for a rotational assignment when the business units were short of resources. (Of course, the managers were more than willing to borrow an R&D person, since they only had to pay expenses.)

In the evaluation, which was conducted with the help of an outside consulting firm, questionnaires were sent to R&D personnel having business unit assignments during the first two years of the program. The goal of the evaluation was to determine what the participants learned, whether they felt the experience was worthwhile, and whether the experience changed their perceptions. Data were also collected from the business unit supervisors about the value of the program. A control group of nonparticipating R&D personnel was identified and asked to complete questionnaires with the same questions about how they viewed the R&D community. The business unit supervisors who took R&D personnel into their groups found that the participants could get up to speed quickly and make a valuable contribution to the groups. These supervisors wanted more people available for assignments. The participants from the R&D community also were pleased with the program.

Other analyses compared the R&D participants' responses with the control group of R&D personnel who did not change jobs and with the business unit managers on rotation to the R&D staff. Several significant between-group differences demonstrated that the R&D participants, more than the control group, appreciated the rewards for collaboration, learned the value of comparing different solutions to problems, believed that competition is fierce in the marketplace, and understood that the R&D community has many opportunities for business success.

Business unit managers on rotation to the R&D staff, compared to their colleagues from the R&D community (program participants and the R&D control group), expressed more appreciation for the importance of an interentity assignment, felt they had a better understanding of the role of marketing and product management in the R&D/product definition process, and were more likely to say they perceived shared values of how people should work together across business units. Data from the first year compared to the second showed that R&D participants in the second year were more likely to believe that work-unit performance is rewarded, that the R&D community's survival depends on discontinuing unsuccessful projects, and that mutual respect is the norm across entities.

These results are only a few examples of statistically significant differences in the study. The questionnaire data and write-in responses yielded a rich set of information that helped in adapting the program over time—for example, by providing participants with a better orientation to the purpose of the program and what to expect, by increasing involvement of business unit managers in choosing participants for jobs in their groups, and by clarifying communications about the value of the program for attracting more people.

While the research design used a control group, there was no random selection of participants to groups. The control group participants were chosen for their similarity to the program participants. There was a control group only for the R&D community, not for business unit managers. There was no premeasure of how people felt before participating in the program; therefore, it was impossible to say whether or why attitudes changed over time. Also, because this was an action research project, data were used to make improvements in the program from one year to the next.

Learning from Available Data

Over time, training departments are likely to generate substantial information about effective adult learning methods and characteristics of effective training program design and delivery. Recently, a major study conducted on U.S. Air Force training programs took advantage of such available data to explore the relationship of student characteristics to course content and training outcomes (Mumford, Weeks, Harding, and Fleishman, 1988).

Each year, the Air Force provides initial skills training to more than 50,000 enlistees in some two hundred occupational specialties. Supported by an Air Force contract, the researchers obtained data for over 5,000 students in thirty-nine of these courses. The following are examples of the variables examined:

Student Characteristics

- Aptitude
- Reading level
- Academic achievement motivation
- Educational level
- Educational preparation
- Age

Course Content Variables

- Course length
- Diversity of material

- Practice
- Abstract knowledge requirements
- Reading difficulty
- Student/faculty ratio
- Instructor experience
- Instructional aids (simulations and practice devices)
- Hands-on practice
- Feedback
- Number of students trained
- Day length (eight or six hours)
- Occupational difficulty

Training Performance Measures

- Assessed quality of performance (achievement test scores)
- Special individualized assistance provided by the instructor
- Academic counseling to remediate poor performance
- "Washback" time (retraining hours)
- Academic attrition (elimination from the course based on poor performance due to insufficient ability)
- Nonacademic attrition (elimination from the course based on poor performance due to lack of motivation)

This list indicates the diversity of variables that may be collected. Some may be obtained from the organization's training department. Biographical characteristics are usually part of the student's employment record or may be collected at the time of training. Course content characteristics may be collected from course developers and from observing course content and delivery. Performance measures may be limited to posttest performance or satisfaction measures.

The Air Force study demonstrated that individual attributes are likely to have a greater positive impact on achievement and motivational outcomes than are course content variables, whereas both sets of variables, when negative, can cause poor academic performance. Of the student characteristics, intellectual, motivational, and adaptational constructs were the most important influences on training performance. Course content variables, such as subject matter and occupational difficulty, were more important to training outcomes than were aspects of program design, such as feedback intensity, instructional quality, and course length, although these aspects did influence training performance as well. (See Mumford, Weeks, Harding, and Fleishman, 1988, for more detail.)

The Air Force study demonstrates the complex, multivariate nature of the training process. These variables and relationships must be taken into account to optimize an organization's investment in training. Such information can be obtained from experimental research designs (as described in Resource C). And they can be obtained from existing data and explorations of relationships, as in the Air Force study. Moreover, a process approach to evaluation of training programs as they operate can suggest ideas for improvement. All these methods of evaluation are necessary for understanding the ingredients for training that maximize learning and ultimately improve job performance and organizational productivity.

Summary

The need for training measurements depends on the client—training managers, instructors, and writers who are responsible for developing and delivering training; department supervisors who send students to training programs; and the students themselves. These clients want to know the effectiveness of training programs in order to evaluate their own success as providers and users of training. Sources of data include students and supervisors describing their satisfaction with the training and their perceptions of its effects on job performance. The registration system provides information on the number and type of students served. Instructional technologists are trained to observe instructors and provide information on their effectiveness. Training managers may learn how to conduct instructor observations as well. Training performance tests are a way to assess the knowledge and skills learned in the training program. The chapter provided examples of ways to collect course evaluation information.

The last part of the chapter described research designs for drawing conclusions from measurements of training effectiveness. This research process entails accounting for or controlling the possible effects of extraneous variables that may affect the data and interfere with the effects of the training. Experimental research designs, such as those described in Resource C, show how to control for these confounds. Another way to understand the training process is to examine relationships among relevant variables, such as individual characteristics and program design elements. An action-research process approach to training does not wait for clear answers about factors affecting training outcomes but rather uses measurements to suggest areas for improvement. The improvements are made, and the training is monitored to show the effects of the changes.

Policy Opportunities and Recommendations

1. Evaluations should be conducted to assess individual and group performance. That is, individual employees need feedback about how well they did. Information on groups of people participating in the training is necessary in assessing the overall effects of the program on performance and organizational effectiveness.

2. Users of training data should help determine what data should be collected, the form of the reports (how the data should be aggregated—by program, by location, by instructor, and so on), and the frequency of reports. One idea is to have a users' council meet periodically to discuss the timeliness and practicality of the data.

3. Training managers should advise their client departments on the meaning and limitations of the data (for example, threats to reliability and validity). They should also recommend how to apply the data—for instance, how to plan for needed training and to enhance the effects of the training.

4. The results of training measurements, particularly indicators of knowledge and skill acquisition, should be fed back to students and their supervisors as soon after the training as possible. To do this requires efficient data systems for collecting, recording, and analyzing training information. These data systems should be integrated—that is, putting all data reflecting an individual's training attitudes and performance on the same data record. This will allow for easier report generation and for examination of relationships among different variables.

5. Whenever possible, multiple training measures should be collected about the same program and should include student opinions, performance tests, and indicators of changes in job performance.

6. Training managers should understand how to apply different evaluation designs to suit the need. Experimental tests are important for trials of new programs in that they can help isolate the effects of the different components of the training on different training alternatives (for example, CBT versus instructor-led). Studies of relationships among elements of training do not hold extraneous variables constant but rather try to measure as many relevant variables as possible and then determine their interrelationships. Action research is the ongoing process of using measurements once the training program is on line so that adjustments can be made that will improve future sessions.

7

Investing in the Professional Development of the Training Staff

Training professionals, just as other employees, are concerned about maintaining their level of expertise. They are also concerned with advancement opportunities—ways to earn more money and to attain higher levels of responsibility. However, the earning power of a training professional working in the training department is affected by the staffing and development policies of the organization.

This chapter examines directions for professional growth and development within the context of an organization's training department. Competency models outlining job skills and requirements for people in different training roles are described, certification of instructors and course developers is discussed, and avenues for continuing education and affiliation with professional organizations are reviewed. Finally, the chapter (as well as Resource D) describes career planning processes and suggests alternative career paths for training professionals.

Staffing Training Departments

Some firms hire training experts—people with advanced degrees in training, education, instructional technology, or related fields. These individuals may have a chance to move into different positions in the training organization, and if successful, they can move into training management and directorship roles.

Other firms may have a few training experts, but the majority of employees in training are on rotational assignments from line positions, having moved into training for the opportunity to learn and practice platform or writing skills. These skills can be valuable in responsible line assignments, for instance, in sales and marketing. The line experience of these employees lends credibility to their position in the education process; that is, as instructors these employees can speak from experience about what is being taught.

For example, Ameritech Publishing in Southfield, Michigan, pulls trainers from the line for two- to three-year rotational assignments. The goal is to "seed" the organization with people who have become adept at developing others—a skill and set of values these individuals will continue to exercise as they move into more powerful positions in the company.

> In the first year, they learn to be evaluators, group facilitators, instructors, and individual development counselors. The second year finds them practicing instructional development, marketing, needs analysis and media development. The best ones stay for a third year and learn skills needed to be a lead trainer, program administrator and program designer. [Gerber, 1988, p. 44]

Generalist managers on rotational assignment to the training department are often the only training staff members having the opportunity to attend courses and to receive challenging, skill-enhancing assignments. In these firms, long-term training staff members are given little opportunity for continued professional growth. In this scenario employees may find their way into the training department by default and stay there for many years, perhaps until they retire. In this case, the firm does not view training as a suitable assignment for high-potential employees and also does not see the need for employees with master's or doctorate degrees in training. Given this lack of attention by the organization, the training department can develop a reputation as a home for "dead wood."

Another scenario is that a training department is staffed with a mix of training experts and experienced line employees. Training managers, especially those in the most responsible positions, are not training experts but are high-potential managers who are being trained as generalists by working in different positions in a variety of departments. These managers bring to the job the ability to organize and direct the department's activities in line with their knowledge of overall organizational strategies. Training professionals who want to advance in the organization must do so by moving out of the training department and into different types of line and staff positions. They may return to the training department, but continued allegiance to training, and the desire to return to training, probably would hamper their careers.

Staffing Policies and Professional Development Opportunities

The difficulty with the last scenario is that training professionals who aspire to increased levels of income and responsibility feel they cannot achieve these career goals without leaving the profession or the organization. While such goals can be attained in consulting firms that specialize in training development, some individuals prefer to work within an organization's training department rather than as external consultants. Internal trainers identify with the organization—its goals and its people. They feel part of the corporate family, and develop long-term relationships with colleagues and the departments they serve, enjoying the results of their long-term efforts. Unfortunately, they may not have the same opportunities for advancement as the people they train.

Early career plateaus become the norm for training experts because training is not viewed as a central aspect of the organization's activities. Young managers identified by supervisors as having potential for advancement are included in the organization's high-potential development program. The program may be run by the training department for the entire organization. Such a program may be geared to training generalist managers, where people in the program are moved through a series of departments to learn different aspects of the organization before they are promoted to the next level of management. Managers who are not in the program may have little chance for advancement in the organization, no matter how expert they are in a particular discipline.

As an example, one training manager responsible for a group of course developers was offered a place in the firm's high-potential development program. Rather than leave the training profession, this individual declined the invitation. In another case, a training manager took a downgrade position because he preferred to be an instructional technologist advising course developers. He felt that management did not allow him to utilize and continue to develop his knowledge of training and development.

To some extent, staffing and development policies in training departments will depend on how the training department fits into the organizational structure. Central training organizations serving a large number of students in different departments can afford to hire and, to some extent, promote training professionals. Small training departments that focus on education in one specific function, such as systems design or sales, are likely to offer fewer opportunities for training professionals. Such departments require that instructors and program developers have knowledge of the subject matter. External training consultants, or perhaps training experts in the firm's headquarters, can provide advice on program design and evaluation. Small organizations may rely almost totally on external training expertise, even for program delivery. Generalist managers may be rotated in and out of training management positions, and program material may be purchased from outside consulting firms or from individual contractors who are hired to develop and/or deliver a specific program.

Lack of developmental opportunities for training professionals limits the ability of the organization to attract and retain competent training experts and may require the organization to hire outside consultants who are expensive and who do not have the knowledge of the organization. One firm was faced with the problem of having key experienced trainers leave because there was little opportunity for advancement. Rather than try to replace them by hiring seasoned training professionals from other organizations, the training director began hiring recent college graduates with degrees in education and instructional technology. The director felt she could attract bright individuals with the latest technological know-how, but she recognized that she would have to invest in instructing them about the organization. She also realized that the return on this investment would be short-lived because these young trainers would eventually become as frustrated by lack of advancement opportunity as their predecessors.

A Recommended Staffing Policy

An advantage of having internal training professionals is that they become familiar with the organization's people, strategies, and methods of operation. When managed properly, this approach can contribute to responsive, cost-effective training. An advantage of using external consultants in training is that they can meet an immediate need and then leave. As needs change, different contractors can be hired who have the requisite knowledge, although this involves a constant search for talent and a high cost for what is only a temporary service.

The advantage of rotating line experts and generalist managers into training is that they bring their knowledge of organizational goals and procedures to bear on training development, delivery, and administration. Presumably, this leads to programs that are highly responsive to the needs of client departments. The advantage of employing training experts is that their knowledge of adult learning and alternative training technologies contributes to cost-effective educational programs that enhance learning, application, and evaluation of the effects of training.

Consequently, a good approach to staffing training organizations is to have a mix of people and to allow multiple career paths. Technicians and managers from line departments should be able to move into the training department, learn several major aspects of training (for example, how to enhance platform skills or learn about course development). These employees may not become training professionals per se, but they will learn much about training and, hopefully, will excel in one area of training. They may return to their home departments with improved communications skills and an enhanced sensitivity to the importance of education. If they desire to make training their careers, and their outstanding performance warrants keeping them in the training department, then they should have opportunities for continued growth and challenge in training.

Harry Bernhard, former program director of advanced management development at IBM, summarized the importance of staffing and development in the training department as follows:

> How a company structures and staffs its T&D [training and development] efforts says a lot about how it views education. . . . A good choice for T&D director is a respected member of the organization, someone with line management experience who understands the company's culture and values as well as its business. . . . For the same reason, put experienced members of the organization—people in line or field positions serving temporary, say, two-year terms as instructors—on the T&D staff. At IBM, 75 percent of the education staff consists of experienced practitioners, passing through the T&D department as part of their own career development.
>
> Seasoned company veterans have automatic credibility. They embody the company's culture, know its procedures, and illustrate by example the qualities and behavior that the organization values. . . . Using line managers as T&D staff—instead of hiring trainers and creating a bureaucracy to serve them—is also a flexible approach. As the need for teachers grows or shrinks, the business can add or redeploy in-house staff quickly.
>
> There is a place for a small core of experienced, homegrown teachers who do not get rolled back into other functions after a stint in the classroom. Some permanent educators are essential to maintain continuity and provide expertise in adult learning theory and course development. But they should be trusted and respected members of the organization, not people who have been put out to pasture on the theory they'll

> do less damage in T&D than elsewhere. [Bernhard and Ingols, 1988, p. 42]

Training experts who were hired into the training department with advanced degrees or substantial training experience and who wish to maintain careers as training professionals should have opportunities for increased responsibility, advancement, and income growth. They should be encouraged to transfer to different jobs in the training organization and should have opportunities to rotate into other types of human resource assignments—such as employment, career planning, and salary administration—to take advantage of opportunities to enhance their supervisory skills and expand their knowledge of human resource development and administration.

Perhaps training professionals will not have as many opportunities for advancement as they would if they were willing to move into other departments and gain a broader view of the firm's operations. However, the value of training expertise and outstanding performance should be recognized by promoting these individuals to senior positions in the training department. This will be more likely when line managers, especially higher-level managers, consider training as a valuable part of the organization and training careers as worthwhile. This situation is likely to occur as high-potential generalist managers rotate into training departments as part of their career development, as they develop a better understanding of the importance of training to the organization's success, and as they move into other departments for developmental jobs, demonstrating the value of human resource development skills. It will also help if training departments share resources with line departments—for instance, borrowing managers to serve as trainers and subject matter experts in program development. In general, training professionals will be valued more as training becomes an integral part of accomplishing the organization's goals.

In addition to fostering opportunities for training professionals to advance, all training staff should be provided opportunities for continuous learning—that is, the chance to learn and perform different roles in the training department. It is crucial that these professionals be allowed to belong to, and participate in, professional associations and to take courses to update their skills and knowledge in learning principles and advanced training technology.

Furthermore, training staff should be encouraged to generate new knowledge in the training field by experimenting with new techniques and evaluating the effectiveness of these techniques. Staff should be encouraged to share the results of these trials with their colleagues inside the firm and in other firms through publications in professional journals and presentations at professional meetings.

Competency Models

Training design principles should be applied to establishing curricula and development programs for training personnel. Such principles involve the same type of front-end analysis required for analyzing performance problems and determining possible solutions. Elements of front-end analysis include identifying job behaviors, skills, and knowledge required for competent performance. This approach requires the development of a competency model.

A competency model describes the major elements of the job and outlines those behaviors and associated individual characteristics (knowledge, skills, and abilities) necessary for acceptable performance and for advanced or high levels of performance as well as those characteristics that are unacceptable. These characteristics are used as a basis for selecting people to fill assignments and for determining what development programs (training courses and job assignments) lead to acceptable and higher levels of performance.

Competency models can be developed for each major role in a training department (for example, instructor, program developer, instructional technologist, educational consultant) and for different levels of training management (for example, training director). (See the description in Chapter Three of these different roles.) The International Board of Standards for Training Performance and Instruction has developed over two hundred skill sets that can be used by designers of learning programs and developers of instructional strategies.

Exhibit 13 provides examples of competency models from the

Exhibit 13. Excerpts from Competency Models.

Instructor Competency Model

Competency	*Behaviors*		
	Unacceptable	*Sufficient*	*Excellent*
1. Applies principles of adult learning	Ignores student apprehension by not allowing questions at the start of the program	Lessens student apprehension by allowing time for questions about goals and methods	Gives students a clear picture of what to expect and allows plenty of time for questions
	Uses one instructional technique	Uses several teaching methods; structures delivery to emphasize learning	Uses methods to match the need; structures delivery to enhance learning
2. Managing course structure and organization	Fails to make transitions between modules as designed	Makes smooth transitions	
	Is rigid in depth of coverage and delivery style	Adjusts coverage and style to match students' needs	Modifies structure to fit the situation yet accomplishes objectives
3. Presentation methods	Presents all content with similar emphasis	Emphasizes main points	Integrates main points into a comprehensive whole
	Does not follow methods prescribed in the instructor manual	Follows instructor manual	Enhances material with examples, anecdotes, role plays, and so on
4. Subject matter expertise	Does not keep current with updates and enhancements	Keeps current with changes in subject matter	Seeks out information about content changes and finds ways to incorporate

Exhibit 13. Excerpts from Competency Models, Cont'd.

Instructor Competency Model

Competency	*Behaviors*		
	Unacceptable	*Sufficient*	*Excellent*
			these changes in training programs
5. Administration and evaluation	Is late with feedback to students on course performance	Gives feedback within the prescribed time	Gives feedback as soon as possible
	Gives incomplete feedback on course peformance	Gives thorough feedback; allows ample time for questioning	Traces trends as a basis for comparison in giving feedback
			Coaches supervisors in how to reinforce students' new skills

Training Manager Competency Model

Managers of program developers and course instructors should have a broad knowledge of the training field, including:

- A basic understanding of adult learning principles
- Knowledge of program design
- The ability to observe and evaluate competent instructor platform skills
- An understanding of how to evaluate the cost-effectiveness of a training program
- An understanding of program evaluation, action research, and experimental design
- Expertise in strategic planning
- An understanding of client department needs
- The ability to give objective performance feedback to subordinates
- The interpersonal skills needed for coaching and developing subordinates
- The insight into how to identify and select talented individuals for the department
- The insight to select staff with the appropriate mix of skills
- The motivation to take time to recognize and reward subordinates' achievements

Exhibit 13. Excerpts from Competency Models, Cont'd.

- The willingness to risk experimenting with new training methods
- The recognition that subordinates want challenging assignments
- The organizational skills to balance meeting client demands with encouraging subordinates to acquire new skills and knowledge.

Overall, the training manager must exhibit general principles of competent management by designing challenging assignments, involving subordinates in making decisions that affect them, providing subordinates with frequent feedback on their performance, offering constructive ideas for development, and providing them with opportunities for improvement. In addition, training managers must be knowledgeable about the training field and what behaviors comprise excellence in training performance.

---

standpoint of the instructor and the training manager. These examples are excerpted from competency models covering many major skills needed by instructors and training managers. For instance, instructor competencies (as shown in Exhibit 13) involve front-end analysis (for example, analyzing course materials and learner information), managing the learning environment (for example, demonstrating effective communications and presentation skills and responding appropriately to learners' needs for clarification and feedback), and evaluation (for example, evaluating student performance and reporting evaluation information).

As Exhibit 13 suggests, competency models may have different formats and varying degrees of detail. Some models specify behaviors (as in the instructor competency model). Other models may simply list desired competencies (such as the training manager competency model). Another approach is to specify desired skills and knowledge areas in addition to abilities. Exhibit 13 includes examples under different categories of behaviors but is not comprehensive. In general, a competency model must be thorough enough to guide selection, training, and appraisal of training professionals.

Generating a Competency Model

In generating a competency model, those employees judged by their supervisors and peers to be highly competent should be identified and then observed and interviewed to distill those abilities and skills accounting for outstanding performance. Less experienced and lower-performing individuals should be observed to identify the low end of competency dimensions. A team of employees should work together on the competency model, so that everyone has input on the model that will be the basis for training and appraisal and that will be used to select and train future employees. Exhibit 14 describes ways to identify highly competent performers, analyze job behaviors, develop the competency model, and apply the model to assess deficiencies in the target population.

The steps for generating a competency model require a good deal of staff time and might require external assistance, which could be costly. Small organizations can apply the same steps, perhaps with a training manager working together with a co-worker. In such cases, less attention might be paid to collecting and analyzing data and more attention paid to identifying what behaviors constitute competent performance and agreeing on the elements of competence for the particular role in the training department.

Competency-Based Certification Procedures

Since many training departments staff program development and delivery positions with people who do not have a training background, some procedure is desirable to ensure that newcomers to training positions have the skills and knowledge needed for the job. In addition, since new programs are continuously being developed and refined, procedures are necessary to ensure that trainers have the expertise they need to develop or teach a specific program. This is no different from the need to establish employee competence in other fields, such as sales, accounting, or general management, and, in fact, the training staff is usually called on to develop procedures for such training and assessment.

Certification is a way to identify employees as professional and is a formal recognition of the individual's accomplishments and abilities. Working in complex disciplines such as training requires keeping current on technical advances. As specialization becomes important in a field, methods to ensure that an individual has the competence to perform tasks related to that specialization

Exhibit 14. Steps for Generating and Applying a Competency Model.

A competency model should consist of a definition of the tasks carried out by those who are competent performers as well as a detailed description of the knowledge and skills that allow these employees to maintain a level of mastery. The steps involved in developing and applying such a model are: (1) identifying the most competent performers; (2) analyzing their job behaviors and personal characteristics; (3) synthesizing this data to generate a description of the various tasks, resources used, and skills and knowledge required for each task; and (4) applying this information to identify deficiencies and to determine training solutions.

Identifying Highly Competent Performers

A highly competent performer is someone who excels in the job, performs at the highest levels, and exhibits mastery of the most important tasks. Nominations of highly competent performers may be obtained from supervisors, resource review committees (groups of supervisors that periodically discuss human resource requirements and make staffing decisions), or top executives. Departmental promotion lists or performance appraisal data are other sources for identifying competent performers.

Analyzing Job Behaviors and Personal Characteristics

A comprehensive job analysis is the foundation of a training needs analysis. The elements of behavior and individual characteristics under investigation will depend on the group of individuals being analyzed. If the competency model is based on a single job in one functional area of training, then elements may be highly specific. If the model is to apply to all those at a certain level across a job function (such as all training managers), then elements will have to be more general. The advantage of the general approach is that the competency model can be applied broadly to many jobs in the department. The disadvantage is that specific task elements may be missed. Training requirements for such specific tasks would have to be identified and addressed as the model is applied to specific jobs.

There are many job analysis methods from which to select, including checklists or questionnaires, frequency counts, interviews, and observations. The checklist method requires the job incumbent to select from a list of behaviors required by the job. A checklist may be augmented by asking for the frequency of each behavior and its importance to the position.

In the interview method, the job analyst asks highly competent performers to describe their jobs. The analyst collects examples of particularly effective behaviors and may also observe the individual and record the frequency of various behaviors.

Exhibit 14. Steps for Generating and Applying a Competency Model, Cont'd.

Part of developing a competency model is the assessment of personal characteristics that distinguish better from poorer performers. Therefore, similar methods should be applied to determine behaviors and skills that distinguish different levels of performance. Supervisors may nominate people who represent these different performance levels, and the observation, interview, or checklist/questionnaire approach to job analysis may be applied to this broader sample of individuals. The results should be a set of behaviors and skills that clearly distinguishes levels of performance.

Synthesizing Results into a Competency Model

Exhibit 13 showed formats for a competency model. When using the competency model as a basis for selection, appraisal, and training, it should be recognized that there are different ways to perform well in the same job. Therefore, equally competent performers may have different strengths and may exhibit different behaviors. Variation in behaviors also may occur when individuals have somewhat different job functions even though they have a similar job title. For example, the work of training program developers will differ depending on the curriculum they are working on and the training technologies they are using.

Applying the Competency Model for Deficiency Diagnosis

Training needs are evident when the knowledge and skills typical of highly competent employees are compared to those of less skilled employees. A diagnostic analysis is necessary to determine the target population's skills and knowledge and to identify deficiencies. Several assessment procedures are possible for deficiency diagnosis, including multiple-choice questionnaires, observation of on-the-job behavior, and simulations.

After deficiencies have been identified, it is necessary to determine whether they can be alleviated with training. Some skills are not easily developed, such as those involving intelligence and decision-making ability. While it may be possible to make major changes in such dimensions, the cost to the organization and the time involved may make such training unfeasible. It may be possible to enhance such individual characteristics and abilities; this is the goal of management development programs on such topics as decision making. Some skills, such as communications ability, can be changed more easily, and an effective training program may lead to considerable improvement. In cases where training and development may not be fruitful, the solution may be to select people who already have the needed skills.

Source: Adapted from London and Stumpf, 1982, pp. 174–179.

are desirable. Unlike licensure, which is mandated by law and meant to protect the public from incompetent practice, certification is applicable to professionals who can practice without being certified (Lee, 1986).

Certification may be a rather strong word for an internal procedure to ensure that people can do the work they have been assigned, and certification is certainly not the only, and perhaps not the best, way to maintain standards. Yet firms are instituting competency requirements (sometimes termed *mastery paths)* and certification procedures (especially in technical fields) to be certain that employees keep up to date with technology and to assure customers that employees are qualified. Certification, in addition to seniority, may be used as a way to evaluate employees when layoffs are necessary.

A training certification process ensures that program developers and instructors are not expected to perform tasks for which they are unqualified and that training personnel are knowledgeable. Such a program helps maintain standards, thereby contributing to meeting client requirements, and is a source of credentials, which are important to trainers when making decisions about students. These decisions may affect the student's pay and future career prospects, and so it is critical for the student and the student's department to feel that training performance evaluations and resulting decisions are made by qualified people. Certification enhances the reputation of the training department as a professional organization with high standards and quality products. Moreover, certification provides a basis for trainers to be proud and self-confident in their abilities.

Training is an area with many diverse aspects. Moreover, the skills required are partially dependent on the particular programs developed and the methods used by the organization. Training professionals may desire certification to enhance their professionalism within the organization. Training directors, particularly of large departments, may also want certification procedures to ensure that standards of excellence are maintained. Each organization must decide on the value of certification and determine what background and experience requirements will be accepted for certification.

Who to Certify. A certification program could be established for line managers who move into training assignments. For example, certification may be important to ensure that line managers transferred to instructor positions are selected for their communications ability and have the opportunity to learn how to be effective trainers. After a period of training, perhaps including practice as a coinstructor, they would be evaluated by training supervisors and certified as qualified instructors. The same process may be applied to personnel who move into course development work from another discipline, with the focus, in this case, on writing skills and knowledge of adult learning. Certification may also be relevant for training experts with advanced degrees in education or instructional technology if the training department wants to be sure that the expert has the skills and knowledge required by the department for a particular position.

The term *certification* is sometimes applied to learning how to instruct or administer a particular training program. The goal, in this case, is to ensure that training staff members have the knowledge needed to teach a particular course. When a company purchases a course from a consulting firm, the consulting firm may offer to "certify" the company's trainers as instructors of the course. This is a quality control check to ensure that the course is delivered as intended.

A training department may establish its own certification process and standards based on competencies developed by training professional societies such as the American Society for Training and Development. Certification should be competency based—that is, it should measure the competencies of an individual against a set of predetermined standards and requirements for competent performance (Lee, 1986). The certification process may require training instructors and developers to demonstrate mastery of a certain body of knowledge (for example, the essential ingredients of a needs analysis, principles of instructional design, and so on) and a certain set of skills (for example, the ability to write an instructional objective, teach a class, conduct a role play, and so on). A competency model may be the foundation for designing learning experiences and for determining criteria for evaluation and eventual certification (Kenny, 1986).

The Consequences of Failure. In some organizations, there is a negative connotation to certification because it carries with it the possibility of failure. Organizations should set policies to determine what happens when individuals do not certify. For example, such employees may be given more training and a second chance at certifying, moved into less responsible assignments, or asked to leave the department or the organization.

To avoid the pass/fail aspect of certification, some organizations prefer to use other terms, such as *mastery path* (London and Mone, 1987). A mastery path is based on the same rigorous foundation of job analysis and competency identification as certification. A standard set of apprentice job assignments and training courses is established. There are periodic checkpoints and a final assessment conducted by supervisors and other judges as well as a recommended time period for completion of each stage. However, achieving mastery may take longer for some people than for others and thus should not be a prerequisite for being able to do certain tasks (such as teaching a course solo). Rather, mastery should be a recognition point indicating that the individual has successfully completed a set of experiences and achieved a high level of expertise.

Professional and Technical Certification. Professional certification refers to a mastery path or certification process that focuses on a general discipline, such as training instruction, course development, or educational consulting. Individuals participate in a training program and series of on-the-job learning experiences that prepare them to handle the major functions in the area of expertise.

Technical certification refers to learning in a specific technical area—such as being certified to teach a specific course or to design computer-based training using a specific software package. Such certification is often built into the design of a new program. For instance, the training department that purchases a particular course from a training consulting firm also may be required by the firm to pay for the department's in-house trainers to attend a train-the-trainer session to learn how to teach the course. Some in-house trainers may be certified as master trainers who can teach others how to run the course.

An Example of a Professional Certification Process. Consider the elements of a certification process outlined in Exhibit 15.

Exhibit 15. An Example of an Instructor Certification Process.

I. Establishing competencies
 A. Institute job-analysis procedures.
II. Selecting staff
 A. Apply the competency model to develop selection procedures that measure candidates on the competencies or on predictors that indicate ability to become competent.
  1. Selection criteria may include demonstrated competence in another setting or having the educational background that suggests competency (such as an advanced degree in instructional technology).
  2. Special assessments may be designed to evaluate competencies, such as role playing by an instructor to demonstrate platform skills.
III. Establishing evaluation responsibilities
 A. Form a team to evaluate the newcomer.
  1. This team may consist of the training manager (the new instructor's supervisor), an experienced instructor who can be a mentor and role model for the new instructor, and an instructional technologist who has advanced expertise in adult learning methods.
 B. Develop assessment procedures and establish time lines for periodic assessment.
  1. Assessments may include observations of in-class performance, students' evaluations of the apprentice trainer, checks on performance in classes on training methods and techniques, and an interview wherein the assessment team asks questions about what the individual would do in certain circumstances.
  2. Each assessment must build up to a final assessment before certification is granted.
 C. Suggest ways the development team can coach the trainer-in-training.
  1. The team members should work with the trainee throughout the certification process to structure job experiences that enhance learning.
  2. The team members should be encouraged to give frequent feedback to trainees. Feedback should occur after interim evaluations as well as at any relevant time during the certification process.
IV. Procedures for the first three months on the job
 A. Formal training
  1. Training may include an instructor's training workshop, courses in instructional design, and a workshop on race and gender issues (to enhance instructor sensitivity to fair treatment).

Exhibit 15. An Example of an Instructor Certification Process, Cont'd.

B. Initial classroom experience
 1. The trainee should observe experienced trainers in class.
 2. The trainee should coteach sections of courses, perhaps by serving as an aid during class demonstrations.

V. Procedures during three to nine months
 A. Continued practice, coteaching, and attending train-the-trainer programs
 B. Continued observation and coaching by the evaluation team

VI. Procedures during the "certification window" (six to nine months)
 A. When the team and the trainee feel ready, the trainee can be evaluated in a final assessment.
 1. The final assessment may be instructing a class solo.
 B. A policy is necessary to determine what happens if the individual does not pass the final assessment.
 1. Additional chances may be possible up to a final cutoff point, perhaps nine months after starting the job.
 2. For borderline individuals (those who are close to certification but do not successfully complete every aspect of assessment), a provisionary certification may be granted, specifying follow-up practice and coaching with another team review after a designated period of time (three or six months).

VII. Procedures during nine to eighteen months
 A. Continue trainee's experience teaching a variety of courses.
 1. The trainee can be assigned to a new role model for additional coaching and to give the trainee a chance to observe a different teaching style.
 B. The trainee should take advanced courses on instructional methods.

VIII. Procedures during eighteen months and beyond
 A. The individual is a fully developed trainer and serves as a role model for others.

IX. Rotating to a new assignment
 A. The training department should establish a policy on the desired length of time the employee should be in a job after certification.
 1. The organization wants to recover its investment in the individual's certification, and this may involve a two- to three-year period after certification.
 2. The next job may be another assignment in training, perhaps as a program developer, or the employee may return to a field assignment.

Note that development does not end with certification. The process outlines the time on the job, from initial apprenticeship through certification to experienced trainer and role model to others. The trainee obtains instruction and feedback from multiple sources. Also, while there is a pass/fail decision for certification, this is not an all-or-none choice. A team of experts comprises the certification board. Borderline individuals are given additional coaching and development until they demonstrate full competence.

The process also includes different methods of learning, including attending training classes, observing experienced trainers, and practicing, with feedback and coaching. Trainees have considerable opportunities to try new behaviors and obtain reactions from students and observers. In addition, the process encourages supervisor-subordinate interaction. The supervisor becomes a coach, not merely a monitor and the source of assignments. Once the trainee has been certified, this coaching relationship should evolve to empowerment. The supervisor should feel confident in the subordinate's abilities, since the supervisor was partially responsible for the subordinate's growth and development. The supervisor must accomplish this shift in relationship, gradually letting go of the coaching role and becoming a mentor and adviser. Feedback should continue as a routine part of this relationship. However, the subordinate should be given the latitude to form his or her own style of instruction and to experiment with new methods.

In a competency-based certification process, the emphasis is on giving those who meet the entry standards the background and knowledge they need to become expert. The newcomers are employees or new hires who demonstrate competence and potential. The goal in some training departments is to use the best performers in the field as role models for recruits. These top performers are expected to progress through the certification process rapidly.

There has been a debate in the training field about the desirability of certification and whether certification processes should be developed by training societies or by training departments for their own use. (See Lee, 1986, for an overview of this debate and the results of a survey of training practitioners' views on certification.) Some training managers believe that certification is impractical and unnecessary because the training department already has in place a training career path and professional training courses for instructors and developers. For example, Hewlett Packard provides a variety of both training skills and technical courses for its instructors. Detailed job descriptions provide a checklist of required skills that are (for all practical purposes) standards, and the company carefully evaluates the impact of its courses. Another view is that certification sets minimum standards and that outstanding performance requires much more.

Some small organizations hire training professionals from universities who have degrees in instructional technology, education, and related fields. In this case, the degree is the credential. While university programs differ in content and while there is no uniform accreditation process in the human resource development field, the content of university programs can be assessed by the potential employer. For this reason, some organizations may want their own testing programs, such as written examinations on training theory and practice and assessments of training behavior using role plays or actual training performance (such as classroom presentation skills).

As it stands, the burden of judging competence is on the training organization, which hires and develops training staff. It is difficult for small training departments, which do not have standard train-the-trainer procedures, to make such judgments. However, training managers can establish standards by developing detailed job descriptions and associated competency models, using input from training societies that have explored and documented competencies for different training roles. (For information, write to the American Society for Training and Development at the address provided in Exhibit 16.) Also, an effort can be made to implement a certification process that will enhance the professionalism of the staff, such as the process for instructor certification outlined in Exhibit 15. The training department should not wait for its clients to complain that the training staff lacks professionalism and competence. Rather, the objective should be to continuously evaluate the quality of training output and the ability of the staff to develop and deliver high-quality training products.

Professional Affiliation

One of the sources of continuous learning and professional identification is membership in a training association. Membership usually is accompanied by receipt of association journals and newsletters and invitations to local and national conferences. Membership provides a means of keeping informed of the latest advances in the field and of what leading-edge companies are doing in training. Exhibit 16 describes several major professional associations and lists others, along with addresses and telephone numbers.

The list of associations in Exhibit 16 is not exhaustive, but it does illustrate the diversity of professional associations available. Several questions for the training manager to consider are:

- Does your organization have a policy or practice for paying for employees' professional association memberships?
- Is attendance at professional meetings considered part of an employee's professional development?
- Does your organization have guidelines on the number of meetings or days an employee may or should attend such conferences?
- Are there ways for sharing what happens at society meetings?
- How do your employees decide to attend an upcoming conference (for instance, by reviewing the published agenda, by receiving input from other society members)?
- Do you encourage employees to contribute papers to professional journals and to make presentations at conferences?

Training managers should answer such questions and communicate these answers in the form of a departmental policy for professional memberships and participation in professional association activities. Exhibit 17 provides a draft of such a policy.

The policies adopted by a training department depend on the particular needs of that department. A centralized training department having members with Ph.D.s or Ed.D.s in instructional technology and other fields of education may encourage its people to be active in professional associations because this helps keep em-

Exhibit 16. A Sample of Training Associations.

Training Associations

The American Society for Training and Development (ASTD). This is the major association of trainers and educators in the United States and has about twenty thousand members. The $120 annual membership fee includes the monthly *ASTD Journal,* the *Buyer's Guide and Consultant Directory,* a copy of *Who's Who* in the field, and access to a computerized data base for information as well as access to an information resource center and national reports on human resources. ASTD annually sponsors a major national conference. Address: ASTD, 1630 Duke Street, P.O. Box 1443, Alexandria, Va. 22313; telephone: (703) 683-8100.

The National Society for Performance and Instruction (NSPI). This professional organization is dedicated to improving human performance in the workplace through a variety of solutions, including training. Its approximately five thousand members in business, industry, government, education, the military, and health care institutions specialize in human performance technology, including education and training, feedback systems, organizational design, incentive systems, personnel selection, human factors, and other methods that provide cost-effective solutions to human resource problems. NSPI has several professional publications that provide examples of applications and that report research and theory development. NSPI also holds a major annual meeting. Address: NSPI, 1126 16th Street N.W., Suite 102, Washington, D.C. 20036; telephone: (202) 861-0777.

The National Association for Industry-Education Cooperation. This is an interdisciplinary group of corporate and public educators that fosters communication and cooperation between public and corporate education. The emphasis is on improving high school and junior college curricula and vocational education rather than higher education. Address: NAIEC, 235 Hendricks Boulevard, Buffalo, N.Y. 14226; telephone: (716) 834-7047.

Association for Educational Communications and Technology (AECT). This association includes experts in electronic training media, such as CBT, interactive video, and satellite delivery. Address: AECT, 1126 16th Street N.W., Washington, D.C. 20036; telephone: (202) 466-4780.

American Society for Personnel Administration (ASPA). This large organization offers broad coverage of personnel issues, some of it focusing on training and related issues, such as professional certification. Address: ASPA, 606 N. Washington Street, Alexandria, Va. 22314; telephone: (703) 548-3440.

Training Directors' Forum. Not a training association per se, the forum is something training directors can attend. Sponsored by Lakewood Publications, publishers of *Training Magazine* and the *Training Directors' Forum Newsletter,* the Training Directors' Forum is an annual meeting where training directors can share information and learn about advances in the field. Address: Lakewood Publications, 50 S. Ninth Street, Minneapolis, Minn. 55402; telephone: (612) 333-0471.

Exhibit 16. A Sample of Training Associations, Cont'd.

Other Relevant Associations

Association for Continuing Higher Education, College of Graduate and Continuing Studies, University of Evansville, 1800 Lincoln Avenue, Evansville, Ind. 47722; telephone: (812) 479-2472.

International Federation of Training and Development Associations, 923 State Street, St. Joseph, Mich. 49085; telephone: (616) 983-1280.

International Teleconferencing Association, 1299 Woodside Drive, McLean, Va. 22102; telephone: (703) 556-6115.

National University Continuing Education Association, One Dupont Circle, Suite 420, Washington, D.C. 20036-1168; telephone: (202) 659-3130.

Society for Accelerative Learning and Teaching, Box 1216, Welch Station, Ames, Iowa 50010; telephone: (515) 292-6509.

Society for Applied Learning Technology, 50 Culpeper Street, Warrenton, Va. 22186; telephone: (703) 347-0055.

Professional Associations Specific to Certain Industries

American Society for Healthcare Education and Training, 840 N. Lake Shore Drive, Chicago, Ill. 60611; telephone: (312) 280-6113.

Council of Hotel and Restaurant Trainers, c/o Sandi Spivey, Denny's Inc., 16700 Valley View, La Mirada, Calif. 90637; telephone: (714) 670-5498.

National Association for State Training and Development Directors, Attn.: Linda Carroll, Council of State Governments, Iron Works Pike, Lexington, Ky. 40578; telephone: (606) 252-2291.

National Society for Sales Training Executives, 203 East Third Street, Sanford, Fla. 32771; telephone: (305) 322-3364.

Society for Insurance Trainers and Educators, P.O. Box 513, Cary, Ill. 60013; telephone: (312) 516-1921.

Symposia on the Training of Nuclear Facility Personnel. Biennial meetings jointly sponsored by the American Nuclear Society and the Oak Ridge National Laboratory, Oak Ridge, Tenn.; telephone: (378) 831-6058.

These and other associations are listed annually in *Training Magazine*'s *Marketplace Directory*, which can be obtained at a library or by writing to Lakewood Publications at the address given above under the Training Directors' Forum.

Source: The association descriptions were adapted from material prepared by AT&T's Corporate Training Support Group.

Exhibit 17. Draft of a Policy to Guide Company-Sponsored Memberships in Training Societies.

Professional training societies and organizations such as the American Society for Training and Development (ASTD) and the National Society for Performance and Instruction (NSPI) have much to offer training personnel. Such associations provide a forum for the exchange of information and ideas on the latest developments in training as well as an opportunity for training professionals to network with other professionals.

Recognizing this, the training department will pay the cost of society membership dues and the expenses related to attending society functions or meetings, under the following conditions:

1. The work of the association must be relevant to the job. Membership must have a demonstrated benefit to the department as well as to the individual.
2. Requests for sponsored membership and for permission to attend society functions at company expense must be approved in advance by the employee's immediate supervisor.
3. Each training manager will determine the number of sponsored memberships for his or her unit and the approved societies, based on cost and relevance to job functions. Approval to attend meetings at company expense will be based on the same criteria.
4. Employees who attend association meetings at company expense will be expected to share what they have learned with others in their units by circulating literature and preparing a formal report or synopsis of sessions attended. This may be an oral report at department meetings or a memo written to colleagues.
5. Renewal of sponsored memberships is not automatic. Rather, each renewal will be evaluated annually to determine the continued worth to the department and to the individual.
6. Employees who wish to publish articles in professional journals or to make presentations at professional societies should obtain permission from their immediate supervisors. Supervisors should ensure that the material is nonproprietary.

Please note that professional association membership and involvement is neither a condition of employment nor a prerequisite for a training position.

---

ployees current. Moreover, training professionals will probably want such involvement to enhance their network of professional contacts and to maintain their interest in the field. For these individuals, membership and active involvement is a motivating factor and a source of identification.

Professional involvement will be less important for people who are on temporary rotation in training departments. For these individuals, subscribing to a professional journal or occasionally having them attend a local or national conference may be sufficient. The value of even such limited involvement in professional associations is that it helps employees develop an idea of the breadth and sophistication of the field and a better understanding of what resources are available for enhancing training effectiveness and for use after returning to the job.

Continuous Learning for Training Professionals

Opportunities for learning and professional growth are as important for training professionals as for other employees. Certification programs, as described above, may be extended to outline areas for further learning and for new job experiences and responsibilities. In addition, training technology, such as teleconferencing and CBT (for example, touch-screen video) can be used to teach new concepts of adult learning and employee development. Training programs may be offered internally, or trainers may be allowed to take courses run by consulting firms.

As an example of continued advanced education for training professionals, the South Australian College of Advanced Education offers courses and a master's degree in distance education using distance education technology. Distance education is conducted and is designed for part-time study in the home or business setting. Students interact with professors, tutors, and other students via electronic media. These educational programs require special skills in organization and management and involve professors and tutors in different kinds of course design, preparation, delivery, and teaching than in face-to-face instruction. The master's program, with courses offered via video conferences, prepares trainers, instructors, and managers in instructional design and the preparation of course material. (For information about the South Australian program, write to Dr. Lorne A. Parker, 2801 International Lane, Suite 205, Madison, Wisc. 53704; telephone (608) 246-3560.) Columbia University has also experimented with courses in instructional technology offered to training professionals via teleconferences connecting company conference rooms with Columbia classrooms.

Another important aspect of professional development is networking—maintaining contacts with other professional trainers in the organization and with professionals in other firms. Internal conferences may be held if the training community is large enough. Such meetings usually include outside guest speakers, internal business unit managers who describe organizational strategy and review what they expect from the training department. AT&T, Hewlett Packard, and Xerox have experimented with a joint conference for their training professionals via closed-circuit television. AT&T regularly runs such "learning-link" conferences for their internal training community. A typical session will include presentations from outside training experts and allow the audience to call in questions.

External conferences also provide a valuable way to keep abreast of the latest advancements and to maintain professional contacts. These contacts keep trainers current on what the competition and leading-edge training departments are doing and also keep trainers current on job vacancies for those looking for an employment change.

Continued communications may be thought of as a part of development and include communications between the training director and his or her staff and between line executives and the training community. Internal conferences are a way to engender such communication. Another is teleconferences via satellite or closed-circuit television, which reach a wider audience of the training community within the organization. Such conferences may address special issues faced by the organization, discuss advances in the field, and give trainers a chance to share their experiences and examples of innovative approaches to training and development.

One training director held a series of "press conferences" during which training personnel from remote locations could call a telephone number and listen to the director's comments. Staff members could also ask questions anonymously by telephoning to special operators. This technique gave the staff a chance to hear about recent training strategies and decisions and to understand the role of training in some upcoming organizational changes.

Career Planning for Training Professionals

Training departments should establish, document, and communicate a professional development policy that is appropriate for them. This policy may specify increasing the number of long-term positions for training professionals by moving these individuals into a variety of different training positions, thus allowing them to move up in the organizational hierarchy along the way. Or the policy may specify having a lean training department, with most instructors and course developers hired as contractors to meet particular needs.

For an example, Resource D provides a sample career planning guide that can help employees in a training department evaluate career options and plan for the future. The guide outlines the organization's staffing and development policies for the training department and also suggests a process and method for training personnel to work with their supervisors to develop career plans.

The training department in Resource D is called the Training and Development Resource Center (TDRC). This department strongly supports staffing instructor and developer positions from line departments. Those who transfer into the training department are not encouraged to make training a career. The policy suggests that employees stay in a training job for two to three years and then move back to the line or into another training position (for example, from instructor to developer) for another two to three years before ultimately returning to the line department.

Once adapted to suit the specific training department, the career planning guide should be distributed and expectations for its use spelled out. These expectations should include a suggested time frame for completing the career planning form. Training managers should use information about demands on the department to guide a subordinate's career plans (for example, pinpointing when it would be a good time for a subordinate to leave from the standpoint of both the subordinate's need for a new assignment and the department's work demands). Individual training plans should be summarized to provide an indication of expected movement of people out of the training department, thus providing input to the training department's human resource forecasting and planning—that is, what and when skills and abilities will be needed.

The career planning guide should be supplemented by other career planning resources, such as workshops run by the training department on self-assessment and career planning. For instance, a workshop might help participants identify career-related values, interests, and skills; seek data and feedback from their supervisors; find sources of relevant organizational career information (job openings in the company and skill requirements for positions in different departments); set realistic career goals; design career plans with action steps; and prepare for career discussions with their supervisors. Other courses may be available for supervisors to help them coach and guide subordinates through the career planning process as well as work with their own supervisors to the same end. Additional courses on résumé writing and interviewing techniques may be as valuable for training professionals as they are for other employees in the organization.

A "People Plan" for Training Staff

Career planning should be part of a department's overall effort to recognize and devote attention to employees' career and job needs. A "people plan" should be part of each manager's annual commitments and objectives. As applicable to training departments as it is to any other unit in the company, a people plan integrates training with other elements of good management. One department in which I was a manager requested that each person with supervisory responsibility have an eight-point people plan. The commitments under each point can be specific to needs of the manager and the group or can be general goals relevant to all managers. The eight points are listed in Exhibit 18, along with examples of commitments.

Managing the Training Staff

Career development is one aspect of managing the training staff. At a recent conference, training directors brainstormed ideas for managing instructors. Many of their ideas apply more generi-

Exhibit 18. A Sample People Plan.

A. Communications
  1. Hold quarterly skip-level meetings.
  2. Frequently communicate and discuss plans, progress, and feedback from others.

B. Development
  1. Provide performance feedback frequently to all direct subordinates and encourage these subordinates to do the same with their groups.
  2. Coach direct subordinates on ways to improve their performance.
  3. Seek feedback from direct subordinates and discuss with them ways to improve supervisor performance.
  4. Attend at least ten days of training and professional development activities during the year (applies to all managers in the group including supervisor). This training will be in support of a training plan agreed to by the employee and immediate supervisor.
  5. Work with direct subordinates to design a leadership development plan for them and assess their performance against this plan.

C. Staffing and career planning
  1. Ensure that every management employee in the group has a written career plan. This plan will be established, revised, and reviewed by June 30.
  2. Move 10 to 15 percent of the employees in the group to new assignments in the training department or elsewhere in the company during the year to enhance the vitality in the group and allow employees to carry out their career plans.

D. Appraisals and feedback
  1. Ensure that every employee has a written appraisal on the previous year's performance by February 15. Also, ensure that every employee has a mid-year appraisal by August 31. Supervisors will review the appraisals with their subordinates on or prior to those dates.
  2. Provide subordinates with informal feedback well in advance of the formal review session.

E. Recognition
  1. Recognize the accomplishments of employees and nominate them for the departmentwide formal recognition awards.

F. Affirmative action
  1. Guarantee equal opportunities and pursue minority and female candidates for all open positions.
  2. Ensure that all hires, moves, promotions, compensation, and other rewards within the group are based on performance and potential.

G. Teamwork
  1. Work closely with peers and encourage all employees in the

Exhibit 18. A Sample People Plan, Cont'd.

---

group to participate enthusiastically in intergroup work teams and activities.

H. Quality and employee involvement

1. Participate in ways to improve the quality of the products and services produced by the group by developing a better understanding of customers' expectations and by communicating expectations to suppliers. Initiate and participate in quality improvement teams to enhance the quality work processes.

---

cally to other training staff, such as course developers. Below are some of their suggestions (from "Guidelines for the Hiring, Evaluation, and Management of Trainers," 1988, p. 4):

Hiring trainers

- Ask job candidates to do a fifteen-minute presentation on a topic of their choice during the job application process.
- Let the training team help conduct group interviews.
- Send candidates to lunch with a staff member subordinate to the position being filled and ask that person about the candidate's interpersonal skills.
- Ask candidates to write captions for captionless cartoons to help determine sense of humor.

Evaluating trainers

- Observe presentations.
- Ask for student opinions.
- Track student evaluations.
- Use items from competency models to set objectives and establish criteria for performance appraisal.

Dealing with problem trainers

- Hold daily status chats.
- Require weekly performance reports.

Preventing burnout

- Use team teaching.
- Enlist line managers and employees to assist trainers and developers.

Trainers in the field

- Visit regularly.
- Use conference calls and teleconferences to maintain contact among the staff.
- Videotape meetings at the home office to distribute to field trainers.
- Send field trainers to seminars.
- Send home office trainers on sabbaticals to the field. (The visits should promote better understanding of what happens in line operations.)

Summary

This chapter described how the staffing policies of the training department influence the development and advancement opportunities open to training professionals. Training departments often create training professionals from line managers who transfer into training. The organization wants experienced line managers who are subject matter experts in the material that must be incorporated into training programs. Job experience in training develops skills, such as oral and written communications, that can be valuable in other functions. Training departments also employ people with advanced degrees in training who identify with the profession. However, these individuals usually have an early career plateau because there are limited advancement opportunities for advancement within training. Thus, the choice for them is to stay in training, move into a line job that will increase advancement prospects, or leave the firm, perhaps for a more lucrative position in a training consulting firm. The chapter recommended the importance of establishing a staffing policy that suits the organization's need for long-term training professionals and for rotational experience for line managers.

The chapter reviewed competency models and certification processes as the foundation for developing training professionals. Competency models specify skill requirements in various training roles. Certification establishes standards and ensures that trainers have the skills needed for their jobs. Certification lends credibility to the training function and increases the training professional's sense of pride and identification with his or her job. Professional affiliation is another way to enhance professional identification. The chapter outlined steps for developing competency models and certification processes and for guiding policies for organization-sponsored memberships in professional associations.

Finally, the chapter emphasized that training professionals should be on a path of continuous learning, which includes learning new skills, practicing these skills, and obtaining feedback on performance. Career planning processes, such as the sample career planning guide in Resource D, suggest alternative career paths for training professionals and the need for planning, coaching, and opportunities for job transfers within the training function.

Policy Opportunities and Recommendations

1. The training department should have a staffing policy that encourages bringing in people with needed knowledge and skills from other departments in the organization. Training should attract highly competent people if training jobs are treated as valuable learning experiences and if employees with several years in training are able to move into other departments in more responsible positions. The training department should not be a repository for employees who have essentially retired on the job.

2. In line with the first recommendation, the organization should view the training department as a place to develop skills that cannot be developed easily elsewhere but that have applicability to other important functions. For instance, training may give an individual a chance to practice writing, platform delivery, and feedback skills—all of which are critical to functions such as marketing and general supervision. As a result, people with several years' experience in training and people with advanced degrees in training should be attractive to other departments in the organization.

3. The training department should recognize that training professionals may want to stay in training, and the department

should want people who are training experts and who identify with the field. The department should provide opportunities for continuous learning, job rotation, and advancement within training. Training professionals should take advantage of the variety of jobs and roles in training that require different skills and should provide different ways to contribute to the organization (for example, as program developer, instructor, instructional technologist, training manager). The department should encourage movement between these positions and offer some opportunities for assuming higher-level positions within training.

4. Competency-based certification processes should be established to increase professionalism and enhance the credibility and overall effectiveness of the training department. Establishing mastery paths is another approach to certification that is less threatening because it does not have the make-it-or-break-it connotation of certification.

5. Training personnel should be involved in the process of designing and implementing the competency models and certification/mastery path processes. This involvement will enhance ownership in the process by the people who run it and are affected by it. Also, such involvement will ensure that the people who know the organization's needs and who are respected in their departments for their expertise and performance are the ones who determine criteria for assessment and who actually perform the assessment and give the feedback. This should be a team effort, so that multiple viewpoints are obtained and no one individual is responsible for passing judgment on others. Outside experts should be a part of the team to increase credibility and to ensure that state-of-the-art concepts of training are incorporated into evaluations.

6. Professional affiliations should be encouraged as a way to encourage continuous learning—for instance, remaining current on advancements in adult learning methods and training technology and knowing what leading firms are doing to train their employees. In addition, training personnel should be encouraged to generate new knowledge and to share that knowledge with their colleagues in other firms through professional societies. The best way to attract and retain the most competent people is to develop a reputation as

an organization on the cutting edge of the field and as an innovator and a place for creative individuals to try out new ideas.

7. All training personnel should be involved in planning their careers, revising these plans periodically, and receiving support and coaching from their supervisors for continuous learning and job movement. A career planning guide, such as the example in Resource D, is one way to foster such planning, clarify expectations, and communicate the department's staffing policy.

8
Linking Training Efforts with Organizational Strategies

This chapter shows how training departments are linked to organizational strategies by helping define organizational initiatives, by designing supporting programs, and by applying these programs within the organization. The chapter also shows how these programs should be applied within the training department to enhance its productivity and ensure that it is in step with overall organizational objectives. Specifically, the chapter describes the development of education policy for the organization; the integration of training with human resource department initiatives; the implementation of quality improvement programs, redeployment, and retraining efforts; and new directions for leadership and management.

Developing an Education Policy

The training department should work with representatives of line departments and with staff executives to develop a training policy (or several policies) in support of the organization's goals and objectives. An organization may have several training policies reflecting the different approaches to development of different groups of employees (for example, R&D staff, workers on the factory floor, line supervisors, and so on). A training policy should outline the importance of employee education and should be endorsed by top executives. The policy might be written by the training department's "board of directors" or the "human resource development committee." (See the outline in Chapter Three of the role of the board of directors in guiding the training department's efforts.) The statement then should be brought to the office of the organization's chief executive officer and the other top officers of the organization for approval and communication to the rest of the organization.

Exhibit 19 provides an example of an organization's training policy. The policy was drafted by training managers and discussed with the board of directors, which regularly reviewed the department's initiatives and guided the department's curricula. Once drafted, the document was brought to the cabinet of the firm's top officers for further discussion, editing, and approval. The policy expresses the importance of continuing education to employees remaining current on advancing technologies and aware of competitive pressures. The statement highlights the need to plan for training and for managers to support their subordinates' development. In addition, the policy emphasizes that employees will be evaluated on how well they progress in their educational plans for the year.

Integrating Training with Human Resource Policies and Programs

Training and development must be integrated with other human resource policies and programs to ensure that the organization has the people it needs when it needs them. (See the discussion in Chapter One of the role of training in meeting human resource requirements.) Such integration requires a conscious effort to design training that fits the organization's strategies. Training managers, together with their boards of directors and other advisers representing the organization's officers and line management, should be involved in forming organizational strategies and in working with other human resource managers to design consistent, integrated programs.

Exhibit 19. A Sample Education and Training Policy in Support of Organizational Strategy.

Goal

Continuing education is the foundation for an innovative growing organization. Lifelong learning is encouraged to enhance employees' contribution to the organization, increase their personal development, and maintain their interest in their work and motivation to be productive.

All employees, together with their supervisors and supported by the training department, are encouraged to plan educational opportunities that will provide the best investment for them and the organization. Education will be a primary means to improve our competitiveness, serve organization needs, and introduce and promote change.

Policy

The organization's most valuable asset is its people—its human resources. Therefore, our policy, consistent with our mission to be the premier organization in our industry, is to

- Ensure that our employees are competent in relevant (that is, current and cutting-edge) technologies, understand our business and our competitors, and work continually to improve the productivity and quality of the organization
- Encourage use of training and development programs as a means to productive and satisfying careers for our employees
- Support the organization's strategic objectives and supporting initiatives and help to make employees aware of these objectives and initiatives.

Responsibilities

1. Each line manager is responsible for communicating the education policy to his or her employees.
2. Department directors are responsible for monitoring the education needs of their departments and for ensuring that these needs are communicated to the training department.
3. The training department's board of directors will include representatives from each major department of the organization and will oversee curriculum review committees to ensure that needed training is available. This includes oversight of technical and managerial courses.
4. Each employee will establish educational goals and a specific education plan. This plan will be discussed regularly (at least annually) with the employee's supervisor.
5. Management will provide sufficient support to allow each employee to carry out his or her educational plan and to make effective use of developmental opportunities.

Exhibit 19. A Sample Education and Training Policy in Support of Organizational Strategy, Cont'd.

6. The organization will establish a minimum number of hours of instruction annually for each employee. (The exact number may vary from year to year, depending on need and resource availability. How this minimum number is met will vary for each employee—for instance, some employees may require more management development while others may require more technical training. The purpose of specifying a minimum number of hours of training is to emphasize the importance of employee development and to ensure that each supervisor is supportive of employees having at least the minimum number of hours per year.)
7. Performance appraisals will include an evaluation of how well the employee accomplished his or her educational goals for the year. Also, performance appraisals for managers will include an evaluation of how well they supported the development of their subordinates.

The following example demonstrates how the training department can further the organization's goal of increasing employees' level of performance.

The Merck Example

Merck and Company, a leading international pharmaceutical firm, implemented new management training programs to improve managers' abilities to develop subordinates, to increase employees' work standards, and to emphasize the company's expectations for excellent performance. In 1985 the new chairman of the firm, Dr. Roy Vagelos, recognized that remaining competitive and becoming the preeminent health care company in the world would require not only the highly qualified technical people already in the company but also people who were motivated to extend themselves for the benefit of the organization. The firm's emphasis had been on technical competence, not on an ability to manage people.

Vagelos appointed an employee relations review committee to examine the company's current policies and programs. Six line vice-presidents, two personnel executives, and the corporate controller sat on the committee (Peris, 1988; London, 1988). They reviewed the firm's existing personnel policies, compared these policies to the literature on effective personnel practices, talked to leading consultants, interviewed three hundred employees, and identified models of excellence inside Merck as well as at other companies, such as AT&T Bell Laboratories, TRW, and IBM.

The task force concluded its work in six months and issued a report with fifty recommendations. This output was communicated throughout the firm in newsletters and via a special videotape. Employees could see that top line managers, many of whom advanced to higher levels because of their technical ability, were involved in the process and committed to changing the organization.

The recommendations included strengthening the employment process by clarifying criteria for filling jobs and improving the interview process by requiring agreement from several interviewers, not just the hiring supervisor. The company improved employee communications and involvement by instituting team problem-solving groups, quality circles, and focus groups. The performance appraisal system was changed to encourage a greater distinction among employees and to provide higher financial awards to exceptional performers. These efforts were combined with an understanding of employee needs and of what it takes to attract and retain the best people in specific fields. This understanding led to such programs as day care and flexible work schedules.

Human resource initiatives at Merck included expanded training and development programs to improve supervisory skills and to communicate the new personnel policies. A training program for new managers was established to reinforce the importance of the manager as developer. A new core curriculum of management courses was implemented to enhance supervisors' skills and prepare high-potential technical staff members interested in moving into management positions. A special program entitled "Managing in Today's Merck Environment" was designed for all sixteen hundred Merck managers in the United States to communicate current trends in the industry and to convey the management style necessary for the firm to remain highly profitable.

Merck's quality improvement effort was also supported by new training for quality team facilitators and employees. A resource improvement steering committee tracked cost savings from employee involvement and productivity improvement efforts. A savings of more than $22 million was realized during the first nine months of 1988.

Merck's training strategies are an integral part of a concerted effort to enhance the company's productivity and competitiveness through improved management practices and supportive human resource policies. The management training department is part of the human resource department, and management training is viewed as a key way to communicate new expectations and to prepare managers to operate in the new environment. Given its human resource development efforts, it is not surprising that Merck was recognized by *Fortune* as one of the top one hundred best U.S. employers.

Supporting and Using Quality Improvement Processes

Many organizations, such as Ford, Motorola, IBM, Xerox, Florida Power and Light, AT&T, and Hewlett Packard, to name a few prominent firms, have instituted quality improvement processes, thereby recognizing the need to compete in a world marketplace. These efforts have gone beyond standard quality improvement processes in an attempt to improve manufacturing operations and encompass how all work is performed in an organization, including finance, sales, public relations, and training. The following subsections discuss the meaning of quality improvement, how training supports quality improvement teams, and how these teams can be used in training departments to improve the quality of education programs.

Defining Quality. There are many ways of defining *quality*. Xerox defines *quality* as "providing our external and internal customers with innovative products and services that fully satisfy their requirements." This view suggests that quality requires meeting customer demands. A more general definition is that quality is "doing the right things in the right way." The "right thing" may be what customers need, what is most cost-effective, or what presents the best image for the firm. The "right way" may be zero defects, no rework, avoidance of unnecessary costs, or preventing wasted resources.

> Quality-oriented companies are known for their ability to connect the whole organization to the customer. The pursuit of quality comes from the top down; it is systematic, it is measured, it is rewarded, and it involves everyone. [Quality-oriented companies are customer focused; they] recruit, organize, train, and reward people on the basis of their orientation to the customer. And when they train, they include all levels of the organization as well as their customers, suppliers, and distributors. ["Gaining the Competitive Edge," 1988]

The Quality Improvement Process. The quality improvement movement views all work as a process—a series of interrelated tasks. These tasks are usually performed by different people who are interdependent. Customer and supplier relationships represent this interdependence. Customers have expectations about the output of the company. Companies have expectations that suppliers provide input. Quality improvement efforts focus on outlining the work process, identifying the relevant customers and suppliers, identifying improvement areas, making improvements, and following up to ensure gains are maintained. For example, IBM's quality improvement efforts involve twelve steps, as follows (adapted from Kane, 1986, p. 26):

1. *Assign ownership* by charging managers to improve the process.
2. *Perform activity analyses* by establishing measurements and the cost of quality.
3. *Document current procedures* by iterating steps with key employees until accuracy is achieved.
4. *Document the process* by developing a flowchart of tasks that are necessary and the people involved.
5. *Determine process requirements and secure customer concurrence* by collecting data from customers about their expectations and testing possible solutions with them to ensure their needs will be met.
6. *Assess the impact of any mismatch* by prioritizing problems

based on requirements and not being constrained by the existing process.

7. *Analyze potential solutions to bring the process into conformance* by eliminating failures by simplifying the process, combining redundant tasks, restructuring, and automating where appropriate; reviewing additional resources, education requirements, and the need for new capital equipment; and pilot testing process changes with specific pass/fail criteria.
8. *Select and implement the best alternatives.*
9. *Update target and measurement criteria for new processes.*
10. *Establish a regular review of the plan by the next level of management.*
11. *Feed back new management control requirements within the organization for monitoring.*
12. *Update managers' performance plans, making plans specific about the requirements for the new process.*

These processes vary from organization to organization, but the major elements and underlying philosophy for work process analysis, improvement, and monitoring are the same. Quality improvement process steps may be undertaken by individuals in reviewing and improving their own jobs, but usually the process is undertaken by quality improvement teams focusing on a specific work process. Employee involvement is the cornerstone of the activity—so all relevant parties will be involved in the improved process and operation.

Instituting quality improvement efforts throughout a corporation can involve a major cultural shift for the organization as a whole as well as a shift in how employees view their jobs. For one thing, managers may not be used to thinking of their jobs as a part of a process nor may they think of the people with whom they interact within the organization as their customers and suppliers. In addition, managers may not be accustomed to getting subordinates and people from other work units to work together to identify problem areas and explore possible solutions. Introducing quality improvement efforts can involve a massive change in some companies—a change that not all employees may be prepared or able to make. As a result, champions of quality improvement will have to communicate their expectations clearly and impose reward structures that recognize successful quality improvement efforts. Also, there should be penalties (for instance, no financial reward or outplacement) for employees who make no attempt to improve low-quality work outputs.

Training and Quality Improvement Efforts. Virtually every firm that has implemented a quality improvement program has seen the need to train employees on what the quality process is, the tools of the quality process, how to lead and facilitate a quality improvement team (QIT), and how to be an effective team member.

The Xerox Example. In 1982 David Kearns, then CEO of Xerox, conceived the idea of "leadership through quality." Xerox needed to bring a renewed focus to its customers. The firm was losing touch with its customers as the industry became more competitive, and the company had begun to take its leadership position in the marketplace for granted. Analyses of the competition indicated that employee involvement and enhanced quality control were keys to success. These concepts were working well in Xerox's partnership with Fuji in Japan.

Once the leadership-through-quality program was established as the vehicle for change, David Kearns turned to training and development to communicate the meaning and essence of this goal to every employee (Bernhard and Ingols, 1988). In 1984 the top management team was trained in the quality improvement process, and the management team actually worked on a quality improvement application. Functional quality managers were appointed at headquarters and in the field offices. Regional managers were trained, as were district managers and salespeople.

Since the inception of the quality process, everyone at the company has taken the same training course in service quality (Bernhard and Ingols, 1988). This training is supported and reinforced by a staff of quality specialists and by quality projects, quality competitions, and a quality suggestions program. This effort has created a common language shared by all employees and has improved communications and provided a common framework for individual and group action.

The Ford Example. The quality process was also instrumental in the turnaround at Ford Motor Company—perhaps the most significant economic recovery in U.S. history (Easterbrook, 1986). In the early 1980s, Ford went for broke in its development of the Taurus/Mercury Sable line. This was Detroit's first attempt at a car with European handling characteristics aimed at the typical family buyer. At a time when Ford was sustaining substantial losses, it invested a record $3 billion into Taurus development. A union-management agreement resulted in an employee involvement program that put production workers into product design and marketing. Different groups of workers, designers, and managers (including top executives) were responsible for different stages during the five-year product development process.

In another case at Ford, workers redesigned the Ford Escort EXP, which was due to go out of production. Management was persuaded to keep the redesigned car in production, thus avoiding layoffs and increasing market share because of the car's popularity with younger buyers. Ford's CEO, Donald E. Petersen, described his view of quality and the importance of training support in a speech to the Society of Automotive Engineers:

> A total quality concept . . . calls for continuous improvement in everything we do, not just design, engineering, and manufacturing. Essentially, everyone in the company is involved in a process that results in a product or service for a customer—whether that customer is a staff or operating function within the company or a car buyer or owner at a dealership. . . . We've got to keep every process in a dynamic condition so that change and continuous improvement can take place.
>
> Essential operating principles and process . . . must be present to achieve total quality. . . . These elements are: (1) management commitment, (2) customer focus, (3) total organization participation through employee involvement and participative management, (4) statistical process control, (5) *education and training* [emphasis added], and (6) removing roadblocks to progress. I assure you, the numbers do not indicate an order of importance—I'd say they're all about equal.

> Education and training are necessary to improve job and interpersonal skills. We must help our employees, and those of our suppliers, to prepare for the new technology, new manufacturing systems, and new management systems that will be required to win the competitive struggle we face. [Scherkenbach, 1925, p. 42]

A Training Curriculum for Quality Improvement. When AT&T instituted its quality improvement program, its training department formed a new group to be responsible for developing and delivering courses and workshops on the purpose and methods of quality improvement. The group designed a series of programs for quality consultants (internal managers who were appointed to these positions as full-time jobs), team leaders (managers who were voted by their fellow team members to lead the quality improvement team), team members, and middle and top managers who might sit on teams and monitor team progress.

Training was essential in communicating expectations and describing what could be accomplished by the quality improvement process. As employees were introduced to the quality process, they were empowered by higher management to identify work processes that could benefit from a QIT effort, to solicit volunteers for the team, and to hold a series of meetings to discuss the quality improvement process. Higher-level managers formed "quality councils" to guide and provide resources for the grass-roots quality teams under their jurisdiction. The quality councils also could form their own teams.

The first training course in the quality curriculum was a half-day introduction to the quality improvement process conducted by specially trained internal quality consultants. The workshop reviewed the elements of quality and the issues generated in its implementation. Also emphasized were the firm's focus on quality, the commitment of top executives, the definitions and meaning of quality, and the meaning of customer-supplier relationships. The course was usually given to work groups as a general introduction.

A three-day workshop was designed and administered by an

outside consulting firm for middle and top managers. Managers participated in their work groups and learned a common language of quality, the principles of quality, and the steps followed and tools used by quality improvement teams. They created an action plan for improving a work process and examined the roles of team members and team leaders as well as their own role as managers of teams.

Team leader training consisted of a five-day workshop, which employees attended after they were elected by their teammates to lead a quality improvement team. In addition to covering the steps and tools of quality improvement, the course introduced team leaders to the concepts of group dynamics and their impact on the team.

Other courses in the program involved analyzing work flows, brainstorming problems, voting on priorities, identifying potential solutions, collecting data from customers and suppliers, and monitoring work to ensure the success of the quality improvement effort.

These training programs were supported by frequent communications in company newsletters about the value of quality improvement and examples of recent team efforts. Brochures and posters conveyed the purpose of quality improvement and the expectation that everyone should be involved. All managers were expected to lead a quality improvement team at least once during a two-year period.

Other support mechanisms included a computerized tracking system to record team efforts so that employees could review what teams were already in progress or had completed work so that improvements in one area could be applied elsewhere. A recognition program awarded commendations to teams for successful outputs and for using the quality process effectively. Some companies track the cost savings from the quality improvement efforts and allow employees to share in the savings.

Applying Quality Improvement Processes to Training. Several chapters in this book have already described how to improve a training department's responsiveness to client needs. Chapter Four showed how to analyze a training gap (the difference between the training needed and the training planned). Chapter Six indicated ways to reduce training costs. One training department formed different quality improvement teams (QITs) to enhance effectiveness. The middle managers and the director of this training department held quality council meetings to guide and provide resources for the QIT efforts in the department. At monthly staff meetings, a QIT leader was invited to present a "quality moment" and to discuss the purpose of the team and how the quality process had been applied. The types of teams and their functions follow:

- *Standardized course material QIT* developed and implemented standardized student and instructor guide formats so that course materials cover major areas in ways that recognize effective adult learning.
- *Instructor development QIT* established one instructor development process for the training department to ensure that all instructors have the same high level of preparation.
- *Training performance testing QIT* improved the process for collecting, scoring, and recording posttraining performance tests for feedback to students and their supervisors.
- *Registration QIT* established a registration process that will maximize customer satisfaction (that is, make it easy for employees to register for courses).
- *Training coordinator role definition QIT* identified a model role for field training coordinators (managers in line departments responsible for identifying training needs and allocating training seats to work groups) and outlined their relationship to the training department.
- *Front-end analysis QIT* established guidelines for the use of job and needs analysis methods prior to the development of training materials.

Redeployment and Retraining

The term *redeployment* refers to transferring employees from their current job functions where they are not needed to new job functions where they are needed. The new job function often requires learning new skills and knowledge. The term *retraining* encompasses both training and education. (Training involves learning to improve on one's present job, while education involves learning how to be qualified for a future job.) As stated in Chapter One, technological change and global competition have highlighted the importance of continuous learning if companies are to be effective now and in the future. For instance, in a manufacturing setting, employees may have to learn new cost-reduction methods, such as greater control over inventory and defects. Workers who do not have needed skills will find themselves unemployed as technology changes and foreign competition closes domestic plants.

When employees are displaced, education in both basic and job-related skills can help them find employment. However, education is not a panacea. Many displaced workers may choose not to participate in retraining programs because they are interested primarily in rapid reemployment and hope to be recalled to work—an unlikely possibility in some industries (such as basic steel), which will not return to previous employment levels (Cyert and Mowery, 1987). Therefore, companies, labor unions, and government assistance programs support redeployment efforts (often involving retraining), job-search training and information, counseling, and relocation assistance. The next several sections examine how organizations use education to redeploy and retrain their work force to meet current and future needs.

Redeployment

Organizations must be responsive to changes in their environments. This means that managers must be aware of these environmental changes and of what skills and knowledge are necessary to create and take advantage of new opportunities. Companies such as IBM and AT&T have been faced with both changing technology and a changing competitive environment and have found that a different mix of employee skills is needed. One strategy is to lay off employees who lack the needed skills and hire people who have the desired education and experience, assuming these people are available. However, this approach involves losing people who are loyal to the organization and who know how the organization operates. Another strategy is to educate current employees and move them into positions that meet the corporation's need.

IBM shifted 21,500 employees from such areas as manufacturing, development, and administration into marketing and programming (Sellers, 1988). The company also redeployed 11,800 employees to sales jobs (marketing "rep" positions and systems engineering positions involving some selling but primarily serving customers as technical consultants). This redeployment increased the size of IBM's marketing force by 20 percent in two years.

Before being redeployed, candidates had to pass aptitude tests and pass several interviews at branch offices, where local managers did the hiring. The training used a variety of methods, including a self-study system called InfoWindow (described in Resource B) that combines a personal computer and a laser video disk in such a way that the computer becomes an interactive TV. Before attending a class at one of the firm's training centers, a trainee in a branch office can use an InfoWindow program to practice sales calls with an on-screen actor who portrays a manager in a specific industry, such as finance or hospital administration. The training system is programmed so that the actor responds differently depending on what the salesperson does.

In another example, AT&T redeployed as many as three thousand members of its technical staff to sales and sales support positions. The immediate need arose because the company was losing its market share in the wide-area telephone service business (for example, WATS 800 telephone numbers) owing to increasing competition. IBM needed more account representatives in the field to maintain and increase its customer base. In addition, other parts of the company found that costs were increasing faster than revenues, and a major cost-cutting effort was required. Employees in overstaffed positions were given the opportunity to volunteer for marketing positions. Many took advantage of the opportunity because they felt marketing experience would be needed for career advancement as the company became more market driven; some used the opportunity to relocate to another part of the country.

Similar to IBM, AT&T employees who volunteered for redeployment were selected carefully using sales assessments. If they failed the first time, they were given some training and then assessed a second time; those who passed were sent to training. For instance, new sales and sales support people received three to four months of intensive training in the company's products and services, selling skills, and the industry in which they would be selling. Training was delivered in a number of ways, including instructor-led courses, computer-based training, and self-paced workbooks, with courses varying in length from one hour to ten days, depending on the subject matter.

In a recent announcement to introduce new technology into its long-distance network, AT&T stated that it would phase out some sixteen thousand jobs between 1989 and 1993 in such fields as engineering, clerical, operator services, and management. The company also stated that it expects to retrain and redeploy as many as possible of those affected, while taking advantage of normal reductions due to retirement and attrition. Working with the Alliance for Employee Growth and Development, a venture sponsored jointly by the company and two of its unions (the Communications Workers of America [CWA] and the International Brotherhood of Electrical Workers [IBEW]), employees will be offered extensive career counseling, preretirement planning, skills training, tuition aid for college, financial planning, relocation counseling, and job-search advice. Alliance committees at over two hundred local sites already provide an array of training and counseling programs, which are often directed toward employee groups in surplus jobs.

Redeployment is not an easy process for an organization or for the individuals involved. Westinghouse Furniture Systems, a national firm specializing in office equipment for small and medium-sized businesses, found this out the hard way. Faced with an eroding market share, the company wanted to woo potential customers who had purchased equipment from competitors. The company had a large staff of telemarketing representatives who made telephone calls to potential customers; these representatives made up the primary sales staff, although there were also account executives who called on customers. The company felt that more personal contact was necessary because its competitors used face-to-face selling. It therefore redeployed a number of telemarketing representatives to associate account executive positions. This larger sales staff needed supervision, so successful account executives were promoted to management positions. Unfortunately, the company failed to provide training for the new associate account executives and sales managers. This failure to recognize training requirements substantially increased the cost of the transition and, of course, cost the company sales.

These examples of redeployment efforts demonstrate that employees with years of experience in other disciplines can be retrained for new responsibilities. However, such employees often need help in understanding their career interests, redefining their skill sets, thinking broadly about career opportunities, and taking action to achieve their goals. In addition, these employees need to believe in themselves—in their abilities to overcome barriers and accept new challenges. Fear of the unknown can hold people back from redeployment. To facilitate the redeployment process and help people recognize their potential, organizations should offer career planning workshops and experiential programs, such as outdoor experiences that pose physical challenges for groups and individuals. (See the discussion later in this chapter of outward-bound sessions as a type of management training.) Other ways to encourage openness to redeployment include involving the employee's spouse in career sessions and taking some of the risk out of the change—for example, by allowing the employee to return to his or her previous job after a trial period on the new job (Samuel M. Sonnett, personal communication, October 12, 1988).

As the growth of the labor force declines (see Exhibit 1), many firms will have to rely on older workers to meet their human resource requirements. The next section describes the potential for continuing education for older workers and is followed by a description of joint union-management education programs and sources of government funds to support such programs.

Education for Older Workers

Today, more than forty-nine million Americans are age 55 and over. As this number grows, more people are retiring from full-time employment earlier (Bove, 1987). Many of these older workers are trading full-time employment for part-time and/or self-employment as they engage in second, third, or fourth careers. Unfortunately, however, some organizations do not view older workers as able to learn, to accept new technologies, or to function in an increasingly competitive environment. Older workers needing to find reemployment often face age discrimination (Sheppard, 1970).

Recently, however, the limited supply of new entrants to the labor force suggests that businesses will become increasingly reliant on the skills and capabilities of older workers. Some companies have initiated programs to attract older workers who might be interested in second careers, often as part-time employees. Other corporate efforts provide financial incentives to older workers to not retire (for example, by continuing to contribute to the pension plan beyond age 65). Moreover, some firms offer courses that upgrade older workers' skills. Job counseling and education for older displaced employees allow the organization to keep loyal, motivated people who know the organization.

A policy study report entitled "The Future of Older Workers in America" recognized that corporations often exclude workers aged 50 and older from training and redevelopment opportunities (Work in America Institute, 1987). The report's recommendations still apply. The report advised that more consideration be given to lateral assignments, job redesign, ease of shifting between functional specialties, and freer movement of employees out of (and then back to) companies to gain experience or training. The report recommended that employers, before hiring a work force for a new plant or office, should first train current employees (including older workers) wishing to gain new occupational skills, change careers, or obtain new assignments. In addition, the report recommended that top management make it known that the training of older workers must not be sacrificed to current pressures, and more concrete benefits and incentives should be offered to older workers for training, self-development, and self-renewal. Training directors should recognize that older workers have different learning patterns than younger workers, make adjustments to accommodate the needs of the adult learner, and take advantage of the older worker's prior experience. The growing labor shortage in many areas of the country and the economic need of older workers have made several alternative work forms attractive to employers and to people approaching retirement. Such alternative work forms include phased retirement designed to permit job retention, with reduced work schedules and prorated salary and benefits (Morrison, 1986). Another alternative is part-time work for a firm's retirees. Wages are monitored to ensure they do not exceed Social Security earning limitations. Such part-time work is effective, since experienced employees can continue to apply their expertise in working with long-standing clients or co-workers.

Training Employees for New Technology

Some firms are faced with a number of employees with obsolete skills. For example, for the last ten years, IBM hired more than twenty-two thousand production workers who had the skills needed to do the jobs for which they were hired. However, these individuals did not have the skills needed to run the high-technology workstations now being implemented in the firm's manufacturing facilities. Rather than lay off these employees, IBM hopes to upgrade their skills.

IBM began this effort by examining training needs. Sixty to 80 percent of the employees required preparatory work before taking college-level courses. Twenty to 40 percent required basic skills, such as reading, and a significant portion had English as a second language. IBM's central training department intends to provide foundation courses in such fields as math, English, and learning how to learn. In addition, orientation courses will be offered in IBM heritage, logistics, manufacturing, and work environment safety. Courses in statistical process control and related fields will prepare employees for workstation ownership. Local sites will offer courses specific to the needs of the site. Employees who wish to go beyond the basic curriculum to take college courses will be offered tuition assistance.

Much of the course material is being purchased from already-existing materials, thereby reducing development costs and start-up time. The material will be adapted to fit IBM's training delivery system. Almost all the courses will be self-paced, using IBM's on-line computer-based training network, InfoWindow. Students will be grouped into classes that will meet periodically for tutoring and interpersonal support. This close monitoring and support throughout the program will be critical to the success of the program. Without this support, employees volunteering for self-paced training are likely to lose interest quickly unless they have unusually high motivation and self-discipline.

IBM estimates that the cost will be about $9,500 per student. If the firm relied on local colleges with traditional instructor-led courses for this program, it would take about twenty years for all eligible employees to attain the same level of education. The self-paced program will take about seven years. The total cost will be slightly more than $200 million. Currently in the initiation stage, the program already includes a number of courses, with many more in development.

A recent research effort by the American Society for Training and Development and the U.S. Department of Labor identified the basic skills employers desire in employees if the firm is to be competitive (Carnevale, Gainer, and Meltzer, 1988). Employees need new skills appropriate to new technology, participative management, statistical quality controls, just-in-time production, and responsive customer service. Employers identified seven basic skill groups: learning to learn; the "3 Rs" (reading, writing, and computation); communication (listening and oral skills); creative thinking and problem solving; goal setting and motivation (including career development); interpersonal, negotiation, and teamwork; and organization and leadership effectiveness. The report's "blueprint for success" describes how to establish programs to deliver workplace basics. Steps include identifying and assessing problems; building support; proposing a plan; performing task analyses; designing and developing the curriculum; and implementing, evaluating, and monitoring the program.

Reemployment Programs

A program to prevent skills obsolescence should have several critical components, including:

- Counseling and guidance to help employees decide what kind of training they need

- An assessment system that allows training gaps to be identified
- A support system, including tuition assistance, time off from work, and recognition for continuing education
- A variety of program options—for instance, availability of training in basic, vocational, general communication, organizational, and management skills (adapted from Gordus, Gohrband, and Meiland, 1987).

Polaroid's Fundamental Skills Program incorporates the above components and focuses on skills employees need to improve their job performance and prepare for job growth. Employees who volunteer for the program are counseled by a member of the human resources group. Assessment tests are conducted, training is offered when needed, and results assessment tests are used to certify employees' skills and qualify them to apply for more advanced positions.

Many companies have begun to fulfill their commitment to employment security not only by retraining employees for new jobs within the company but also by helping employees find good jobs elsewhere. Some workers are not interested in retraining and may prefer vocational counseling for help finding a job. Major union-management agreements have, in effect, extended the practice of "outplacement" (that is, counseling and job search assistance) of managers to apply to bargained-for employees as well. For instance, at Pacific Bell, a Training Advisory Board developed a system that keeps workers informed about job growth and decline and provides opportunities for continued education. Employees expressing interest in jobs outside the company are entitled to, and provided with, outplacement services (Work in America Institute, 1987).

General Electric implemented a program at its site in Columbia, Maryland, to retrain displaced workers for alternative employment in the area because opportunities are not available within the company. The program is managed by a reemployment center, funded jointly be GE, the State of Maryland, and the federal government (Hickey, 1987).

Union-Management Education Programs

In corporations where there is a union presence, continuous learning programs are most likely to succeed when the union is involved. In fact, a policy of continuous learning can be conducted in a unionized workplace only if the union is involved, since collective bargaining issues (for example, job descriptions, work rules) are always involved in continuous learning efforts. (See London and Bassman, 1989, for descriptions of union-management training at Ford and GM.)

One joint union-management effort is the Enhanced Training Opportunities Program (ETOP) sponsored by the International Brotherhood of Electrical Workers (IBEW) union and AT&T. Training committees consisting of representatives of local employees survey employees about their interest in learning new skills, such as computer programming. Some programs focus on remedial reading and writing skills. ETOP funds are then used to establish computer labs and other training programs on the company premises. The program is not targeted toward surplus employees. Rather, the goal is to enhance employee marketability through courses that provide practical hands-on experience. Employees apply for various courses, and applications are accepted by seniority (older employees having the first chance).

In another example, the operator services department at AT&T worked with union officials to provide learning opportunities for operators who might be displaced by new technology. The new technology—voice-activated automatic response equipment—would reduce the number of operators required. The company and the union wanted to encourage current operators to learn new skills that would make them more marketable for other positions within the company or for jobs outside the company. Rather than wait until there were surplus conditions, the program offered the training two to three years in advance and gave the operators a sense that they were in control of their careers. Career-planning workshops helped operators decide areas of interest in relation to those areas likely to have job openings.

The Alliance for Employee Growth and Development program mentioned earlier (which sponsors programs such as the Enhanced Training Opportunities Program and the operator services educational effort) arose from the 1986 national bargaining agreements between AT&T and its unions. The Alliance program receives $6 million in annual funding and has secured an additional

$2 million in government funding for displaced worker programs. The program enhances individuals' employment security by helping them keep their skills current and develop new skills. The activities of the program are driven by local needs—for example, a union representative in the field may seek help because of an impending downsizing. A local committee of an equal number of union and management employees (six to eight in all) is formed to work with program staff in assessing employees' needs, deciding what types of programs are needed, and identifying local sources for these programs, such as community colleges. The local committee schedules training sessions, signs up employees, and tracks their progress, while the program pays the vendor. Between 1986 and 1988, about twenty thousand employees were involved in Alliance-sponsored programs.

Another example of union involvement in education is the Labor Employee and Training Corporation, a nonprofit job training venture established in California by the United Auto Workers (UAW) union, with corporation directors representing union and management (B. Lee, 1988). The corporation has retrained thousands of workers in new skills and found them jobs inside and outside the auto and aerospace industries. The corporation has been successful in placing workers in the New United Motors Manufacturing, Inc. (NUMMI) plant in Fremont, California. This is a joint venture of three partners: General Motors, Toyota, and the United Auto Workers union. In fact, the UAW was instrumental in designing the plant's revolutionary team production system run by the workers themselves. Workers are responsible for seeing that no car on the assembly line moves on to the next station unless every job is done perfectly. Teams of workers handle related assembly operations and are encouraged to devise ways to do the work more easily and efficiently.

Legislation and Government Support

The turmoil that the American workplace has experienced in recent years due to increasing foreign competition has resulted in lowered profits for many industries and corresponding loss of employment for scores of workers. This situation has prompted government concern in the form of proposed legislation to remedy the negative effects of job loss. Although legislative efforts have taken many directions, we will concentrate here on education and related issues.

The Job Training Partnership Act (JTPA) of 1982 replaced the 1973 Comprehensive Employment and Training Act (CETA). JTPA works through locally based program delivery for remedial education, training, and employment assistance for disadvantaged youth and adults and for dislocated workers. The program also funds federally administered activities, such as the Jobs Corps and research on labor statistics (such as the Labor Market Information System). A 1986 amendment allocates funds for displaced farmers and displaced homemakers.

Title III of JTPA, now updated by the 1988 Economic Dislocation and Workers' Adjustment Assistance Act (EDWAAA), deals specifically with dislocated workers. The intention is to assist experienced workers who have permanently lost their jobs due to technological displacement, foreign competition, or other changes in the economy. The act provides federal funds for state-administered employment and training services for reemployment. States have broad authority over who is served, how the program is planned and administered, how resources are distributed, and what services will be provided. Programs can be organized in reaction to crisis situations (such as plant closings), tailored for specific industries statewide, or targeted at high unemployment areas.

Funds are provided for a broad range of services, including job search assistance, training (for example, basic, remedial, and literary education; entrepreneurial training; and occupational skills training), supportive services (for instance, commuting assistance and financial and personal counseling), programs conducted in cooperation with employers or labor unions to provide early intervention in the event of plant or facilities closings, and relocation assistance. About 80 percent of the people served by JTPA programs received counseling, and about 60 percent received job search assistance. Training was provided to less than 50 percent of recipients.

In general, JTPA-funded programs had about a 69 percent placement rate in helping dislocated workers. Unfortunately, most new jobs paid less than the prior employment, and, in addition, JTPA programs fell short of the need. About 1.5 million people are dislocated each year, and of these, about half find new employment through normal channels on their own. JTPA provided $200 million in 1988 for dislocated workers, enough to serve between 160,000 to 210,000. About $950 million would have been needed (five times more than actual funding) to serve the 750,000 people who required assistance. EDWAAA will have about $280 million in 1989, but more money should be available in later years to help dislocated workers.

JTPA has met with mixed reviews. Training professionals have charged that employment and education legislation in this country does not seriously address the problems of displaced workers caused by unemployment, recession, and new technologies. Government tends to create public jobs to give unskilled workers employment but does not train them for higher-skilled jobs in the private sector (C. Lee, 1983). A 1986 assessment of JTPA concluded that while JTPA was effective in training and placing the best of the unemployed in jobs in the private sector, only 48 percent of the dislocated workers placed under JTPA received some form of training (U.S. General Accounting Office, 1987).

The new EDWAAA specifies that states must create a "rapid response" dislocated worker unit (DWU) to respond quickly to plant closings and mass layoffs, to work with employers and unions in promoting labor-management cooperation, and to give technical assistance to grant receivers ("Dislocated Workers," 1989). Under the sixty-day advance notice law, employers closing a plant or making a mass layoff must give sixty days notice to the state rapid response unit. The unit must provide (1) one-on-one services within forty-eight hours to employers and employee representatives after a plant closing or mass layoff is announced; (2) promote formation of labor-management committees; (3) help select worker representatives if no union is present; (4) work with government agencies to avert plant closings; and (5) help assess feasibility of workers or others buying the closing company.

Some experts feel that retraining is more effective when provided to active workers in order to maintain their employability and that retraining for displaced workers is not as effective

(Condon, 1984). Companies that have attempted to redeploy current employees to new positions recognize that these employees are loyal to the company. An effort can be made to match skills to job specifications, and this will, in some cases, lessen the need for training.

Examples of Government-Supported Programs. One innovative state program, the California Employment Training Panel, was established in 1983 to provide funds for schools and employers to retrain the unemployed and workers likely to be displaced. The panel was set up with funds previously designated for unemployment insurance. The idea was that unemployment insurance payouts would be lower ultimately if fewer people were unemployed. The goal was to move people into careers, not dead-end high-turnover jobs. Research through December 1987 found a significant increase in earnings and a substantial reduction in unemployment for panel trainees (Employment Training Panel, 1987).

In New York State, a Job Training Partnership Council assesses growing labor-force shortages and occupational mismatches in different regions of the state and provides support for retraining. For instance, the council, working with the New York State Department of Social Services and a Job Corps facility in Oneonta, New York, provided on-site day care and living accommodations for young welfare mothers learning employable skills. The council and the State Education Department created a Skilled Worker Emeritus Program. Using Vocational Education Act funds, the goal of the program is to identify workers with outstanding or unique skills who are willing to engage in direct training and curriculum design with local programs so that their expertise can be passed on to the next generation of New York workers. In another case, the state's School and Business Alliance brings business and schools together to ensure that students are being educated for employment in today's work force. This group holds regional training conferences to encourage more businesses and schools to form alliances to address their respective needs.

A principal goal of such state programs is to attract businesses to the state and enhance regional economic development. For instance, the New York State Education Department coordinates an

Employer Specific Training Program that provides funds for training employees in specific skill requirements. Another state-supported program, Workplace Literacy, provides adult basic education, English as a second language (ESL), and high school equivalency instruction as well as courses for employees who need specific job skills, such as algebra, computer literacy, and communications skills. Some of this training is provided by the state's ACCESS (Adult Centers for Comprehensive Education and Support Services) centers, where a full range of training services is available, including basic skills, life skills instruction, and workplace literacy instruction; state-of-the-art occupational training; job development and placement; and comprehensive career counseling.

An example of government support for corporate-sponsored productivity improvement occurred at AT&T's Montgomery Works plant in Illinois, which employs over one thousand people. A training program was developed to meet the needs of a renovated and automated factory and required employees to deal with increasing complexity in their jobs. The training plan called for about 150 courses. Processes such as just-in-time manufacturing required the assembly worker to use a new set of skills, including problem solving and creativity, as part of a team. Courses covered topics in product design, quality, and computer science for engineering, professional, and management employees. The program was partially funded by the Illinois Department of Commerce and Community Affairs, which awarded grants totaling almost $600,000. The program also received $10,000 from the Prairie State 2000 Authority.

In another example, General Electric moved an aircraft engine electronic controls manufacturing operations into the empty half of an outdated electric motor factory in Fort Wayne, Indiana (Smith, 1988). The objective was to reduce the technology drain by establishing a high-tech operation in an old facility. Six hundred and thirty production workers were selected and retrained, with 50 percent of the training costs coming from JTPA funds. The training was developed in conjunction with a local university. Training included an overview of the firm's business philosophy as well as technical training and hands-on practice sessions.

Obtaining Outside Funds for Employee Education. Applying for government funding for employee education requires knowing what programs exist, and in some cases, lobbying government agencies for programs that provide financial support. In addition to federal and state grants, there are numerous private foundations that may support employee education in partnership with organizations. The goal of these public and private agencies is to increase employment security and productivity and thereby contribute to the economy and raise the overall standard of living in the region.

The key to successful grant writing is not to convince the funding source of the magnitude and importance of the problem but rather to demonstrate that the funding source will meet its needs by supporting the proposal (Dianna Dickson, personal communication, March 8, 1988). The granting agency allocates funds in accordance with the purpose for establishing the source of funds—for example, in the case of the 1982 federal Job Training Partnership Act (JTPA), Title III of the act is designed specifically to help dislocated workers find new jobs.

Local training managers must use their own initiative to seek funding sources and develop proposals that meet the organization's needs and those of the funding agency. As an example, one manufacturing plant in the Midwest during the almost three-year period from mid 1984 to early 1987 obtained $1,700,000 from JTPA, $358,000 in tax credits for redeployment of employees, and $37,000 from a veterans' program. In another case, the U.S. Department of Education provided an organization with funds for reimbursement of wages for course developers and instructors, wages for graduate student interns in instructional design of approved courses, and reimbursement for costs of printed materials—in total about $300,000 for one year.

In addition to applying for government funds for employee education, training departments should partner with local governments to support education in the community. This aid may be in the form of financial grants to local school systems, donations of computer labs and other equipment, tutoring programs, and summer internship programs for high school students. The goal is to increase the likelihood that young people in the organization's labor market will gain the basic and technical skills needed by the organization.

Leadership and Management Development

The last several sections of this chapter on redeployment and educational support have focused on programs for occupational employees and lower-level managers. This last part of the chapter examines how the training department contributes to formulating and communicating directions for leadership and management development.

Training managers will be called on to design management and executive training courses, which should be part of broader development programs that include job experiences and assignments. The content of these programs should be related to the management style required by the organization to accomplish its objectives. Consequently, these training and development programs should be strategically focused and should be developed jointly by training professionals, human resource experts, and the organization's top managers. The following sections describe ways training experts help managers conceptualize needed changes in management style and design education and communications programs to support these changes.

Establishing Directions for Skill Development

An increasingly competitive environment requires new ways of managing. Given the fast pace of change and the need for rapid responses, managers must be given as much decision-making discretion as they need. Moreover, in tight economic times, the need to reduce expenses and cut people, including middle managers, has often increased the span of control for those who are left. Therefore, managers cannot double-check every problem and decision with their bosses. As managers' responsibilities increase, so does the responsibility of their subordinates.

Recognizing this new environment, AT&T's Learning and Development Organization outlined the general outputs required of every manager, with the understanding that managers had to decide how to achieve the outputs for which they would be accountable. The outputs and underlying philosophy were published in a set of documents called the *Managing for Excellence Library,* which was a set of booklets covering the firm's business plans in general terms; important managerial outputs required to accomplish the human resource component of the business plans; competencies required to produce these outputs; and recommended goal setting, appraisal, feedback, and career management processes and resources.

The concepts set forth in these documents were developed with input from line managers. The important outputs specified in the model were (1) establishing performance goals, (2) developing positive interpersonal relationships within work groups, (3) fostering networks and positive working relationships (alliances) among groups, (4) designing challenging jobs, and (5) achieving performance goals. The set of skills needed to achieve these goals included problem solving, decision making, leadership, organization knowledge, strategic thinking, creative thinking, understanding people and groups, and communications.

A training curriculum was established to offer courses in these skills. For instance, a course for new supervisors covered observation skills, problem analysis, understanding people and groups, and expressive communications. Some of the training programs were self-paced, allowing students to order from a library of audio- and videotapes. Other courses were traditional classroom training. Materials in the *Managing for Excellence Library* supported the curriculum and included self-assessment tools to help employees evaluate their skills and performance appraisal forms that asked managers to specify their development plans and also to evaluate their job performance. Organization effectiveness consultants in the personnel department were available to help work groups understand and apply the concepts set forth in the *Library*.

In all, the *Managing for Excellence Library* was distributed to over forty thousand managers, and it went into a second printing. However, the program was not an instant success. Some managers viewed it as cumbersome; others were frustrated by the lack of structure and asked the organization effectiveness consultants to spell out step-by-step what they should do. Evaluations showed that more than three-fourths of the managers thought the material was valuable and that they used it. Several departments used the concepts as the foundation for career planning programs and efforts to increase professionalism—for example, encouraging people to evaluate their own skills and to evaluate their subordinates on the managerial skills outline provided in the *Library*. In some departments, the *Library* became the symbol for how the company managed people, specifying desired outputs but allowing managers the freedom to define what the outputs meant to them and then to determine how they would achieve the outputs.

Overall, the *Library* helped establish directions for employee development during a time of change and uncertainty. It was developed by the training department in conjunction with human resource managers, line managers, and top executives and became the foundation for the firm's management training curriculum. Thus, the curriculum was directly related to the strategic objectives of the organization for changing management style. Moreover, the curriculum was supported by other human resource processes, such as performance appraisal, which also incorporated the philosophy of the *Library*.

Supporting Directions in New Leadership Style

Three years after the *Managing for Excellence Library* was introduced, one major unit of AT&T developed a new set of leadership dimensions to guide the behavior of all managers and to serve as criteria for performance evaluation and promotion. Called the "leadership platform," the dimensions were generated by the vice-presidents in the department. These dimensions were refined by members of the training and personnel departments and incorporated into various human resource and training programs.

The dimensions were clustered into four groups:

1. *Builds teams and alliances and manages relationships* (for example, develops quality, strength, and breadth in relationships, has the ability to form coalitions, knows when to involve higher management).
2. *Creates a motivating culture—an "inspired level of performance"* (for example, leads by example, empowers people, communicates and translates corporate strategies in a meaningful way, builds teamwork, develops people).

3. *Implements programs* (for example, achieves results, manages large teams effectively, manages complex issues effectively).
4. *Demonstrates strategic and intellectual leadership* (for example, is future focused, possesses broad business skills, knows "our business," stays in tune with customer needs, is able to see the "big picture").

Recall that the *Managing for Excellence Library* focused on building effective working relationships and meaningful jobs. The *Library* was developed just after the company's divestiture, and the purpose was to describe a style of management that would promote effective and unifying working relationships after the feeling of separation and lack of control that had accompanied the Bell system breakup. The *Library* told managers to take control; outputs would be measured, and it was up to each manager to decide how to achieve the important outputs. In this sense, the model empowered managers, presenting them as enablers. This role was specific to middle managers, who were responsible for translating leaders' directives into actionable goals and helping subordinates achieve these goals.

In comparison, the leadership platform argued that all levels of managers are leaders. The platform emphasized the importance of setting strategic directions, empowering others, and generating commitment and excitement about the corporate mission. While the *Library* was a communications vehicle (with booklets describing the management model [the outputs], the associated management training curriculum, appraisal methods, and other human resource policies), the platform merely consisted of a set of phrases. A plan was needed to convey the concepts of the platform to all managers and to inculcate them into managers' actions.

This communications process was accomplished in several ways. Of course, the dimensions set forth in the platform were published in company newsletters, along with stories about their purpose. In addition, a document was developed by training department members to outline critical incidents that would be indicative of behavior that reflected the platform dimensions. This was used by vice-presidents, who wanted help fleshing out the dimensions they had generated.

For example, one critical incident was a manager meeting one-on-one with a key subordinate to consider performance results for the quarter and future directions for the department. A manager who followed the platform would (1) ask the subordinate to evaluate his or her own performance compared to objectives (thus empowering the subordinate), (2) ask how the performance results supported the organization's goals (translating vision into organizational goals), (3) discuss problems encountered and how they might be resolved (creating change and managing conflict), and (4) discuss the subordinate's role as team member (building relationships).

Another critical incident dealt with personal image conveyed in all interactions (that is, the extent to which the manager conveys values, establishes the culture, sets the tone, defines the norm, and clarifies the direction in ways consistent with platform dimensions). The list of behaviors indicated that such a manager would (1) take work time for self-development and encourage others to do so; (2) balance work and nonwork life; (3) coach, sponsor, and mentor others; (4) recognize that casual comments can influence subordinates' priorities; (5) listen attentively; and (6) handle emergencies in a calm, determined manner.

The list of critical incidents and behaviors was given to higher-level managers to be used for self-analysis and as a checklist for periodic reference and self-evaluation against the platform guidelines. The platform dimensions were also incorporated into a performance appraisal form that asked supervisors to evaluate their subordinates and discuss with them areas needing development. In addition, the platform was used as a basis for making promotions to middle and top management. Several promotions of young managers to important positions demonstrated that the officers intended to reward people who demonstrated the qualities set forth in the leadership platform.

Also, the dimensions were used as the basis for an upward feedback appraisal. Developed by the training department, this was a form that asked subordinates to evaluate their supervisors on the platform dimensions. A rating was based on a five-point scale for each dimension. Subordinates completed the forms anonymously and sent them to an outside consultant for coding. The consultant prepared a confidential report for each manager, with at least three subordinates responding. (Less than three could reveal the identity of the respondents, because the feedback report indicated the range of scores on each dimension.) Managers were not required to share their results with their supervisors if they did not want to, because the intention was to use the results for development. However, after people got used to the process, top management wanted to use the results of future administrations for appraisal purposes—that is, a part of managers' evaluations would depend on how they were viewed by their subordinates.

Another developmental vehicle was a leadership course for middle managers based on the leadership platform. The course provided a series of learning experiences using multiple training methods, such as video, behavioral exercises, case discussions, and group discussions (Edward M. Mone and Jill Havrilla, personal communication, September 29, 1988). For instance, the module on "Vision: The Direction Component of Leadership" communicated the role and value of a leader's vision. The module covered definitions of vision and mission and ways to create and communicate this vision. A module entitled "Empowerment: The Energizing Component" examined what leaders should do to enhance working relationships and build motivation within the work group. Activities included a group discussion, which revealed the need for leaders to reward empowerment, innovation, and quality performance in the group. A module on team building used a videotape of leaders discussing their successes and failures in establishing teams. Also, participants in the course developed a team-building strategy, and small groups worked on case exercises.

In summary, the leadership platform was a new direction for management development, stemming from the top corporate officers and refined, developed, and spread throughout the organization with the help of the training department. Training managers became involved in projects that went beyond typical courses to help with other personnel processes, such as upward feedback. Thus, the training department was recognized as having expertise in how to change managers' behavior, and education was viewed broadly as a combination of communications, evaluation, and educational efforts. Indeed, the particular dimensions in the platform were probably less important than how the dimensions were generated, since top managers and training and human resource professionals were all involved in thinking of better ways to lead and manage the organization. (For other ideas about how to challenge executives to realize the need for change in leadership behavior, see Veltrop and Harrington, 1988, who suggest that leaders should become adept at creating shared values, planning and leading transitions, performing organization and technical systems analysis, learning how to learn, developing a proactive environmental focus, and aiding process facilitation and design.)

Management Forums

The training department can also help educate managers on organizational strategies and environmental trends by designing and coordinating an employee forum, which will help keep managers current about the industry and the organization. Usually lasting several days to a week, such a forum would host industry leaders and top officers of the organization as speakers. Department heads from different units in the organization might be asked to describe major efforts and new directions in their areas. Groups of thirty to fifty mid- and higher-level managers would attend each session of the forum, and sessions would continue until all managers in the target group had attended. An example referred to earlier in the chapter is Merck's special program for managers, "Managing in Today's Merck Environment."

Another example of a forum is AT&T's business directions series. This was created to increase lower-level managers' awareness of their role in the company; to enhance their understanding of, and commitment to, the firm's strategies; and to ensure that they understand how the marketplace and the economy is changing. The overall goal was to help managers understand how their individual success is linked with the success of the business.

The business directions series examined such topics as corporate strategy, profitability, people management, teamwork, customer satisfaction, and quality. The program was designed by human resource and line managers representing all units in the company. The sessions brought people together from different parts of the business, giving them a chance to interact with one another as part of the learning experience.

Lasting two and a half days, the workshop/forum included planned exercises, informal discussions, and videos about financial issues and new corporate initiatives, as described by key managers from across the business. These, together with in-person presentations and question-and-answer sessions with a few top executives, provided key issues for discussion and debate. Participants also received an overview of the full range of the firm's products and services.

Workshop modules focused on the company's financial health, an overview of the responsibilities of the different business units in the company, the meaning of quality improvement and how the quality improvement process can be applied to every job, and how to manage people in a changing work environment, with an emphasis on ways to encourage employee involvement and development. A concluding module helped managers think about their role in shaping their own future and the future of the organization. They were asked to incorporate what they had learned into actions that would have an impact on their own day-to-day activities, the activities of their co-workers, and senior management.

Another type of management forum was used by a firm that had recently experienced severe retrenchment in its work force. The firm wanted to foster teamwork and a sense of challenge and excitement in the people who survived the downsizing and who were responsible for implementing a new product line and radically new work procedures. The program, called "Project Miracles," combined a focus on personal health and well-being with outdoor team exercises. Work groups participated in the week-long program. The purpose was to help people have a better sense for how to control their lives and have more energy by taking care of themselves physically. Also, the program helped managers develop a sense that they all cared about the success of the company and that they could trust one another. Management felt that the program was critical in helping change managers' attitudes from depression and being overwhelmed by seemingly impossible work demands to enthusiasm and a feeling that their goals were achievable. Indeed, the product and work process changes did result in a dramatic financial turnaround. Project Miracles was viewed as a facilitating factor. The executives felt so strongly about the program that they eventually sent all employees through it, even sending hourly workers through an abbreviated version. In general, training was important to the firm's transition, and an average of $5,000 a year per person was spent on this training.

The cost-benefit of such programs should not be ignored. The costs for development (such as video production) tend to be high. Also, the costs for delivery are usually high, especially if the forum is held at an executive conference center. Usually, a "live-in" arrangement is desirable because it provides time in the evenings for informal discussions and networking among participants. An "outward-bound" program, such as Project Miracles, run by a consulting firm costs from $1,500 to $2,000 per person, not including travel, food, lodging, and salaries. The benefits of such a program are intangible, especially since the topics do not focus directly on each person's specific job, and how the new knowledge is transferred to day-to-day activities is not always clear. Nevertheless, top management generally views the benefits as worthwhile if the firm can afford the cost. In general, the organization hopes to gain the following:

- Managers who are able to represent the organization well as they interact with people in other firms and in the community
- Managers who share the same broad objectives and sense of mission
- A sense of team spirit and belonging in the organization
- An increased sense of loyalty and a belief in the importance of the organization's success (which may reduce turnover—and associated costs—of valued employees)
- Managers in different departments who can understand each other (thus decreasing unproductive turf battles and increasing coordination between interdependent departments)
- An increased willingness of managers to move between units and to accept people into their groups from different units
- A sense of corporate mission that will guide managers' decisions and actions (for example, how to allocate resources, what to

communicate to subordinates, when to spend time and resources on continuous learning for themselves and their subordinates).

Summary

This chapter demonstrated how training programs can and should be integrated with other human resource functions to support the overall strategy of the organization. This is especially critical in the areas of education, redeployment, and quality improvement. Many of these programs may be joint union-management initiatives that require cooperation and flexibility on the part of the training department. The training department should be proactive in seeking external funds for retraining. The training department should use continuous learning and quality improvement programs to develop training professionals and enhance the quality of training development and delivery. Finally, by fostering leadership and management development, training can play a role in changing behavior to match new directions for the organization.

Policy Recommendations and Opportunities

1. Training managers should work closely with the organization's human resource staff to develop compatible, mutually supportive systems and programs. For instance, appraisal and promotion criteria should be based on skills and outputs that are important to the organization's success, and training programs should support the development of those skills.

2. Given the importance of training in developing strategically focused programs, the training department should be a model for using these programs. Training professionals should use the career planning tools, appraisal methods, quality processes, and continuous learning courses that they have designed for the rest of the organization. As training managers "walk as they talk," they gain an appreciation for what programs are working and what programs need improvement.

3. Training managers should be on the lookout for ways to improve the quality of training operations, and they should apply quality improvement methods to create improvement opportunities.

4. As suggested in the discussion of the importance of professional development in Chapter Seven, training professionals should take advantage of chances to acquire new knowledge and skills, thereby enhancing their awareness of the organization's needs and making them more marketable for other positions within the organization.

5. In unionized organizations, the training department should work with labor relations managers in designing joint, bargained-for education programs. The training department can play a key role in making these programs successful by understanding employees' needs as well as the organization's requirements and providing responsive programs.

6. Leadership and management courses should be designed to reflect the strategic direction of the organization—that is, the type of leadership style that will enhance the organization's objectives and contribute to individual motivation and professional growth. Too often, a leadership curriculum is merely a menu of topics covering general skills, some of which may be the latest management fad. A leadership curriculum should communicate how top executives want the organization to be managed. Also, the programs should be linked together by a common theme and consistent message.

7. Training managers should recognize their role in formulating strategic organizational directions. The training department may be called on to develop a curriculum in an area that is important to the firm, such as quality or leadership, but the direction may not be articulated well. Training managers can facilitate thinking about and discussion of strategic directions and then can create supporting educational programs.

8. As the organization changes, the need for new and different management development programs will emerge. Training managers should not be so wedded to existing programs that they resist new efforts or maintain old programs until they are useless. Rather, training managers should be on the cutting edge of organizational change and be the first to recognize the need for new supporting strategies.

9

Future Challenges for Employee Education, Training, and Development

Several trends point to an increasing training gap in the United States. A recent policy study sponsored by the U.S. Department of Labor and a number of private organizations (such as Citicorp, IBM, AT&T, Xerox, and General Motors) concluded the following about a U.S. training gap:

> Although educational attainment is improving within the labor force entrant population, the large remaining gaps in attainment among whites, blacks, and Hispanics are a cause for concern. . . . The quality of basic skills training for U.S. labor force entrants is lower than that provided to the labor force entrants of other nations (for example, Japan). Significant deficiencies in the quality of such training for U.S. labor force entrants relative to other nations will impede the ability of this nation to generate and adopt new technologies with sufficient speed and effectiveness to remain competitive in the world economy. [Cyert and Mowery, 1987, p. 143]

Several other trends emerged from a recent survey of technical training conducted by the U.S. Department of Labor and the American Society for Training and Development (reported by Carnevale and Schulz, 1988). This study suggested the following:

- Job growth between 1989 and 2000 will be in technical areas. Moreover, technological advancements mean that skill requirements are increasing on the job.
- The quantity and quality of entry-level workers is declining.
- Academic learning (in schools and colleges) is not sufficiently applied, and applied learning does not meet basic academic standards.
- Highly technical workers receive the training they require; however, blue-collar technical employees do not. As a result, the United States does well at developing new products but has trouble getting these products through production and into the marketplace quickly.
- New styles of management give workers more freedom to structure their jobs, which often involves working in teams to improve the work process. Therefore, employees require higher levels of interpersonal, teamwork, negotiation, and organizational skills.
- Managers do not receive the training they need in new technologies, and they lack the management skills required to manage semiautonomous work teams (such as knowing how to provide leadership while empowering subordinates or knowing how to facilitate work groups by providing structure and support).

Another point to consider is that while participative work structures and the use of more varied skills can mean more satisfying and meaningful work, there is an increasing social conflict between a smaller number of highly skilled workers having up-to-date skills and those workers with little education and little hope of getting it (Howard, 1985). Put another way, there is an increasing gap between the "haves" and the "have nots."

This book has shown that organizations will be competitive by meeting customer requirements and by improving work processes to produce high-quality products and services. Training and education are the foundation of successful quality improvement efforts, participative work structures, and customer responsiveness. Employee training also plays a critical role in redeployment efforts, retraining programs, and reemployment assistance programs. In addition to designing and delivering training programs, training departments facilitate learning by teaching people how to learn and by coaching supervisors on ways to support development. Training departments provide the resources managers need to develop training programs that meet local needs. The training gaps noted above will be overcome as organizations supply these resources to their employees and as employees are encouraged to understand the value of education and their responsibility for their own education. Also, these gaps will be reduced as organizations recognize their responsibility to, and vested interest in, the education of future entrants to the labor force and support community education efforts.

Unfortunately, this will not be an easy process; many employees will drop out (minorities and older workers being the most likely casualties), and economic conditions will influence the number of employment opportunities. However, the challenge for corporations, unions, and government will be to cooperatively provide the resources to meet changing skill requirements and increase U.S. competitiveness in world markets.

Summary of Major Points

This book described ways to enhance the effectiveness and to reduce the cost of training development and delivery. Organizations increasingly will need to provide employees with advanced skills and knowledge as job requirements continue to become more complex and the labor force becomes less prepared to meet these skill requirements. Corporate education should take into consideration how adults learn if managers are to design cost-effective training and development systems. Advanced training technologies will be integrated with, and in many cases take the place of, traditional instructor-led, face-to-face classroom training. Training organizations will need to establish close working relationships with their clients of training, including the product and service developers, organization leaders, and human resource experts supplying the content of training and the students, employees, and supervisors who require advanced skills and knowledge. The training department must develop strategic plans that link training to organizational needs. In the process, training managers should analyze costs and ensure that training methods are competitive and effective in meeting intended goals. In addition, training managers should maximize the development and professional growth of instructors, program developers, instructional technologists, and other training experts.

Training managers have multiple roles in organizations, as educators, evaluators, leaders, strategists, change agents, consultants, and futurists. These managers must be attuned to external trends and forces as well as to internal human resource requirements and, in addition, know the business their organization is in and be experts in training methods and technology, adult learning, and the management of people.

Other training professionals—such as instructors, program developers, and instructional technologists—also must be effective in the same roles as training managers. These professionals must know who their customers are (for example, students and line managers) and be aware of, and be prepared to meet, their customers' expectations. They must develop close relationships with their suppliers—subject matter experts, their colleagues in the training organization, and vendors from whom they purchase program materials. Moreover, they must know what behaviors and outputs they must produce to be successful and to develop as professionals.

The training department must be closely linked to the goals of the organization and must be considered by top executives and line managers as vital to the organization's success. If not, the training department will be viewed merely as providing a commodity that can be purchased as well from an outside vendor as from an internal source—the chief determinant being who can deliver the product (for instance, education) most cheaply. The training department's added value lies in knowing the organization and how training professionals can work with other departments to enhance individuals' and the organization's chances for success.

Therefore, customer satisfaction should be the major criterion of a training department's success. The latest training technology, the most comprehensive courses, the least unit cost, and the most rigorous evaluation will mean little unless training is truly an integral part of the organization's strategy. Training managers should educate line managers about the returns from investing in the development of the firm's employees. All management must recognize the importance of continuous learning—not only for meeting immediate business needs but for being prepared for future demands.

Quality, then, is meeting customer demands and doing the right things in the right way. For example, training should be based on problem analysis and a determination of job requirements. Alternative solutions to meeting organizational needs should be considered along with training. Solutions should be adopted based on cost-benefit analyses. Training may be part of a larger solution—for instance, improving productivity by hiring more people, increasing selection standards, and improving the skills of current employees.

Training can be a critical part of major organizational initiatives, such as redeploying staff, introducing new technology, and being responsive to marketplace demands and changes. The training department can be a partner in developing these initiatives—that is, in establishing organizational direction, implementing change, monitoring effectiveness, and redirecting or fine-tuning the course of action.

Responsiveness is a key to a training department's success. Program materials must be flexible to meet client requirements, and training must be available when and wherever it is needed. Self-paced learning technologies, such as computer-based training, videos, interactive video disk, as well as printed job aids, are essential tools in an environment having multiple clients with differing needs. Training thus becomes modularized, with different levels of complexity and varying depths of learning available to suit different educational requirements. Training professionals not only must be proficient in these alternative technologies and be able to incorporate them into training programs but must be able to educate employees in how to use these technologies.

Training Challenges

This section considers several challenges for training organizations: taking advantage of new training technology, cooperating with other institutions to make maximum use of training, providing global training, integrating employee training and external customer training, focusing on the education of employees in high-impact jobs (that is, jobs critical to the organization's success), linking management and technical education, and taking a systems approach to educational processes (that is, recognizing the multiple inputs, throughputs, and outputs and their interrelationship).

Technological Advances. New technology presents many challenges to educators, allowing instructors to take full advantage of adult learning principles by providing hands-on experiences in realistic environments. Learning can be accelerated—for instance, by using simulations in ways that give the student control over the learning process (as discussed in Chapters One and Two). Consider, for example, an on-line computer data base that allows an employee to rate him- or herself on a set of skill dimensions. These ratings are compared to the average of ratings made by supervisors and peers about the employee. The employee then receives a summary of the results, recommendations for appropriate training programs, and the option to register for courses. The computer provides instant access to CBT, video disks, and remote classrooms via PC teletraining. Such integrated learning systems are under development. (See, for examples, Chute, Balthazar, and Poston, 1988).

Training departments must find ways to use such technology cost-effectively, and training professionals must learn how to use advanced technology to develop as well as to deliver training. No doubt the cost of program development using computer technology will be lowered as program developers become more expert in its use. Also, unit costs of delivery will be lower when more people are willing to take advantage of self-paced, computer-based training.

Corporate-University Partnerships. Many organizations are taking advantage of the knowledge that resides in educational institutions. Corporations sponsor internship programs in instructional technology as a way to keep on the leading edge of new advances in training technology. Corporations sponsor research to improve the effectiveness of new training methods and to attain a better understanding of adult learning and also work with colleges and universities to develop and run training programs.

In addition, corporations are increasingly aware of their stake in the educational levels of today's students—the future source of corporate managers, engineers, professionals, and blue-collar workers. Many corporations support education in communities by providing funds, resources, and people to public schools to help prepare young people before they enter the labor market. For instance, Ford Motor Company is initiating a pilot urban schools program in Detroit, Cleveland, and Chicago to attract minority and female students into math and science. In Detroit, the Board of Education, local universities, foundations, parents, and corporations formed the Pre-College Engineering Program to prepare minority students to pursue bachelor's degrees in science or engineering.

Some firms with mutual training needs band together in consortia to develop a common curriculum or a common delivery system, such as satellite broadcasts. For example, in southern California, Hughes, Northrop, and several other aerospace firms developed a curriculum and contracted with a network of community colleges to provide courses to employees (Chmura, Henton, and Melville, 1987). In another case, the National Technological University was established by partnerships of more than fifty firms and twenty-three engineering schools. Satellite technology was used to provide courses from these schools to engineers in their corporate classrooms.

An example is the master's degree program in optical sciences offered by the University of Arizona to students at Kodak. Students enroll through the National Technological University. Courses are taught in Arizona, while students at Kodak take courses at their work site in Rochester, New York. This program was created for Kodak and other industrial sponsors because there is a critical shortage of engineering graduates with an optical science specialty and because few universities offer degrees in this area.

The University of Arizona has found no difference in the performance of students who take courses via satellite compared to those in a traditional classroom setting. However, some of the disadvantages of satellite courses are that there is less student interaction, there are logistical difficulties involved in mailing homework and exams, and on-campus students believe they are penalized because the professors gear the classes to television students. The advantages for television students are that they can take the classes at their work site, they can view a videotape of a lecture if they miss a class or if they want to double-check their notes, and they often use what they learn on the job as they go through the program.

Other such "electronic university" arrangements allow employees to receive credit for courses taken at home from universities around the country, with access to professors via electronic, computer-based mail. Students can leave questions for professors, and professors can give exams via computer. Students learn from textbooks and from written lectures delivered via computer text. The cost of the program may be paid by the student's employer as part of a tuition assistance program.

Small organizations can benefit especially from a training consortium that will offer programs generally developed by large corporations. Training directors of small organizations should find ways to work with one another to share resources. For instance, two firms could agree to work together on a leadership training curriculum. Each firm could develop a course and then trade with the other firm. Introductory material and minor revisions can help customize each course to the special needs of a particular firm. Training directors must have the initiative to search for such opportunities and also must convince top management of the value of such cooperative efforts. Such joint efforts should also be considered by large organizations and also by smaller training departments within these organizations so that overlap in training can be avoided and resources conserved.

Global Training. Consistent with the trend toward a world economy and the globalization of business, training departments may operate internationally. One firm may have training departments in Singapore, Brussels, and Rio de Janeiro. These centers may operate independently, providing training to in-country nationals in the language of that country. Training centers may also be responsible for training expatriates (citizens of other countries who are transferred to a foreign location). Training (including language training) is needed to help these expatriates adapt to foreign cultures and to repatriation.

The training department should be involved in determining how foreign assignments fit with management career goals and development programs for high-potential managers. Foreign assignments should be structured to be meaningful experiences, for example, giving managers autonomy to make a substantial contribution and support in dealing with a different culture. The program should also specify desirable positions for those returning from foreign assignments.

Too often, organizations emphasize preparation of individuals selected for a foreign job and ignore those returning from foreign assignments. These individuals and their families need support in adapting to changes in their home country, and they also need rewarding jobs to come home to so that the foreign assignment is a stepping stone to more responsible positions. Such support will attract more high-potential managers to international assignments.

A headquarters' training department may be responsible for ensuring the consistent high quality of training in all training locations across the globe—a difficult task owing to language and cultural differences. Courses may be designed to deliver similar messages, such as the values of the firm. Doing this will require recognizing cultural differences and interpreting the firm's mission and values in a way meaningful to employees in other countries.

International organizations are likely to have training organizations in different parts of the world. These departments need to develop programs to suit local needs, including regional language requirements for classroom and self-paced courses. However, these departments can draw on materials designed by other training departments in the organization. Firms such as IBM have a central training support department that provides some training materials for adaptation (including translation) by its foreign training facilities.

Integrating Employee Training and Nonemployee Training. Companies have a vested interest in training their suppliers to provide high-quality products and services and on-time delivery. In addition, training external customers has become a line of business for some organizations. In some cases, the same training designed for employees is offered to the firm's customers, suppliers, partners in joint ventures, and franchisees. In other cases, special training programs are designed for these external employees—for instance, training that keeps customers informed of the latest advances and of the company's products and services. These programs are generally free of charge to customers when the intention is to educate and advertise at the same time. Many firms use innovative techniques to reach their customers, such as videos that describe products to consumers in retail stores and satellite communications that reach employees of other companies.

Customer training is an area for showcasing the firm's products and for using the most effective and efficient methods (that is, the clearest communication, the best use of adult learning methods, the most efficient use of time). Some of the programs designed for external customers are valuable for employees as well. In fact, firms that fail to recognize this may develop redundant training programs for these audiences. For both audiences, attention should be paid to whether the message has been communicated—that is, whether the training has been successful.

Targeting High-Impact Jobs. While it is important to offer educational experiences to all employees (such as courses in management skills consistent with organizational strategy), special attention should be given to high-impact jobs. For instance, IBM has identified more than eighty key jobs, according to Barry Arnett, an IBM training manager (Arnett, 1988). These jobs may include key positions in marketing and service, especially those involving direct customer contact. Job analyses should be used to fully understand the requirements of these jobs, and current employees should be assessed to ensure they have the needed skills. Where training gaps exist, educational programs should be designed to give current employees and new employees the training they need.

Focusing training resources on high-impact jobs should maximize return for each training dollar. Clarifying skill requirements for these jobs will inform job incumbents and their managers about what is important to achieve mastery and will also make it possible to track the impact of training on unit and organizational performance, which is important, given that these positions are closely tied to the organization's financial bottom line.

Linking Management Development and Technical Education. Technical education should include information on the interface between the technology and the people using it, including demonstrating that the technology is flexible and can be adapted to suit the users' needs. Also, technical training should include how the technology will affect work standards, performance evaluations, and the structure of work—for instance, how it affects the employee's job challenge, how people have to work together to use the technology, and how supervisors will monitor performance. The human component should be an integral part of demonstrating and providing an opportunity for employees to use the new methods and procedures. (For a more detailed discussion of the human component of introducing new technology, see the description of the introduction of a new monitoring system for telecommunications equipment and the implementation of a new electronic office mail system in London, 1988.)

Taking a Systems Approach to Employee Education. A good way to summarize the interaction between the training department, organizational objectives, and student needs is a system of closely interrelated processes and programs. Top management provides strategic direction; the training department provides the up-front job analyses, program design, and delivery mechanisms; and the employees assume responsibility for utilizing educational resources. The value of the systems perspective is that it recognizes that training does not occur in a vacuum but must be tied closely to major organizational actions and directions. A major organizational change, such as introducing a new technology, is likely to spark the need for training. Even layoffs may mean more training for the people who are left, because they have to do more than before (or because, in union firms, "bumping" rules may put more senior people into jobs they have not performed before).

Goals for More Effective Employee Training

There are several goals for meeting the educational needs of employees and their organizations, and these include ensuring that training professionals (1) encourage diversity and breadth of background and experience in the training staff, (2) encourage managers to support their employees' education, (3) use training resources wisely (especially important for small training organizations), (4) help employees learn how to learn and how to solve problems and make decisions, and (5) be flexible in response to changing organizational requirements.

Encouraging Work-Force Diversity. Organizations can benefit from a diverse force of training professionals in other ways than meeting employment and affirmative objectives. Attracting minorities to the training profession and women to technical training (since women already have a prominent role in management training) will help match the increased diversity in the work force and help the training department understand employees' educational backgrounds and learning habits. Also, a more heterogeneous staff of training experts will help the training organization respond to educational requirements in different cultures, both in the United States and in different countries in which the firm operates. As training becomes increasingly recognized as at the heart of organizational strategy development and implementation, more people will be attracted to the field. More women and minorities can be attracted by corporate intern programs and corporate-sponsored scholarships for undergraduate students in education and graduate students in such advanced fields as instructional technology and distance learning.

Empowering Managers to Be Responsible for Their Subordinates' Training. As discussed in Chapter Eight, new styles of management can empower employees to use their expertise, make decisions, and be accountable for the consequences of those decisions. The difficulty managers have in empowering subordinates is that empowerment means the manager must let go of control and authority. Training professionals need to empower local field managers and their staffs to be responsible for their own department's training and long-term education. The training department should provide the resources to make this possible—programs, counseling, advice, instruction, and so on. However, training experts may fear losing control over the quality of the training products and may be concerned that the value of their position as professionals thus will be lessened.

However, just as managers must learn that empowerment makes them more responsive to their subordinates' needs for support and direction, training professionals must learn that empowering local managers will make the training department more responsive to its clients' requirements. Empowering managers to be responsible for their own development means that training programs must be sensitive to how the skills and knowledge being taught will be applied and how this will enhance employees' personal growth. Training professionals will be rewarded for these efforts by increased demand for their services and by line managers' recognition that training contributes to the strategic direction and ultimate success of the organization.

Allocating Training Resources Wisely. As indicated in Chapter Two, there are a multitude of training options in terms of media and content. Small training departments do not have the luxury of making mistakes (for example, developing an expensive video disk program only to find it is not effective). No organization wants to make mistakes, but large organizations can afford to experiment with new technologies and presentation techniques.

Small training units must experiment with ways to provide just the right training when it is needed. Joining a multicompany consortium is one way to do this; other ways include customizing off-the-shelf vendor programs or learning from competitors who make presentations at training conferences or write articles in professional journals. In addition, small training departments should engage the cooperation of the organization's managers and work groups to conduct skills inventories, performance audits, and training needs analyses. Field managers can be used as subject matter experts in program development and instruction, thereby not only reducing training costs but also increasing managers' commitment to, and involvement in, their own education.

Teaching Strategy, Problem Solving, and Learning to Learn Skills. Rather than merely teaching narrow skills, training programs should provide employees with a conceptual foundation for analyzing problems, making decisions, and learning on their own. Employees must have the basic skills to make the most of technological enhancements. Also, employees must be able to view problems from the customer's perspective. This means knowing how to recognize what is important to the customer and how the products or services sold to the customer fit into the customer's operation. This analytical orientation can be conveyed using simulations and hands-on practice with the firm's products and services. Training is a vehicle for helping employees understand how the quality of their work makes the organization successful by increasing customer satisfaction. As indicated in the first chapter, training is a way to communicate corporate strategies and to demonstrate how the employees contribute to corporate goals.

Remaining Flexible in the Face of Changing Skill Requirements. Training departments, and, in fact, the U.S. educational system as a whole, has been very sensitive historically to skill demands resulting from technological and economic changes (Cyert and Mowery, 1987). Corporate training departments, for example, have been able to gear up quickly to provide training for redeploying engineers to sales positions. Universities expand or reduce degree programs depending on the demand for certain professions, such as robotics and aerospace engineering. Fortunately, this flexibility makes it unnecessary to try to forecast long-term training requirements, which is difficult, given the changing environment and poor forecasting methods.

Training departments must make a conscious effort to remain flexible. It is easy to become wedded to a narrow, structured method—for instance, a model for conducting performance analysis or a particular mode of instruction—but such rigidity can be the "kiss of death" if the client believes a different approach is necessary. As facilitators and catalysts, training personnel must be open to new and changing demands and must constantly explore, debate, and experiment, bringing new knowledge and ideas to bear on new problems. Training is a field in which creativity and freshness can be applied to technological advances and discoveries about adult learning. The field is an exciting combination of art and science made practical. Remembering that training is a dynamic process will increase a training department's chances of success.

Policy Opportunities and Recommendations

1. Training professionals should educate the organization on how important education is to the organization's long-term viability and vitality. Training managers can ensure this link by

adopting policies that contribute to effective use of training resources and by taking direction from top management and developing programs that contribute to accomplishing organizational goals. In this sense, education becomes an intervention for organizational change that is facilitated, implemented, and, in some cases, initiated by the training department. Moreover, the training department should be professional and responsive to their customers' needs for new directions and for solutions to problems

2. As the work force becomes less stable, with less job security and people changing jobs, and sometimes careers, more frequently, organizations can attract top talent by offering the opportunity for professional growth and development. The training department should help make employee learning a cornerstone of the organization; this will enhance the firm's reputation as a good employer. Thus, continuing education aids competitive advantage by ensuring that the organization has the people it needs when they are needed.

3. While training content is driven by business need and top executive expectations, learning is the responsibility of each individual. Therefore, the training department should design flexible programs that allow employees to control their own learning. The goal should be to foster self-awareness, self-growth, and meaningful career direction. This may mean offering the same program content in different media, thereby providing employees with learning options that suit their needs and learning preferences. This also suggests the value of creating hands-on learning environments and experiential tools that can be used in the workplace as well as in training centers.

The goal of this book has been to show that a training department can implement these recommendations cost-effectively by developing and following operations plans that are tied to the organization's needs, using advanced technology training methods, tracking unit costs, and evaluating training success. Consistent with the view of training as part of an organizational system, the organization determines training requirements, the training department provides the resources, and individual employees assume the responsibility for learning, with the support of their management. Finally, training assignments should be viewed as opportunities for the development of high-potential employees—both training experts and generalist managers. This will enhance the reputation of the training department and involve all employees in the educational process.

Resource A
Administrative Functions

The planning and administration of training functions require efforts similar to other operations in the organization, involving staffing, developing personnel, allocating funds and other resources, tracking expenses, evaluating performance (both individual and departmental), and communicating to employees and to customers and suppliers, whether internal or external. This resource examines these functions and how they enhance training goals and apply to training departments, from the standpoint of my experience as manager of planning and management systems. Some functions unique to training—for instance, program scheduling, employee registration, and the operation of a number of administrative support systems—are critical to the operation of a training unit. Data systems are required to link training requests and enrollments to training records. Data bases are necessary to track student opinion of courses and student performance during and immediately after the program as well as later on the job.

Administrative Functions and Goals

In 1987 I became the manager of planning and management systems for a major, nationally deployed training department. The department as a whole employed about seven hundred people and provided technical training to about forty-five thousand people. A training organization of this size is usually found only in the largest companies and government agencies. However, the administrative functions I describe below are still carried out in smaller training departments, although there will be fewer resources devoted to each activity and perhaps more reliance on vendors and consultants for some functions (such as data systems and catalog design).

I reported to the director of the department, which had been formed recently by the merger of two other departments that served separate divisions of the company. When these divisions merged, the training units also merged. My position was created to handle the variety of administrative tasks needed in the new department. Some of these tasks, such as budgeting and staffing, had been done by others in the separate departments. Other functions, such as communications, were new to the training department. All the functions would take on a different form to fit the newly merged training organization.

Training Administration Functions

The following is a list of administrative functions I established and major projects and objectives associated with each. Each function had at least one manager and in some cases two or three support staff.

Budgeting and Financial Tracking. This function organized the budgeting process and also tracked expenses, providing accurate and timely reports using the company's financial data systems. Financial analyses were conducted to identify and track unit costs and check reasonableness of expenses. A related function was to develop and monitor the capital equipment budget and to process equipment orders.

Staffing and Personnel Measurement. This function processed requests for job evaluations, job advertisements, and payroll changes as new people were added and as others transferred to other departments. The function issued monthly reports tracking employee moves within the training department and between the training department and other departments in the organization. Employee movement within the training department was forecast, progress on equal employment opportunity and affirmative action was reported, and service anniversaries were reported to the director and published in the department newsletter. The function maintained the department's organizational chart and issued monthly updates of names, addresses, and telephone numbers to the employee directory.

In addition, this function administered the company's appraisal process in the department for midyear and end-of-year performance review, established employee ranking and rating procedures, administered the company's compensation plan, and was also responsible for coordinating office space. The function also organized employee recognition programs (rewarding outstanding employee contributions with nonfinancial awards) and developed a career planning and professional development process for the employees in the department.

Business and Operations Plans. This function coordinated the department's business plan in conjunction with the organization's overall business plans and the plans of the departments served by the training unit. The function coordinated the development and tracked the implementation of training operations plans, assessing how these plans accomplished business objectives. The function developed an ongoing process for forecasting training needs in the company and in external client groups (other companies that sold or purchased the company's products and paid for training on those products). In addition, the function tracked new technology and service developments, assessed their effects on training needs, and informed those responsible for training program development.

Operations Measurements and Reports. Working with the administrative systems function (described below), this function generated monthly reports on indexes of training effectiveness and efficiency, including number and types of programs developed, instructor classroom days, client satisfaction (from course evaluation questionnaires and client telephone opinion surveys operated by other managers), instructor platform time (time spent teaching), days spent by instructors as "key instructors" (assisting in the course development process, such as a trial of a new course), classroom facilities utilization, and student days.

Communications. This function published a newsletter, communicated product announcements and organizational change announcements to training department employees, coordinated training program announcements to customers, and prepared presentations (such as speeches for the director). The function managed communications products (such as the course catalog, descriptions of curriculum paths, and updates in these documents) and consulted with training managers on the design of all training department publications, including training manuals and materials. In addition, the function worked with the training personnel function (described above) to implement an employee recognition program.

External Training Coordination. This function enhanced the training department's commitment to serve external clients by effectively negotiating with external clients and training department delivery managers responsible for providing training. The function involved delivery managers in developing policies and procedures and in reviewing the effectiveness of external client training. This function cooperated with other training departments in the company to develop and implement centralized systems for a single point of external client contact for scheduling, registration, and course announcements. The function generated a monthly tracking report on the amount of training provided to external clients, associated income, and the amount of training required but not yet met.

Executive Support. This function assisted the training director in scheduling meetings, preparing material for corporate reports, and scheduling and managing the agenda of the training board of directors' meetings. The function coordinated and produced the training department's monthly tracking report for the director and the director's supervisor. The report consisted of data on expense-to-budget tracking; number, type, and location of training programs developed and delivered; personnel moves; and descriptions of major accomplishments and special projects. Also, the function coordinated the department's quarterly and annual accomplishments report, which was compared against the department's business plans and commitments. Another function related to executive support included developing the agendas for a variety of monthly staff meetings (for example, meetings of the director and those reporting directly to the director and meetings of the midlevel managers throughout the country responsible for training development and delivery).

Administrative Systems Operations. This function operated the registration system and the training records data base, tracking student day usage and generating reports on employee training for the department's monthly tracking report. Other reports were generated to meet the specific needs of client departments to track their employees' training. The reports also were used by program delivery managers and program development managers to track volume of use, unmet demand (registration requests and waiting lists), instructor platform time, and other indexes by curriculum and training site. The function established a regular series of useful reports and customized reports to meet specific needs of client departments and training managers.

Administrative Systems Development. This function developed new data systems to meet needs as they arose and identified more effective ways to provide data systems. Projects included the following:

- A program development tracking system so course and program developers could record their progress on each project
- A data base to integrate data from course evaluation questionnaires and performance tests
- A system requesting employees to check the accuracy of their training records and make corrections in these records
- An on-line course catalog that could be updated easily and that could be accessed by employees and their supervisors
- A software system to help training managers schedule instructors to teach classes, based on course demand, instructor expertise, and the availability of instructors and facilities.

Special Projects. This function conducted special projects as needed, including the following:

- An analysis of training needs in the organization compared to the existing training resources and plans (the gap analysis described earlier)
- A team comprised of line managers from customer organiza-

tions and of training managers that worked to reduce the training gap
- A team that worked to reduce unit costs of training (described in Chapter Five).

Commitments of the Administrative Staff

The motto of my administrative functions group was "Customer Satisfaction Through Responsiveness," which indicates that the group served multiple clients—the director, those directly reporting to the director (senior training managers), and customers of the training department. The group contributed to customer satisfaction by providing information on training use and effectiveness and by supporting the staffing and professional development needs of the department. The development of employees in the group was another important goal and involved ensuring that group members had appraisals, received performance feedback reviews, and had written career plans. That is, the same programs that applied to other members of the department had to be applied to members of the administrative staff.

Accomplishments

Each quarter, I wrote a list of accomplishments, with input provided by each manager in the group. Progress was made on the major new initiatives, such as the training records data reconciliation. We prided ourselves on working as a team to enhance the interfaces within the group (for example, between measurements coordination, reports coordination, reports generation, and administrative systems). We also tried to enhance linkages with clients internal to the training department—the various development and delivery managers as well as the top managers. We did this by responding to requests as rapidly as possible and by attending staff meetings and coordinating overall departmental meetings. We found that clear and frequent communications are key to maintaining such relationships.

Barriers to Effective Operations

Despite our accomplishments, there were numerous barriers to overcome and problems to solve. Recognizing and analyzing these barriers may help others involved in training management recognize and prevent potential problems.

Burdening the Field with Requests. Because we were the director's staff, we were often in the position of requesting data from an already overburdened field staff. Some data could not be obtained from our administrative systems and required time-consuming manual data collection. The need for this data usually arose from a particular request from the director that had to be responded to immediately. Indeed, the director felt that we were not generating enough information fast enough on the many possible measurement indexes to give a thorough indication of the department's performance. Moreover, because many requests for information were not routine and could not be anticipated, we had to act in an emergency mode, or at least with the feeling that time was of the essence, and we needed the field to do so as well. Examples of requests included the need for a report on numbers of registered students who cancelled or who did not show up for courses. Other data and information requests were routine but required constant reminders to the field, such as the need for updates on special projects for the monthly tracking report.

The requests for information led to the impression that we were creating work for the field trainers rather than serving them. In one case, our director wanted to know how many people had received performance appraisals and reviews from their supervisors. All managers had committed to ensure that every employee would have an appraisal and review and that the personnel manager on the administrative staff would collect copies of the appraisals and the director would review a sample of them. Several reminders were necessary to get the managers to send their appraisals to our central office.

The issue we faced was one of balancing responsiveness to the training department's top management with responsiveness to the field groups. Clearly, we needed to do both even though these two objectives occasionally conflicted. There was no single or completely satisfying solution to this dilemma. We handled the issue by recognizing it, bringing it up at staff meetings, trying to limit our emergency requests to true emergencies, and devoting time to training managers' needs as well as top management's needs.

Occasionally, we would question the director about whether a set of reports was absolutely necessary to be certain that he was clear on the amount of work and the costs involved. Sometimes the director would revise or cancel a request that was optional or when costs outweighed need. Fortunately, the director was open to discussion and feedback from subordinates. Without this understanding, our group might have been perceived solely as a watchdog, and relationships would have degenerated. As it was, we were able to maintain an effective equilibrium despite occasional minor conflicts.

As administrative staff, we were considered part of overhead costs, as was the entire training department in the corporation. However, most departments and top officers viewed employee training as critical to accomplishing their objectives. For this reason, when most departments were requested to reduce their overhead expenses, training was first required to reduce its unit costs but not its overall expenses. The goal was to deliver more training for the same amount of money. (Methods for unit cost reduction are discussed in Chapter Five.) As part of the firm's effort to cut expenses, we eventually needed to reduce our direct costs of training administration and then to reduce overall training costs.

The problem with reducing administrative costs was that we were being asked to do more and more with less and less. This is not an unusual problem in corporate America today. One quick way to reduce costs was to shed our temporary employees. To do this without burdening our permanent staff beyond reason required prioritizing and doing fewer projects. This was extremely difficult because our clients' number of requests determined our work load. Doing less meant saying no, and this was difficult for a department devoted to responsiveness.

Nevertheless, we did make progress by discussing this dilemma with our clients and obtaining their help in setting priorities. This process took considerable time, and we learned that it is far easier to establish new functions than it is to reduce inflow of work.

Improving Quality and Morale. The work overload as well as normal personality conflicts required us to devote attention to group morale. One way to attack the work-load problem was to examine the quality of our output and the efficiency of our work processes. My entire group went through an introductory course on quality improvement. We held a group meeting with the theme "Energy Through Quality" to discuss the meaning of quality, how other organizations provided quality customer service, and ways we could improve. Several groups identified improvement areas, such as faster ways to procure capital equipment for classroom demonstrations and computer simulations and faster processing of payroll change reports by eliminating redundant steps. Also, as a group, we planned a course called "Managing Individual Effectiveness" to help us cope with the heavy work demands. Doing this together also served as a team-building event.

Dealing with External Training Issues. Having external customer registration as one of the administrative functions posed other dilemmas related to being a go-between. The training organization's major objective was to serve internal clients, but taking time to train external clients channelled resources away from this goal. Thus, there was considerable negotiation with the delivery training managers to ensure that external customers were allocated places in courses. External training also required interfacing with the development training managers who had to modify courses to suit external clients' needs and determine what courses were proprietary and not open to external customers. The desire to balance the needs of external training with development and delivery was the reason the function was placed in the administrative section of the department.

After six months of managing external training registration, the head of training delivery and I agreed to move the funtion to the delivery unit. We hoped that if a delivery manager was responsible for external as well as internal training scheduling, external training would receive a higher priority. The delivery manager who assumed responsibility for the function would also have to deal with policy issues, even though these were more remote to normal delivery functions.

Additional Support Functions

There were several support functions that were not part of my administrative group. One was the counseling, scheduling, and registration group, which was part of the delivery organization. This group was run by a manager in another city who had clerks in several geographical locations who answered client training questions, scheduled courses for client groups, and registered individuals for prescheduled courses.

Another support function was the group of instructional technologists that consulted with program developers on methods and media for presenting material. (See the description in Chapter Three of this role.) In addition, several instructional technologists were responsible for developing measurements that would later serve as the data my group would process and use as the basis for reports. This included the course evaluation questionnaires; pretests to ensure that students had prerequisites; posttests to evaluate students' learning and to allow some employees to waive a program if they could pass the test without taking the course; and follow-up telephone surveys on students' attitudes about the program three and six months later, as well as supervisor opinions about the students' application of new skills and knowledge.

Use of Office Automation in Training Administration

Training administrators should investigate applications for advanced technologies. Chapter Two and Resource B show the use of advanced technologies for delivering training (such as self-paced computer-based training and computer networks). Similar technologies can be applied in training administration. Desktop publishing can be used for program announcements. Course catalogs can be computerized via disk or on-line systems. Program developers can work via computer with subject matter experts and instructional technologists to improve use of resourses. Computers can collect course evaluation information and pre- and posttest data directly from students and calculate student reports as well as reports of usage (numbers of students participating in the training) and training effectiveness. Training materials can be stored in computer data bases and provided to students via computer, eliminating the need for paper manuals. (Course manuals can be provided on computer disks and taken home by students for use as job aids.) As other examples, computers can track equipment orders, vendors used to provide training materials and programs, employees who have provided subject matter expertise to the training department, employees who have served as instructors, and the progress of projects under development.

Given the potential of computer applications to training support, a training department is likely to need a variety of computerized systems, which should be integrated to work together. An example of systems relationships is shown in Figure 4.

Ideally, these systems will work together in an interlinked set of data bases. The number of people served will determine the complexity of these systems. In small organizations, these processes

Figure 4. Interrelation of Systems to Be Computerized.

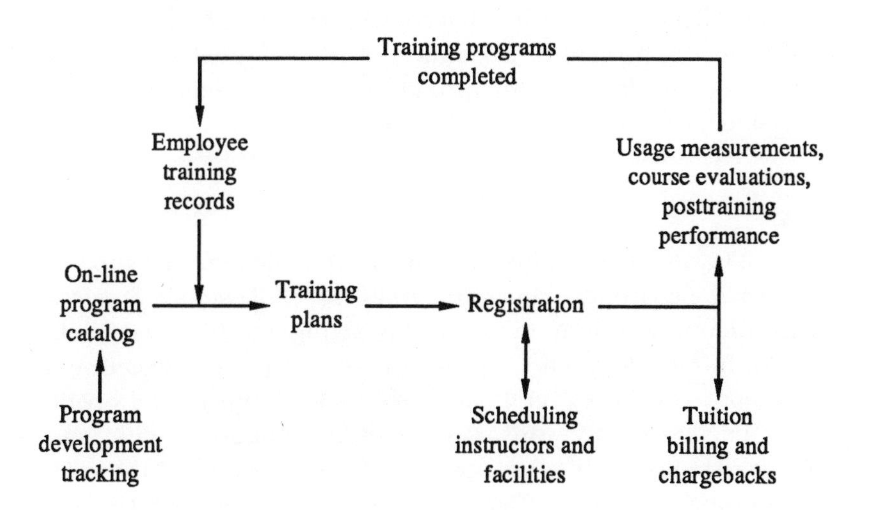

may be managed manually or with a few PC-based support systems. In large organizations, large-scale computer systems are necessary.

One special project undertaken by my systems people was the establishment of an integrated computer system architecture for the training organization. The goal was to ensure that computer systems supporting training met user needs. Users included client departments needing training data to plan future training and to track employee skills and knowledge levels as well as training managers who were held accountable for training expenses and who allocated training resources to meet client needs. The integrated architecture was based on the business plan for the training department, and the focus was on work processes, not computer systems per se (for example, the process of registering an employee for a course, tracking whether the employee completed the course, and updating the employee's training record).

In general, systematic planning for training information systems should begin with an analysis of current systems and should include interviews with users of data to determine the types of systems required and the expectations users have for these systems. The interviews we conducted identified concerns about ease of access to data, timeliness and accuracy of data, and the ability to link systems (for example, to tie the registration system to the personnel data base to ensure that courses completed became part of the employee's permanent personnel record). Our goal was to work toward creating data bases that could be integrated and drawn on as needed to answer questions and perform tasks.

Summary

This resource outlined administrative functions that support a training department, including staffing, professional development, planning, communications, budgeting and financial tracking, training effectiveness measures, registration, instructional technology consulting, and data systems development and operations. The key to successful training administration, as with most jobs, is responsiveness to the needs of multiple clients—in this case, the training director and managers of training development and delivery.

In addition, training administration must be cost-effective, which means that training administrative functions should be limited only to what is necessary. Moreover, managers responsible for training development and delivery should be involved in administrative processes as long as they are not burdened to such a degree that they cannot get their jobs done. Administrative managers should be largely coordinators, so that administrative work, such as planning, is done by the managers who need the output. Following this approach should help limit unit training costs and enhance the value of training administration.

Finally, training administration should be positioned as a resource to all relevant clients within the training department. The administrative staff should be apprised of their responsibility to be responsive to client needs. The training director should recognize that his or her subordinates on the administrative staff must balance needs of multiple clients and should obtain a performance review from them as input for evaluating the performance of the staff.

Resource B

Premier Training Programs: How IBM and Motorola Do It

This resource describes how two major companies, Motorola and IBM, operate their employee training units. This information is valuable for serveral reasons. These firms are known for their excellent training opportunities, so how they develop and deliver training is important to other companies in the same industries as well as to firms in different industries. Of course, the approaches of these two companies are shaped by their specific needs—needs that may not apply to other organizations.

Different published sources provided the information on Motorola and IBM (which was collected and coordinated by Barbara Bell and Nina Barbato). Since much has been written about their training efforts, these firms provide a good example of the types of comparative data that are readily available for training managers who are willing to compile data from different sources. The cases are vignettes of recent major developments and trends in the two companies.

Training at Motorola

Expense and Force Budget

Motorola spent about $44 million on training in 1988—about 2.5 percent of its annual payroll and 1 percent of sales (Gray,

1988; Therrien, 1988). The figure jumps to $90 million when employee wages and benefits are included along with training expenses. In terms of training staff, about eight hundred employees have full-time training duties throughout Motorola (Doyle, 1986) and call on about three hundred and sixty subject matter experts for advice on training directions and content. The firm purchases services from about two hundred training vendors.

Amount of Training

Motorola has about ninety-six thousand employees (Therrien, 1988; "The *Fortune* 500," 1988), and the company provides each employee with about three and a half to five days of training per year (Brody, 1987; Wagel, 1986).

Organization Structure and Training Content

The company operates the Motorola Training and Education Center (MTEC)—a centralized headquarters training facility. (See the description in Chapter Three of the center.) As one Motorola employee in computer systems stated:

> [Employees] can take courses on almost any topic at the center. There's training in management, engineering, manufacturing, marketing, and sales, among other subjects. There's also a wealth of data processing here. The majority of the courses are mainframe-based, ranging from applications to specific products. . . . We're moving into the PC arena soon, with the opening of the "electronic library" at the center, as well. [Galazan, 1986, p. 43]

Motorola's vice-president and director of training and education, A. W. Wiggenhorn, described the intended quality of Motorola's programs as follows:

> All MTEC programs are benchmarked against the best performers in the world. They are designed to build

> the specific knowledge, behavior, and skills that have proved to make the difference between average performance and real success on the job. [Wagel, 1986, p. 5]

In addition to the centralized training facility, each major business unit (communications, semiconductors, automotive/electronics, government electronics, and information systems) has its own training department that determines its training needs and develops and delivers training programs (Galazan, 1986).

On a corporatewide level, the firm's chief operating officer works with an advisory board to decide on training priorities. Training is then designed and delivered by the Training and Education Center or by the business units. Some training is purchased from vendors and outside institutions such as colleges. Business units are under no obligation to use the Training and Education Center, thereby encouraging the center to be competitive in its pricing and responsiveness to business unit needs. One of the training courses teaches managers how to develop competitive benchmarks against which they can measure the performance of their departments. Motorola publishes a monthly newsletter, *Opportunities,* which informs employees about training programs and services throughout the company.

Motorola's management institutes are two-week forums designed to educate engineering, sales, manufacturing, and operations managers in the concepts and strategies necessary to support the company's goals. Sessions during the forum focus on the key elements of world-class manufacturing competition. Managers are encouraged to apply a proactive management style that takes a "big picture," "macro" systems approach emphasizing cost, resource efficiency, quality, delivery, and flexibility.

The corporate training facility is the Galvin Center for Continuing Education in Schaumburg, Illinois, a two-story, 88,000-square-foot facility that can handle 556 students at once. It has thirteen classrooms, twenty-eight break-out rooms, and a 180-seat auditorium. It houses several major training laboratories, including a personal computer lab, a computer-aided design and manufacturing lab, a robotics lab, and a semiconductor development systems lab. There is also a satellite earth communications station and an advanced audiovisual system. The corporate training center also uses classrooms at several community colleges in Phoenix, Arizona.

Training at IBM

Budget

IBM's training budget is more than $1 billion per year—larger than the annual budget of Harvard University (Sellers, 1988). The cost of training is actually about twice as much when student salaries, travel, and lodging associated with attending training are considered. About 52 percent of IBM's training is directed to IBM's customers. Thus, IBM spends about $500 million per year in training its 389,348 employees ("The *Fortune* 500," 1988; Galagan, 1989).

Amount of Training

IBM provides about four million student days per year for employees, averaging slightly less than ten days per employee per year. About 30 percent of IBM's student days are in self-paced learning, much of which is computer based. IBM's goal is to drive down the cost of training while increasing its effectiveness. Advanced technology training methods are the key.

Organization Structure and Training Content

Management Training. IBM has several central training facilities; its management training center is located in Armonk, New York, near its corporate headquarters. The center is part of the firm's Personnel Department. IBM has thirty-seven thousand first-line managers, fourteen thousand middle managers, and sixteen hundred executives. The typical IBM manager receives about forty hours of management training per year.

The management development center provides a series of developmental experiences for managers as they move up in the organizational hierarchy. New first-level managers attend a one-week "New Managers' School" within thirty days of their appointment. Self-study courses and other management training are used as managers gain more experience. Experienced managers attend a one-week management school every few years. Topics covered with lower-level managers include techniques of management; higher-level managers focus on decision-making skills. High-potential middle managers—those on an "executive resource list"—attend a three-week advanced management school focusing on the external forces affecting the company.

Every three years, IBM designs a new three-week program for its executives—for example, a class at the Armonk center, an outside leadership program at a university such as Harvard, a public affairs program at the Brookings Institution, or a humanities program at the Aspen Institute. The Management Center at Armonk is staffed by top-performing functional managers who are assigned to the center for a two-year job rotation (Braham, 1987).

Functional Training. IBM recently reorganized its training unit, consisting of many independent training departments, to include a strong central education staff to provide common programs and to ensure that training matches corporate strategies as well as the needs of IBM's lines of business (Galagan, 1989). This new system helps control training quality and limit the cost of training by sharing resources and providing more self-paced training.

IBM's training staffs are split into two major groups, IBM U.S., with its own vice-president of education, and IBM World Trade, which includes education departments servicing the four world territories, the Americas Group, Asian-Pacific, Africa and the Far East, and Europe. A small corporate headquarters staff includes a corporate strategy and programs director group to coordinate training among IBM organizations. Four types of training groups report to IBM's U.S. Education Department, including customer executive education (providing overviews of IBM's products and services to executives of major customers), industry education (educating customers on applications of IBM's products), management development (described above), and twenty-six training groups in IBM's plants and laboratories.

IBM has a large educational facility outside Atlanta, Georgia. One of the programs offered is sales education for employees from a variety of functional disciplines, with emphasis on increasing sensitivity to the firm's product line and awareness of competition in the marketplace. Courses in the program cover finance, marketing, and an overview of the company's major product lines. The classes are competitive, and tests are administered throughout the nineteen-day program. One exercise in the class is to prepare and present an executive briefing on a product or service.

More than 40 percent of IBM's education for its service technicians (those who install and maintain computer equipment) is provided by interactive computer systems, thus eliminating the need for travel and keeping customer engineers in branch offices ready to respond to customer calls. The service education center in Atlanta includes a state-of-the-art media center and video production studio for creating sophisticated instruction materials, from video- and audiotapes to interactive, computer-based training programs.

The company's technical education organization has major centers in Belgium and New York, which are responsible for technical information transfer and curriculum development for manufacturing and development engineers, scientists, programmers, product planners, and technical managers. IBM's International Finance, Planning, and Administration schools in Belgium, New York, and Hong Kong provide functional and business management education to finance and planning employees. The Information Systems Education Facility in Dallas and worldwide regional education centers provide a broad range of entry-level through advanced training for programmers, computer operators, telecommunications personnel, and information systems managers.

Advanced Training Methods. IBM uses a mix of training methods (Conference Board, 1985). By 1990 the firm hopes that 50 percent of its instruction will be computer-based, 10 percent will be delivered by satellite, and 40 percent will be instructor-led. The company started its satellite broadcast network in 1985 to deliver technical courses on such subjects as operating systems, office systems, and data-base management ("IBM's Video Education Network," 1987). In 1988 it had two hundred and fifty downlinks reaching sales, marketing, and technical personnel at about three hundred field offices and marketing centers. The network broadcasts more than six hours of training programs daily, with programs lasting from one to five days. In 1987 about half of the total twenty-two thousand plus participants in the satellite training programs were customers, and the company plans to provide this training directly at customer locations.

In addition to video broadcasts of product announcements and updates, IBM's Interactive Satellite Education Network (ISEN) offers programs delivered by instructors at eight broadcast sites to fourteen classroom sites around the country. Using PC teletraining technology, each student has the capability of communicating with the instructor and seeing computer-generated graphics. Classrooms are equipped with video display and student response units (one for every two students). The instructor can broadcast from IBM's Technical Training Center in Thornwood, New York. The studio classroom is manned by a production technician who has remote control over cameras in the classroom, including an overhead camera to show visuals prepared by the instructor. The student response units allow the instructor to ask questions of all students who respond with a yes or no or with a number on a scale. The computer instantly computes and displays the distribution of responses, allowing the instructor to determine the students' understanding of the material as the class progresses. Also, students at remote sites can interrupt the instructor to ask questions. Test scores indicate that student comprehension is as good or better with satellite courses as with an instructor present in the classroom.

IBM has another internal training network for R&D labs and for plants (Shaw, 1988). In 1988 this network ran eighty to one hundred classes, and more than ten thousand employees attended. Several of the company's education facilities have advanced technology classrooms (ATCs) that allow an instructor to orchestrate presentation media (such as PC graphics, audio- and videotape, and video disk) and to respond to student questions (using a hand-held remote control device or a podium with a built-in, touch-sensitive panel). Students respond to the instructor's questions using individual electronic keypads. The microcomputer system immediately tabulates all student responses, displays a graph of responses, and compares these to responses of previous classes. This information increases student attention, promotes learning, and helps program developers examine responses and revise courses for more effective learning.

IBM's InfoWindow program uses interactive video disks for self-directed learning. Computer equipment includes touch-sensitive screens, graphic overlays, and simulations and makes education available at the student's convenience. The company's Discover/Education courseware delivers self-study product training to customers directly on their IBM systems.

Cost Comparisons. The justification for increasing the use of advanced technology to deliver education came from a detailed cost study (Galagan, 1989). In general, IBM discovered that it costs an average of $350 a day to train each student using a central classroom at one of the education institutes. More than half the cost is for transportation and living expenses. Classroom training at IBM plant sites around the world costs an average of $150 a day for each student. Courses carried by satellite from a central classroom to distant sites around the U.S. cost roughly $125 a day per student. Self-study, whether computer, video, or print based, costs $175 a day.

Using more advanced delivery techniques, IBM produced 13 percent more education in 1987 at a 6 percent lower cost per student day, according to Barry Arnett, an IBM training manager (Arnett, 1988). The company is building a satellite training network in Japan that will save a billion yen per year by reducing the costs of travel and lodging. (Other aspects of IBM's approach to education are covered elsewhere in this book.)

Resource C

Choosing the Best Training Evaluation Methods

This resource examines measurements that vary in degree of objectivity and research designs that vary in degree of rigor (the extent to which they accurately account for the effects of training). The purpose is not to encourage the most rigorous research design at all times. Rather, the goal is to help researchers choose evaluation methods that meet the needs of the situation (that is, take into account practical considerations about time availability, ease of measurement, and how important it is to isolate the effects of a particular program). Also, the purpose is to help the sponsor of the research understand the limitations of the measurement and research design.

Levels of Measurement

Several types of measures are possible:

- Satisfaction with the training
- A test of knowledge or skills acquired during training
- A demonstration of behaviors learned in training
- Performance on the job
- Department or organizational effectiveness.

The more distant the measure is from the time of the training and from the concepts taught in the training, the more difficult it is to attribute the performance measure to the effects of training. The most important measures (from the standpoint of the performance of the organization) will be affected by more extraneous factors than will measures that are closely tied to the training in time and concept. Nevertheless, the goal of training evaluation is to determine the effects of the training on outcome measures that are important to the operation of the organization.

Research designs try to isolate the confounding factors by holding extraneous variables constant in order to determine the pure effects of the training. Since this purity is difficult to accomplish, evaluation involves recognizing the potential confounds, given the practical limitations of the research.

Levels of Research Design

The following examples of research designs vary in the type and timing of measurement, the random assignment of employees (students) to groups, and the use of comparison and control groups. (In comparison groups, different training methods are employed from those used with the group being tested; comparison groups may not have students with equivalent experience and abilities. A control group is one in which training is withheld altogether, at least until the study is completed.)

These different research designs do not represent a pure continuum from the least to the most rigorous. Different combinations of design elements affect various threats to validity. For example, random assignment will help eliminate bias due to student differences; control groups help eliminate the effects of continuing job experiences (disregarding training as an explanation for training effects). The more control of possible confounds in the research design, the more valid (that is, the fewer threats to internal and external validity) the results will be.

Statistical Significance. Statistical tests should be applied to determine the significance of between-group differences. In addition to calculating statistical significance, researchers should calculate the proportion of variance due to a significant effect—that is, how much variation in the data is due to the effects of the training program. A difference in performance between two groups may be statistically significant because there is a greater difference between the groups than there is variation in scores within each group, given the particular sample size. However, the proportion of variation between groups relative to the total variation may not be very high. Stated another way, a large enough sample size may result in statistically significant differences between groups but not a very high proportion of variance accounted for. Proportion of variance is an indicator of the practical significance, or usefulness, of the effect.

Types of Research Designs

1. *Posttest* (no comparison groups, no random assignment, least rigorous)

Description: Measures are collected after the training and only for the group receiving training.

Example: The data in Exhibit 20 reflect posttraining results for all students taking a particular course during one quarter of the year. Multiple measures were used, including a satisfaction questionnaire, a test of training content, and a telephone survey of supervisors asking about improvement in job performance.

Information gained: The results suggest that the training was effective, although the training department and the students' supervisors would like to see more improvement in job performance. There is still some room for improvement in almost all the other measures, except that just about all supervisors plan to continue sending students to this class. This information, along with data on how many additional employees are eligible and how many supervisors can send from their groups at one time, will be helpful in planning future sessions.

Threats to validity: The results do not show whether another course or different course material would have been more effective. Also, although the supervisors note improvement in job performance, it is not known how much improvement there has been or whether the improvement will be maintained. Since these data are based on supervisors' perceptions, the supervisors may have been

Exhibit 20. Example of Posttraining Results from Posttest Research Design.

Course: Advanced Technician II	*Date*: Fourth Quarter
Number of sessions: 10	*Total number of students*: 150
Satisfaction Questionnaire	
	Percent Favorable
Overall course effectiveness	88.1
Overall instructor effectiveness	94.9
Recommend course to others	86.8
Training Performance Test Results	
	Percent Passing
	87.0
Supervisor Perceptions of Student Job Performance Following Training	
	Percent Favorable
Notices improvement in performance	70.2
Plans to send other employees	99.0

biased by the knowledge that the employees in question attended the class. Therefore, they may expect a change in performance, or possibly they assigned students to tasks that allowed them to demonstrate higher performance.

When to use: This research design is an excellent start for tracking the progress of a training program. The information can lead to insights on the training process and suggest ideas for improvement—as long as program administrators realize that the results may be influenced by multiple factors, including the training.

Comparing different groups as more people attend the course: Eventually, data can be compared at different points of time (for example, for the results of training at the end of each quarter over a two-year period). Sudden shifts in the data may be indicative of a change in the effects of the training. For instance, a new instructor may cause a dip in the instructor-satisfaction measure and the performance measures. Or a new work procedure may make the training less necessary, resulting in little change in performance after the training. Supervisors may consider the training less valuable over time, not because the course content is less applicable but because they are tired of the scheduling difficulties involved in sending employees to the program.

Collecting additional data: The possible causes of a particular finding need to be fleshed out by collecting explanatory data. When a problem seems evident, as judged by a change in the regular data, focus groups or one-on-one interviews may be held with former students and supervisors about the class and its usefulness on the job. The purpose of this supplementary analysis is to elicit likely explanations, thereby avoiding conclusions based on the numbers alone.

2. *Pretest, posttest* (no comparison group, no random assignment)

Description: In this design, data are collected from the students before they take the course and may be data about course expectations or a test of current knowledge or skills. The goal is to determine, more precisely than with a posttest measure alone, whether there was an improvement in performance and whether the class met the initial objectives.

Example: Consider the report shown in Exhibit 21, which is from the course described in the first example.

Information gained: Certainly, the data suggest that the training improved test performance. To some extent, the pretest scores were so low that some movement upward would not be difficult to achieve. The curriculum managers and supervisors would need to judge whether the posttest improvement is adequate and the extent to which instructors should strive for better performance in the future.

Exhibit 21. Example of Pretest Report.

Course: Advanced Technician II	*Date*: Fourth Quarter
Number of sessions: 10	*Total number of students*: 150
Average Pretest Performance	*Average Posttest Performance*
20% correct answers	85% correct answers

Threats to validity: Since employees were not selected randomly for the training, presumably those who needed it most were the ones chosen. However, the training may be more or less effective for other groups. As an example, consider fast learners who already have a solid basis of knowledge. Performance could be about the same if the instructors repeat information the students know already. However, performance could be higher if the instructors recognize the advanced level of the class and provide more in-depth information or more difficult problems as class examples. What would result from this approach is an empirical question that can be determined only with comparison groups.

When to use: Pre- and posttests are good ways to determine the qualifications of students entering the class and to calibrate the training content to the level of the students. In an action research paradigm, instructors would examine precourse tests and vary their teaching approach to meet students' needs. However, in other cases, instructors may try to maintain standard course content because of the need to ensure everyone has the same level of skill and knowledge when they leave the class, even if some students have the potential to learn more. Data across several groups (for example, the above data for one quarter) can be used to determine the skill levels of entering students and to change the standard course content if necessary.

As indicated above, the pre-post comparison is a useful indicator of whether the course content is acquired by students as intended. However, it remains unknown whether this performance might change further over time and whether students' knowledge at the start of the course might have been at a low level because of lack of opportunity to use the skills or knowledge on the job, in which case the course is really a refresher.

Multiple time-line data: One way to answer such questions is through multiple time-line data before and after the program, as shown in Exhibit 22, with alternative, comparable forms of the test.

These data show some decline in test scores from T_1 to the time of training a year later. Perhaps the employees in this student group had an earlier course that provided some information covered in the later course. Or perhaps the students had a chance to see some

Exhibit 22. Example of Multiple Time-Line Data.

Average Percent Correct Responses						
Time 1	$T_1 + 6$ *months*	$T_1 + 12$ *months*	$T_1 + 12$ *months*	$T_1 + 12$ *months*	$T_1 + 18$ *months*	$T_1 + 24$ *months*
28	22	20	Training	85	70	62

relevant skills demonstrated on the job. However, the early scores were not high, at least going back one year.

The posttraining scores indicate another decline in test scores, perhaps due to lack of use on the job because the work does not require use of the skill or perhaps because the technology changed somewhat.

3. *Pre- and posttests* (one or more comparison groups)

Description: This research design compares different types of training—for instance, using different training technologies all covering the same content with the same learning objectives. The goal is to compare the effectiveness of the different training methods or to compare which methods students prefer. Of course, random assignment of students to groups would help ensure that the training method influences the results, not that the results are influenced by students' backgrounds, skill levels, or aptitude for, or interest in, different training methods.

Example: Suppose a study compares three different types of training: instructor-led classes; instructor-led classes combined with video demonstration; self-paced, computer-programmed instruction without the video; and self-paced, computer-programmed instruction with the video. Consider the possible results shown in Exhibit 23.

Information gained: The data indicate that all four programs increased test performance. The self-paced CBT with video resulted in the highest scores. Statistical tests would be necessary to determine whether the 92 percent average score for CBT plus video is significantly higher than the other groups. Additional comparison groups would be necessary to determine the effects of video

Exhibit 23. Possible Results of Comparison of Pre- and Posttraining Assessment.

Training Methods	*Test Performance Percent Correct Responses*	
	Pretraining	*Posttraining*
Instructor-led	20	72
Instructor-led combined with video demonstration	22	75
Self-paced, computer-programmed instruction without video	21	80
Self-paced, computer-programmed instruction with video	23	92

alone. Other groups could be added to examine the effects of alternative ordering of training modules in the program (for example, introducing video early in the training or at the end).

A study using a similar research design to compare alternative training technologies was conducted by Chute, Bruning, and Hulick (1984, cited in Chute, Balthazar, and Poston, 1988) (as described in Chapter Two).

Threats to validity: The study does not take into account possible differences due to the amount of time spent in training. Employees using the self-paced package can review the material as long as they want and see the videotape several times if they desire. Controlled conditions could be imposed to ensure that all students followed the self-paced training in a standardized order and length of time. However, then the advantage of the flexibility of self-paced training to meet students' needs is lost. Flexible use could be compared to structured timing to examine differences in learning. Thus, once a threat to validity has been identified, it is possible to design a study to hold it constant or to vary it to study its effects.

When to use: Comparison group designs are an excellent way to demonstrate the impact of alternative training methods. However, each alternative procedure compared adds a number of possible confounds to the design (for instance, effects of different ordering of information presented to students, effects of different lengths of time available for learning, effects of instructor style when multiple instructors are involved).

4. *Pre- and posttests* (comparison and control groups with random assignment)

Description: This is one of the most comprehensive research designs because it provides evidence of change due to training as compared with control groups not receiving the training. One control group can be measured twice, with the same interval between measurements as the groups receiving training. Another control group can be measured once. Comparing these two control groups tells whether early measurement affects later test scores independent of the training (that is, practice effects).

There is still the possibility that pretesting may sensitize students to what is important in the training and thereby interact with the training. Therefore, a group trained but receiving no pretest would be necessary as well to compare to those groups trained and receiving pretests. Once again, random assignment of students to groups ensures that students with certain levels of ability or interest are not systematically placed together in certain groups.

Example: The example shown in Exhibit 24 has four comparison groups and two control groups. The data are arranged to best demonstrate the design of the study.

Information gained: These results suggest a possible sensitizing effect from the pretest, with higher posttraining test scores for groups that were tested earlier than those that were not. Also, there may be a practice effect in that the control group, which was tested twice, improved the second time. Consequently, some of the improvement in the training groups' performance is due to the early testing. (It is assumed that alternative forms of the test have been determined in pilot testing to be equivalent in difficulty and coverage of the topic.)

Threats to validity: Time devoted to instruction may vary for the two training groups. Also, the video may raise issues for class discussion that are not brought up in the instructor-led-only training. This would represent an interaction between the effects of video and the instructor-led format that could be tested by a control group using the video alone.

Another, less systematic test would be a follow-up study consisting of interviews with students about the class and video or an observation study. Interviews and observations add a number of

Exhibit 24. Example of Four Comparison and Two Control Groups.

Average Pretest Performance	*Training*	*Average Posttest Performance*
22%	Instructor-led	78%
24%	Instructor-led plus video	85%
(no pretest)	Instructor-led	68%
(no pretest)	Instructor-led plus video	76%
22%	Control group (no training)	35%
(no test)	Control group (no training)	21%

potential confounds, such as the student's desire to impress the interviewer or observer, that may influence the validity of the data. However, the goal here is not to isolate these effects but to obtain some additional information that will suggest reasons for the results in the main study, not determine conclusively what caused a particular finding.

This study, as well as the one in Exhibit 23, does not speak to the external validity of the data. That is, will the results carry over into job performance? Follow-up data on job performance are necessary, and follow-up testing would be useful to determine the lasting effects of the training on the skills and knowledge acquired. Here, again, control groups with no training would be necessary to determine whether skills and knowledge are acquired on the job and not related to the training.

When to use: This research design provides incremental information beyond that available from the previously described designs. Control groups are usually not difficult to obtain, since cooperation must be gained only for taking the test. Control group participants can be given the training at a later time to ensure that all employees benefit from the training.

Random assignment may be difficult to accomplish because of scheduling difficulties and supervisors' needs to control their own subordinates' assignments to training. However, random assignment can be made a routine part of the training evaluation, and supervisors can be led to expect the process when a new program is being introduced.

Sample size: In all the above examples, it is important to ensure an adequate sample size so that the study has sufficient power to demonstrate reliable effects. There are ways to calculate the sample size for a certain level of power; however, researchers will often have to take what they can get in terms of participation. (See a standard statistics text such as Cohen and Cohen [1975] or Winer [1971] for such tests.)

The constraints of the class will determine class size. A study should include multiple classes, each of which follows a standardized process as much as possible. Self-paced training is a matter of including enough students, each of whom works independently.

A good rule of thumb about sample size is to have five to ten times the number of variables and measures in the design. In the last example, there are pre- and posttests times six groups (or twelve different variables—including the no-pretest groups in this count). This would be a total of about sixty to one hundred twenty people (ten to twenty within each group). It is a good idea to have about the same number of students within each group to ensure equally reliable data across the study. However, statistical tests can take group sample size differences into account. (For more information on training evaluation, see Phillips [1982] and Kearsley [1982].)

Resource D

Designing Career Plans for Training Professionals

What follows is a sample career planning guide for employees of one organization's training department, here called the Training and Development Resource Center (TDRC). This document provides suggestions that can help training professionals formulate similar career plans and, more specifically, it

- Clarifies the meaning of development
- Outlines the skills and knowledge that different jobs in TDRC help develop
- Suggests possible career directions within and outside of TDRC
- Includes a question-and-answer sheet on TDRC staffing policies and expectations.

The career planning form (Exhibit 25) should be completed by all employees. The career planning guide is based on the following assumptions:

- Experiences within TDRC enhance your knowledge and skills.
- The knowledge and skills acquired from a TDRC experience are marketable.

Exhibit 25. Career Planning Form.

Name: ______________________ Social Security number: ________
Current position: ____________ Time in position: ________ months
Supervisor: ____________________________________

Use additional pages if necessary to answer the following questions. Please attach your résumé to this form.

Recommended developmental actions (training courses, job experiences, supervisory training, and so on):

Career plan (next job options—list department, line or staff position, headquarters or regional assignment, organizational level, work function, and target date for move, and include up to three possibilities):

Mobility (indicate willingness to relocate, desired locations, time availability, and any restrictions on movement to another city):

Long-term career goals (indicate work functions and organizational level you aspire to five years from now):

General comments:

Employee's signature: ____________________________ *Date*: ________
Supervisor's signature: ____________________________ *Date*: ________

- TDRC encourages job movement to enhance employee development, maintain vitality in the training department, and instill an appreciation of expertise in training within the line organization.

Development has both short-term and long-term implications. In the short term, development refers to acquiring the knowledge and skills to do your current job better. This may mean correcting weaknesses, enhancing strengths, or acquiring new abilities—for example, by attending training classes or taking on different or special job experiences or tasks. Or development may mean fine-tuning your technical skills.

In the long-term, development refers to preparing to make a contribution to the company in the future. Long-term development implies preparing for a job change—within the same department or to a different department, at the same level or at a higher level.

In the short and long term, development may be focused on improving technical skills or improving managerial and leadership skills. The direction of development will depend on your needs, as determined by you and your supervisor.

Recording Development Plans

The performance appraisal form completed each year by your supervisor has a space asking for your development plans. The response generally depends on the results of the performance appraisal. If the appraisal indicates low performance, then movement to a different job or remedial training may be indicated. If the appraisal indicates average performance, development plans may suggest new and different job experiences or advanced training to enhance current job performance.

If the appraisal indicates that you are exceeding expectations or have outstanding performance, then development plans may focus on ways to increase job challenge and maximize your accomplishments. This may be through a new or expanded job assignment, possibly (although not necessarily) a job at a higher level.

The career planning form should be an extension of the development information on the performance appraisal form. The career planning form asks you and your supervisor to agree on

- *Recommended developmental actions* (training courses and job experiences that enhance your marketability for other jobs)
- *Your next job options* (with space to list up to three possible next jobs in terms of the department, line or staff, headquarters

or region, level, work function, and target date for the job change)
- *Your mobility* (whether you are willing to relocate to a different geographic location, when you would be willing to move, and any restrictions you have)
- *Possible time lines* (indicating work functions for one or more possible career paths one to four years from now)
- *General comments* you or your supervisor might want to add
- *Your signature* and *your boss's signature* (indicating that you both agree with the plan)
- *Your résumé.*

Uses of the Career Planning Form

The form should be a guide for you and your supervisor to indicate when you should take various classes and when you should prepare for a job change.

Data from the forms will be available to the training director and training managers to calibrate the degree of turnover planned for the organization as a whole and to evaluate whether managers are acting on their commitments to develop their subordinates. All information provided will be treated as confidential, and summary reports of plans across employees will be prepared without divulging individual plans.

Skills Developed in the Training Department

This section considers skills that may be developed from some of the major positions within TDRC. While reading this section, think about the skills developed in your particular job. *Instructor positions* are especially valuable for

- Building self-confidence
- Sharpening verbal and interpersonal skills
- Influencing group dynamics (controlling and managing a group)
- Dealing with interpersonal conflicts
- Presenting ideas coherently

- Being a good listener
- Being a role model for students (demonstrating the technical know-how and interpersonal ability needed for effective working relationships and customer interface).

Course developer positions are especially valuable for

- Learning project management skills
- Learning negotiation skills (negotiating with either external or internal supplier or customer groups)
- Managing relationships
- Communicating effectively (both orally and in writing)
- Being creative and resourceful
- Delivering a product on time
- Increasing depth of knowledge and resourcefulness (by focusing intensely on specific technologies).

Instructional technologist (IT) positions are valuable for

- Learning how to apply IT skills to technical disciplines
- Applying educational techniques to real business needs
- Gaining operational and business experience
- Becoming acquainted with the firm's products and services
- Developing and refining new training technologies (CBT, PC teletraining, and video for use in training and job aids)
- Convincing others about the value of IT techniques
- Applying evaluation methods and communicating the results to enhance organizational performance.

Other types of positions within TDRC include:

- Educational consultant
- Course registrar and counselor
- Quality consultant
- Administrative support
- Clerical support
- Site manager
- Delivery manager
- Curriculum manager

Some of the skills listed for the instructor, course developer, and instructional technologist apply to many TDRC job functions. However, other skills and knowledge may apply as well, such as

- Learning methods for needs analysis, planning, and counseling
- Learning to match the requirements of the customer with the resources of the training organization
- Applying quality principles (such as, the customer comes first, quality improvement never ends, problems may be prevented through planning, all work is part of a process, and quality happens through people)
- Learning facilitation and team-building skills
- Improving customer interface skills
- Applying business skills and knowledge (such as finance, strategic planning, people management, staffing, coordination, delegation, supervision, prioritizing, and project tracking)
- Expanded knowledge in technical areas.

Career Options and Timing of Assignments

An assignment within TDRC is generally rotational, especially for instructors, course developers, educational consultants, delivery managers, site managers, and curriculum managers. These positions require a background in line or subject matter expert positions.

A single assignment within TDRC may last two to three years, after which the person moves back to his or her home department or to a position in another department. If a person moves between disciplines within TDRC (for example, moving from teaching technical design courses to teaching advanced products courses), or between functions (for example, moving from instructor to course developer), he or she may stay in TDRC for four to six years.

TDRC wants the best people, and so the sending organization often wants these people back. However, the skills developed from assignments within TDRC prepare the individual for a number of career options.

Career Options

Consider the following examples of career options:

1. One immediate career option might be a second job within TDRC, probably at the same level. For instance, a course developer might move to another course developer job in a different discipline, or an instructor might move to a course developer's job.
2. Instructors and course developers are likely to return to field positions or subject matter expert staff positions, because these positions are usually the sending organizations, and a buy-back agreement usually is arranged before the individual enters TDRC. However, as suggested in number 1, movement within TDRC can prepare the person for a job in another part of the firm.
3. Educational consultants and quality consultants are also likely to move back to their home departments.
4. Instructional technologists may have opportunities to move into other training organizations in the organization. Their TDRC assignment may prepare them for a more responsible position, perhaps in another training department in the firm (for instance, sales training) or in the human resource department.
5. A TDRC assignment may prepare an individual for a job in marketing (a technical consultant's position requiring product knowledge and customer interface skills) or an assignment in human resources (a job requiring people skills or an understanding of the business and of corporate strategy).
6. An experienced, high-potential instructor or program developer may receive the polish needed for promotion to the line or field or, possibly, for a promotion within TDRC. Instructor and developer positions provide opportunities for visibility to higher management and give the individual a chance to demonstrate outstanding performance and the potential to perform well at a higher level.

Consider the following possible career paths (Figure 5):

Figure 5. Possible Career Paths.

1. High-potential technician → instructor → course developer → field staff or line position

2. First-level employee → course developer / subject matter expert → program developer in new discipline → headquarters subject matter expert

3. Line manager → instructor → educational consultant → site manager → line manager

4. Recent IT graduate (in TDRC) → program developer (in TDRC) → instructor → trainer/consultant (sales training department)

5. Personnel staff manager → instructor (teaching customer interface skills) → staff supervisor (sales branch office) → sales account executive

6. High-potential line manager → training site manager (in TDRC) → curriculum manager (on important new data services project) → manager (in data services organization)

Need for Planning

Figure 5 shows *possible* career paths that may occur because the individual and management realize the value of skills developed.

Some jobs are more "migratable" than others—that is, a similar job may exist in another department, making the overlap in skills obvious and increasing the individual's apparent ability to do the job. Other positions are less migratable. Skills developed may be relevant to other positions, but the positions may involve different job functions.

For instance, technical expertise and communications skills may be similar in instructor and sales consultant positions. However, managers of sales consultants in the marketing department are unlikely to look for former instructors from the technical training department to fill sales consultant jobs. (They may look to the sales training department, however, for candidates.) Nevertheless, the technical instructor considering a marketing position can prepare for a sales consultant position by taking marketing courses and applying for sales consultant positions in the company.

Career planning is important in preparing for one or more career options. Also, because of the critical skills developed in TDRC, TDRC employees should consider a broad array of career options within training and from training to other organizations within and outside of the firm.

Mobility

Geographic territory and ability to relocate can be a barrier to some career options. For instance, training sites may not be located near course development offices. Instructional technologists may be located in two training sites but not at the firm's corporate headquarters location in another state, thereby limiting opportunities for visibility of instructional technologists, thus requiring them to relocate for a corporate headquarters job (assuming they want to move into a position other than IT).

Some people may wish to consider the possibility of relocation to expand career options. Others may wish to take advantage of the diversity of opportunities available in or around their current locations. Returning to your previous organization may be perfectly desirable after a stint in the training department. On the other hand, many company locations offer considerable variety of opportunity within different departments. You will have to exercise your initiative to identify these opportunities.

Supervisor Support

Managers have several key roles in helping subordinates develop and carry out career plans; among other things, supervisors

- Foster self-confidence by creating opportunities for achievement and by rewarding good performance
- Enhance insight by
  - providing performance feedback
  - coaching and advising subordinates how to improve their performance and seek new opportunities
  - sharing information about organizational events, policies, and job possibilities.
- Encourage commitment to the job, department, and company as a whole by
  - supporting professional growth through training and new job experiences
  - encouraging job movement and, when appropriate, encouraging advancement.

Supervisors are able to attract the best people to their groups when they develop a reputation of sending the best people to other departments and when high-potential job candidates know they will be developed if they enter the department.

Career Planning Sessions

Supervisors should meet with each subordinate to discuss the subordinate's career plans. Supervisors should be a sounding board for the feasibility of the subordinate's career ambitions, which means

- Providing accurate information about job opportunities and the direction of the business
- Providing direct and honest feedback about the subordinate's potential.

The focus of the career-planning session should be on the

- Subordinate's need for development, given the direction the firm is taking
- The skills needed to take advantage of opportunities within the firm
- The subordinate's strengths and weaknesses in relation to realistic career directions
- The subordinate's career interests and ambitions.

Questions and Answers

Does career planning mean I have to change jobs?

No. Career planning, at least in the short run, can focus on development needed to improve job performance and can ensure that you are prepared to do the job well in the future (given expected changes in technology and the business). However, when you think about the long term (two to five years out), you should be thinking about your next job. If you have been in your job for more than three years, you should definitely be thinking about your next assignment.

Suppose I like training. Do I have to move out of TDRC?

Training supports this firm's business. We do not make revenue directly on training our employees (although we recognize that training makes our firm more competitive). Therefore, a majority of TDRC employees are on rotational assignments and will return to line or staff assignments in their sending departments or will move to jobs in other departments, as the above examples of possible career paths indicate. Some employees may stay in TDRC longer because they are training professionals (for example, instructional technologists). However, even for these individuals, job movement is necessary for new challenges and for better advancement opportunities.

What type of people does TDRC want?

TDRC wants to attact the best people in their fields, which means people who are competent in technical and managerial skills and, for instructor positions, people who can be role models for students. TDRC must develop a reputation as a developer of people. Good people come to the training department because they grow professionally, and when they leave, they move into more challenging, exciting jobs, sometimes at higher levels.

Are there opportunities for high-potential managers in training?

Yes. TDRC has key jobs in all positions, including expert instructors who are called on to deliver special programs to executives and course developers who contribute to defining strategic products and services. Instructional technologists, who convince clients and course developers to apply leading-edge technology, and educational consultants, who help clients develop training plans to match their department's business strategies, are also in critical positions. In addition, special TDRC work groups, often in conjunction with field organizations, provide important and visible job opportunities. Examples include a work group to develop operational indicators of training effectiveness and another to implement solutions to increase training in the company.

Are there promotional opportunities within training?

Yes, there are some. Last year there were instances of instructors and course developers promoted to training management assignments. TDRC wants to encourage promotional opportunities from training into other departments. Most departments within this company try to do the same. Professional development and organizational vitality come from developing people and generating opportunities for them in other units rather than from promotions within narrow disciplines. There will still be promotions within training. However, these individuals will have to demonstrate broader technical skills, general managerial skills, and competitiveness comparable to high-potential employees in other departments.

What if my boss isn't interested in my career plans?

Supervisors who are not interested in their subordinates' career plans are not doing their jobs. All TDRC supervisors are expected to develop career plans with each of their subordinates. However, career planning and carrying out those plans are primarily your responsibility. Supervisors should provide the resources (opportunities for training and professional development), but it is up to you to take advantage of them.

How far out should I plan my career, and how specific should my career plans be?

Of course, the farther out you go, the more difficult it is to specify the type of position you want, let alone the exact job. In general, career options should include general career directions or job "families," not specific job assignments. The more specific you are in planning your next assignments, the less the particular jobs are likely to be available to you when you want them. On the other hand, planning for a position in a job family makes more sense because it provides flexibility and direction in preparing for the future.

You should plan several career paths and evaluate them for feasibility and differences in the training required. It may be that several different paths require very similar preparation. This will give you maximum flexibility to accomplish your career goals while accommodating the needs of the business.

In addition, you should plan for the short term (the next two years) and the long term (three to five years out). Short-term planning should include training plans and job experiences for increasing your current performance, correcting weaknesses, and enhancing strengths and might also include alternative job moves, especially if you have been in your current assignment for several years. Long-term planning should include alternative career plans, specifying logical sequences of job families and organizational levels.

What happens after I write a career plan?

Writing a career plan is just the start of development. Carrying out a career plan requires commitment on the part of the subordinate and the supervisor. The subordinate must be willing to undertake the training and job experiences specified in the career plan. The supervisor must help by providing the time, resources, encouragement, and contacts to help make this happen. Furthermore, career planning is not a one-time event. You must revise your career plans periodically (at least once a year and perhaps every six months) based on your interests, your progress, and the opportunities available to you.

References

Ackoff, R. *Creating the Corporate Future.* New York: Wiley, 1981.

"Adult Learning Needs." *Performance and Instruction,* 1988 (Feb.), 49.

American Society for Training and Development. *Consortium Study of Corporate Training.* Alexandria, Va.: American Society for Training and Development, 1986.

American Society for Training and Development. *Gaining the Competitive Edge.* Alexandria, Va.: American Society for Training and Development, 1988.

Arnett, B. Unpublished presentation at AT&T's Learning Link Conference, Holmdel, N.J., Oct. 5, 1988.

Ballman, G. *Training/HRD Department Audit Kit* (Special version for respondents to the 1987 U.S. Training Industry Survey). Minneapolis: Lakewood Research, 1987.

Bernhard, H. B., and Ingols, C. A. "Six Lessons for the Corporate Classroom." *Harvard Business Review,* 1988 (Sept.-Oct.), 40–47.

Blacker, F., and Brown, C. "Evaluation and the Impact of Information Technologies on People in Organizations." *Human Relations, 38,* 213–231.

Boudreau, J. W. "Economic Considerations in Estimating the Utility of Human Resource Productivity Improvement Programs." *Personnel Psychology,* 1983, *36,* 551–576.

Bove, R. "Retraining the Older Worker." *Training and Development Journal,* 1987 (Mar.), 77-78.

Brachman, R. J., and Henig, F. H. "The Emergence of Artificial Intelligence Technology." *AT&T Technical Journal,* 1988, *67* (1), 3-6.

Braham, J. "Cultivating Tomorrow's Execs." *Industry Week,* July 27, 1987, pp. 34-38.

Brody, M. "Helping Workers to Work Smarter." *Fortune,* June 8, 1987, pp. 86-88.

Buchanan, B., II. "Building Organizational Commitment: The Socialization of Managers in Work Organizations." *Administrative Science Quarterly,* 1974, *19* (4), 533-546.

Bureau of National Affairs. "Training Facts and Figures." *Bulletin to Management,* Washington, D.C.: Bureau of National Affairs, 1986.

Carnevale, A. P., Gainer, L. J., and Meltzer, A. S. *Workplace Basics: The Skills Employers Want.* Alexandria, Va.: American Society for Training and Development, 1988.

Carnevale, A. P., and Schulz, E. R. "Technical Training in America: How Much and Who." *Training and Development Journal,* 1988 (Nov.), 18-32.

Cascio, W. F. *Costing Human Resources.* New York: D. Van Nostrand, 1982.

Cascio, W. F., and Silbey, V. "Utility of the Assessment Center as a Selection Device." *Journal of Applied Psychology,* 1979, *64,* 107-118.

Casner-Lotto, J., and Associates. *Successful Training Strategies: Twenty-six Innovative Corporate Models.* San Francisco: Jossey-Bass, 1988.

Cheek, L. M. "Cost-Effectiveness Comes to the Personnel Function." *Harvard Business Review,* 1973 (May-June), 96-105.

Chmura, T. J., Henton, D. C., and Melville, J. G. "Corporate Education and Training: Investing in a Competitive Future." Report no. 753. Palo Alto, Calif.: SRI International, 1987.

Chute, A. G., Balthazar, L. B., and Poston, C. "Learning from Teletraining." *Journal of Distance Education,* 1988 (Oct.).

Chute, A. L., Bruning, K. K., and Hulick, M. K. *AT&T Communications National Teletraining Network: Applications, Benefits, and Costs.* Cincinnati, Ohio: AT&T Communications Sales and Marketing Education Center, 1984.

Cohen, J., and Cohen, P. *Applied Multiple Regression/Correlation Analysis for the Behavioral Sciences.* New York: Wiley, 1975.

Condon, M. "The Ins and Outs of Displacement." *Training and Development Journal,* 1984, *38* (2), 60–65.

Conference Board. "Trends in Corporate Education and Training." Report no. 870. New York: Conference Board, 1985.

Cook, T. D., and Campbell, D. T. "The Design and Conduct of Quasi-experiments and True Experiments in Field Settings." In M. D. Dunnette (ed.), *Handbook of Industrial and Organizational Psychology.* Skokie, Ill.: Rand McNally, 1976.

Cronshaw, S. F., and Alexander, R. A. "The Selection Utility Model as an Investment Decision: The Greening of Selection Utility." In *Proceedings* of the forty-third annual national meeting of the Academy of Management, Dallas, Texas, August 1983.

Cross, K. P. *Adults as Learners.* San Francisco: Jossey-Bass, 1981.

Cullen, J. G., Sawzin, S. A., Sisson, G. R., and Swanson, R. A. "Cost-Effectiveness: A Model for Assessing the Training Investment." *Training and Development Journal,* 1978, *32* (1), 24–29.

Cyert, R. M., and Mowery, D. C. *Technology and Employment: Innovation and Growth in the U.S. Economy.* Washington, D.C.: National Academy Press, 1987.

Datan, N., Rodeheaver, D., and Hughes, F. "Adult Development and Aging." *Annual Review of Psychology,* 1987, *38,* 153–180.

Deming, W. E. "Western Managers Must Make Drastic Changes." *Executive Excellence,* 1987 (Feb.), 1.

"Dislocated Workers." In *AFL-CIO Reviews the Issues.* Report no. 30. Washington, D.C.: AFL-CIO Economic Research Department, 1989.

Doyle, B. "Staying Ahead of Change—Motorola's Investment in Training." *Data Training,* 1986 (Oct.), 17.

Drake, Beam, Morin, Inc. Briefing on "Voluntary Windows for Early Retirement Incentives." New York: Drake, Beam, Morin, Inc., 1987.

Easterbrook, G. "Have You Driven a Ford Lately?" *Washington Monthly,* 1986 (Oct.).

Employment Training Panel. *Report to the Legislature, State of*

California. Sacramento, Calif.: Employment Training Panel, 1987.

Feuer, D. "Training Magazine's Industry Report 1988." *Training Magazine,* 1988 (Oct.), 31-34.

"The *Fortune* 500." *Fortune,* April 25, 1988, p. 41

Galagan, P. A. "IBM Gets Its Arms Around Education." *Training and Development Journal,* 1989 (Jan.), 35-41.

Galazan, P. "Focus on Results at Motorola." *Training and Development Journal,* 1986 (May), 43-47.

Gerber, B. "The Care and Feeding of Trainers." *Training,* 1988 (Aug.), 41-46.

Gill, M. J., and Meier, D. "Accelerated Learning Takes Off at Bell Atlantic." Washington, D.C.: Bell Atlantic, 1988.

Godkewitsch, M. "The Dollars and Sense." *Training,* 1987 (May), 79-81.

Goldstein, A. P., and Sorcher, M. *Changing Supervisory Behavior.* Elmsford, N.Y.: Pergamon Press, 1974.

Gordon, J. "Who Is Being Trained to Do What?" *Training Magazine,* 1988 (Oct.), 51-60.

Gordus, J., Gohrban, C., and Meiland, R. "Information Series Number 322." ERIC Clearinghouse on Adult Career and Vocational Education. Columbus: Ohio State University, 1987.

Graddick, M. M. "Corporate Philosophies of Employee Development." In M. London and E. M. Mone (eds.), *Career Growth and Human Resource Strategies.* New York: Quorum, 1988.

Gray, B. J. "Motorola's Workers Go Back to School." *Human Resource Executive,* 1988 (Nov.-Dec.), 32-34.

"Guidelines for the Hiring, Evaluation, and Management of Trainers." *Training Directors' Forum Newsletter,* 1988, *4* (9), 4.

Guzzo, R. A., Jette, R. D., and Katzell, R. A. "The Effects of Psychologically Based Intervention Programs on Worker Productivity: A Meta-Analysis." *Personnel Psychology,* 1985, *38,* 275-291.

Howard, R. *Brave New Workplace.* New York: Viking Penguin, 1985.

Hickey, J. V. "Brightening the Job Prospects of Displaced Workers: General Electric Company's Columbia, Maryland, Reemployment Center." Scarsdale, N.Y.: Work in America Institute, 1982.

Hunter, J. E., Schmidt, F. L., and Coggin, T. D. "Problems and Pitfalls in Using Capital Budgeting and Financial Accounting Techniques in Assessing the Utility of Personnel Programs." *Journal of Applied Psychology,* 1988, *73* (3), 522-528.

"IBM's Video Education Network: Lowering the Price of High Quality." *Uplink,* 1987 (Winter), 6-9.

Kane, E. J. "IBM's Quality Focus on the Business Process." *Quality Progress,* 1986 (Apr.), 24-33.

Kanter, R. M. *The Change Masters: Innovation for Productivity in the American Corporation.* New York: Simon & Schuster, 1983.

Kearsley, G. *Costs, Benefits and Productivity in Training Systems.* Reading, Mass.: Addison-Wesley, 1982.

Kenny, J. C. "HRD: Better Service Through Credentialing?" *Public Personnel Management,* 1986, *15* (4), 451-458.

Kirpatrick, D. "Four Steps to Measuring Training Effectiveness." *Personnel Administration,* 1983, *28* (11), 19-25.

Knowles, M. S. *The Adult Learner: A Neglected Species.* Houston, Tex.: Gulf, 1978.

Kolb, B. A. *Learning-style Inventory.* Boston: McBer, 1976.

Kolb, D. A., and Baker, R. J. "Personal Learning Guide: A Practical Guide to Increasing Your Learning from a Training Program Workshop." Dallas, Tex.: Richard J. Baker, n.d.

Komanecky, A. N. "Developing New Managers at GE." *Training and Development Journal,* 1988 (June), 62-64.

Latham, G. P. "Human Resource Training and Development." *Annual Review of Psychology,* 1988, *39,* 545-582.

Lee, B. "The GM-Toyota Team: Worker Harmony Makes Nummi Work." *New York Times,* Dec. 25, 1988, sec. 3, p. 2.

Lee, C. "Retraining America: Solutions or Sugar Pills?" 1983, *Training, 20* (5), 22-29.

Lee, C. "Certification for Trainers: Thumbs Up." *Training,* 1986, *23* (11), 56-64.

Lee, C. "Training Budgets: Neither Boom Nor Bust." *Training,* 1988, *25* (10), 41-46.

Lee, C., and Zemke, R. "How Long Does It Take?" *Training,* 1987 (June), 75-80.

Lewin, K. *Field Theory in Social Science.* New York: Harper & Row, 1951.

London, M. *Developing Managers: A Guide to Motivating and Preparing People for Successful Managerial Careers.* San Francisco: Jossey-Bass, 1985.

London, M. *Change Agents: New Roles and Innovation Strategies for Human Resource Professionals.* San Francisco: Jossey-Bass, 1988.

London, M., and Bassman, E. "Training and Retraining: Contributions to Career Growth, Continuous Learning and Organizational Strategy." In I. Goldstein (ed.), *Frontiers of Industrial and Organizational Psychology,* Vol. 3. San Francisco: Jossey-Bass, 1989.

London, M., and MacDuffie, J. P. "Implementing Technological Innovations: Case Examples and Guidelines for Practice." *Personnel,* 1987 (Nov.), 26-38.

London, M., and Mone, E. M. *Career Management and Survival in the Workplace: Helping Employees Make Tough Career Decisions, Stay Motivated, and Reduce Career Stress.* San Francisco: Jossey-Bass, 1987.

London, M., and Stumpf, S. A. *Managing Careers.* Reading, Mass.: Addison-Wesley, 1982.

Lorenzo, R. V. "A Computer-based Employee Skills Inventory System." In M. London (ed.), "The Role of the Industrial/ Organizational Psychologist in Business." *Journal of Managerial Psychology,* 1988, *3* (2), 5-9.

McCall, M. W., Jr., and Lombardo, M. M. "Looking Glass, Inc.: An Organizational Simulation." Technical report no. 12. Greensboro, N.C.: Center for Creative Leadership, 1978.

Madlin, N. "Computer-based Training Comes of Age." *Personnel,* 1987, *64* (11), 64-65.

Mandel, T. F. *Corporate Education and Training: Investing in a Competitive Edge.* Palo Alto, Calif.: SRI International, 1987.

Manz, C. C., and Sims, H. P., Jr. "Leading Workers to Lead Themselves: The External Leadership of Self-Managing Work Teams." *Administrative Science Quarterly,* 1987, *32* (1), 106-129.

Mervis, C. B., and Rosch, E. "Categorization of Natural Objects." *Annual Review of Psychology,* 1981, *32,* 89-115.

Morrison, M. "Work and Retirement in an Aging Society." *Dae-*

dalus, Journal of the American Academy of Arts and Sciences, 1986 (Winter), 269-294.

Mumford, M. D., Weeks, J. L., Harding, F. D., and Fleishman, E. A. "Relations Between Student Characteristics, Course Content, and Training Outcomes: An Integrative Modeling Effort." *Journal of Applied Psychology,* 1988, *73* (3), 443-456.

Nadler, L., and Nadler, Z. *Developing Human Resources.* 3rd ed. San Francisco: Jossey-Bass, 1989.

Peris, J. S. "The Role of Human Resources in Companies Today." Presentation at the symposium "Human resources: The Emerging Corporate Entity," sponsored by Kranz Associates, Valley Forge, Pa., Sept. 28, 1988.

Phillips, J. J. *Handbook of Training Evaluation and Methods.* Houston, Tex.: Gulf, 1982.

Piore, M. J., and Sabel, C. F. *The Second Industrial Divide.* New York: Basic Books, 1984.

"Quick Fixes Must Be Part of Training Manager's Repertoire." *Training Directors' Forum Newsletter,* 1988, *4* (3), 1-4.

Rosow, J. M., and Zager, R. *Training—The Competitive Edge: Introducing New Technology into the Workplace.* San Francisco: Jossey-Bass, 1988.

Saari, L. M., Johnson, T. R., McLaughlin, S. D., and Zimmerle, D. M. "A Survey of Management Training and Education Practices in U.S. Companies." *Personnel Psychology,* 1988, *41,* 731-743.

Saljo, R. "Learning about Learning." *Higher Education,* 1979, *8,* 443-451.

Scherkenbach, W. W. "Performance Appraisal and Quality: Ford's New Philosophy." *Quality Progress,* 1985 (Apr.), 40-46.

Sebastian, P. "Labor Pains: Buffalo, N.Y., Shows How Workers and Jobs Get Out of Alignment." *Wall Street Journal,* Sept. 16, 1988, p. 1.

Sellers, P. "How IBM Teaches Techies to Sell." *Fortune,* June 6, 1988, pp. 141-143.

Shaw, S. "Keeping Pace with the Training Needs of IBM's Employees and Customers." *Business,* 1988 (Winter).

Sheppard, H. L. (ed.). *Toward an Industrial Gerontology.* Cambridge, Mass.: Schenkman, 1970.

Smith, P. S. "General Electric, Fort Wayne, Indiana: High Tech

Comes to the Rust Belt." In J. Casner-Lotto and Associates (eds.), *Successful Training Strategies.* San Francisco: Jossey-Bass, 1988.

Sonnenfeld, J. A., and Ingols, C. A. "Working Knowledge: Charting a New Course for Training." *Organizational Dynamics,* 1986, *15* (2), 63-79.

Stephan, E., Mills, G. E., Pace, R. W., and Ralphs, L. "HRD in the *Fortune* 500: A Survey." *Training and Development Journal,* 1988 (Jan.), 26-32.

Stumpf, S. A. "Business Simulations for Skill Diagnosis and Development." In M. London and E. M. Mone (eds.), *Career Growth and Human Resource Strategies.* New York: Quorum, 1988.

Taylor, M. "Learning for Self-direction in the Classroom: The Pattern of a Transition Process." *Studies in Higher Education,* 1986, *11* (1), 55-72.

Therrien, L. "Motorola Sends Its Work Force Back to School." *Training,* 1988, *23* (11), 67-79.

Tushman, M. L., Newman, W. H., and Romanelli, E. "Human Resources Special Report." *The Career Center Bulletin,* 1985, *5* (2), 6-13.

U.S. Bureau of the Census. *Statistical Abstract of the United States.* Washington, D.C.: U.S. Government Printing Office, 1987.

U.S. Bureau of Labor Statistics. *Handbook of Labor Statistics.* Washington, D.C.: U.S. Government Printing Office, 1987.

U.S. General Accounting Office. *Dislocated Workers: Local Programs and Outcomes under the Job Training Partnership Act.* Washington, D.C.: U.S. Government Printing Office, 1987.

Van Maanen, J. "Breaking-in: Socialization to Work." In R. Dubin (ed.), *Handbook of Work, Organization, and Society.* Skokie, Ill.: Rand McNally, 1976.

Veltrop, B., and Harrington, K. "Roadmap to New Organizational Territory." *Training and Development Journal,* 1988 (June), 23-33.

Wagel, W. H. "Building Excellence Through Training." *Personnel,* 1986, *63* (9), 5-10.

Wanous, J. P. *Organizational Entry: Recruitment, Selection, and Socialization of Newcomers.* Reading, Mass.: Addison-Wesley, 1980.

Wiggenhorn, A. W. "This Is the Motorola Education and Training

Center." Unpublished presentation, Motorola Education and Training Center, Schaumburg, Ill., 1988.

Winer, B. J. *Statistical Principles in Experimental Design.* (2nd ed.) New York: McGraw-Hill, 1971.

Work in America Institute. *Training for New Technology,* Part 2. *Toward Continuous Learning.* Scarsdale, N.Y.: Work in America Institute, 1985.

Work in America Institute. *Training for New Technology,* Part 4. *The Continuous Learning/Employment Security Connection.* Scarsdale, N.Y.: Work in America Institute, 1987.

Youngblood, P., Tanner, M., Poston, C., and Chute, A. *An Evaluation of the Client Teletraining Network.* Cincinnati, Ohio: AT&T Communications Sales and Marketing Education Center, 1987.

Index

A

B

C

D

E

I

J

K

L

M